J. E. H. Foster
2d Lieut. 3d Cavalry

A Brave Soldier & Honest Gentleman

LT. JAMES E. H. FOSTER IN THE WEST, 1873–1881

By Thomas R. Buecker

Nebraska
STATE HISTORICAL SOCIETY

Nebraska State Historical Society Books / Lincoln

Portions of this book are
based on and drawn directly
from the illustrated journal
of James E. H. Foster, which
is owned by the Museum
of Nebraska Art, Kearney,
Nebraska, and which are
published here with the
permission of the Museum of
Nebraska Art, which retains
the copyright on all material
drawn from the journal.

ISBN 978-0-933307-34-6
The paper in this book
meets the guidelines for
permanence and durability of
the Committee on Production
Guidelines for Book
Longevity of the Council
on Library Resources, Inc.

Library of Congress Control
Number: 2013941414
Printed in the U.S.A.

Book design by Nathan Putens

For my parents.

Contents

Illustrations

Publication of this book was made possible by The Ronald K. and Judith M. Stolz Parks Publishing Fund established at the Nebraska State Historical Society Foundation, and use of this Fund for this purpose is made in memory of Wayne Kemper Parks (1909–1995) and Hazel Virginia Hill Parks (1911–1991), lifelong Nebraskans who were born on Madison County farms, were married on March 19, 1930, and were farmers in Madison and Pierce counties.

J. E. H. Foster
2d Lieut. 3d Cavalry

Introduction

This book is about James E. H. Foster, a cavalry officer who served in the frontier army during the post-Civil War period. Since the days of his youth, James wanted to be a soldier. After under-aged enlistments in the Civil War, and service as a staff officer in the early Pennsylvania National Guard, he applied for and received a commission in the regular army, in a profession where many were called and few chosen.

His adventures and duties while on frontier service portray a promising young officer, whose life and career were cut short by the rigors he had faced on the western plains. An examination of the life of this extraordinary soldier firmly secures his place in history and contributes to the legacy of the army in the West.

* * *

During the early 1870s, the Army of the United States was a small force, reduced by Congress and scorned by a population that had recently suffered through four long years of Civil War. In the view of many Reconstruction politicians, maintaining a larger army in time of peace presented an unnecessary strain on the American taxpayer. From 1870 until the Spanish-American War in 1898, the authorized strength of the army stood at twenty-five thousand men. And, until the end of Reconstruction in 1877, one-third of that number was stationed in the southern states.

On the other hand, there was war in the West. As the white population of the country continued and increased its incursions into the new states and territories of the Trans-Mississippi, plains tribesmen likewise continued and increased their resistance. Years of bitter hostilities between the whites and a variety of nomadic, western tribes bore witness to the dramatic struggle for supremacy on the plains. On the Northern Plains, the conflict saw hard fighting between the Lakota Sioux, Cheyenne, and Arapahoe, and the scattered units of cavalry and infantry of the U.S. Army, stationed at small forts and posts across Nebraska, Wyoming, the Dakotas, and in Montana.

The officer corps commanding the army in the West was a proportionately small fraternity of men at arms. As a consequence, the Indian War army provided military commanders from the Civil War through the turn of the century and beyond. Men who were junior line officers during the 1870s were wearing stars and leading brigades and divisions during the Spanish war. A few officers, such as Charles King and Hugh Scott, were actually still on duty during the First World War.

For the large part, the officer corps was composed of excellent, dedicated officers. While many were talented individuals with other offerings to the public, others were inventors and entrepreneurs, men with achievements beyond the profession of arms. The accomplishments of certain officers are well known. Henry Martyn Robert graduated fourth of his class at West Point in 1853. He was a major of Engineers in 1876 when he compiled his first rules of order. Charles King, an 1866 graduate, began his writing career as a captain of the Fifth Cavalry. A highly successful writer, he authored over sixty books and novels to become known as the "Chronicler of the Frontier Army." A prime example of an officer/entrepreneur was Anson Mills, who served as an infantry captain in the Civil War, and in the west as a Third Cavalry troop commander. He invented and held patents for the woven cartridge belt adopted by many armies, and retired as a brigadier general in 1897.

On occasion the army recognized the skills and interests of its officers, and sent them on leaves of absence from their regular duties for service in non-military roles. For example in 1873, Lt. Edgar Z. Steever, Third Cavalry, was detailed by the Secretary of War for duty with the Palestine Exploration Society, to map the Holy Land. Second Lieutenant Frederick Schwatka, also of the Third, is well remembered for his polar explorations in the latter 1870s, where he demonstrated that white men could survive in Arctic regions by adopting the native way of life. But, what is perhaps less known is that he was admitted to the Nebraska bar in 1875 and a year later received a medical degree from Belleview Hospital Medical College in New York.

Outside of the army's primary role of providing protection and a sense of stability in the West, its officers made other contributions to the national and western experience. As part of their direct duties Corps of Engineers officers and topographers surveyed and mapped heretofore unexplored lands. In addition to establishing routes of travel, they made notes of the agricultural potential and natural resources of the new regions, opening vast areas for settlement and development.

Army officers frequently had contact and interactions with the various tribes of native peoples as part of their regular duties. Some officers took great interest in observing native cultures and religions. Lt. John G. Bourke, another Third Cavalry standout, who served as an aide to Gen. George Crook, filled numerous notebooks with information gathered on his own on southwestern and northern Plains Indian tribes. After graduation from the Point in 1876, William P. Clark likewise took great interest in Plains Indians and organized units of scouts for service with the army. After the end of the northern Plains wars, both men were put on detached service as the first government ethnologists.

But all in all, the basic purpose and responsibility of officers was to command the army. Many officers were career men with long years of service in company or field grade ranks. Others, like Mills and Robert, were promoted to brigadiers before retirement. In the later years of retirement, old officers would sit around in the Army and Navy Club in Washington, basking in the glories of past deeds, and remembering those of deceased comrades.

However, the idea of military service has always attracted young men who dreamed of leading companies of soldiers and brave deeds, always ready and willing to serve, reaffirming the country's abiding faith in the line army. While some had the inclination for military life despite having never served, others had experienced a taste of the profession of arms and its dangers. One of those young men was James Foster.

* * *

Like other members of the officer corps, Foster contributed during his period of active service. He proved his worth as both a leader of men in combat and in his proper execution of less exciting administrative tasks and assignments, the unglamorous mechanics of the military profession. He also was a talented individual through other venues, extra-curricular to his military obligations. Although he remains relatively unknown to historians and the general public, his name appears literally hundreds of times in the military record, documenting his successful military service.

Foster's first duty station was Fort McPherson in western Nebraska. Shortly after he arrived there, he began to record his army experiences.

Foster was well-educated and a good writer and kept at least one journal to record his activities, which fortunately survives today. The first part of his journal recorded vignettes of his experiences in Nebraska. While at times reading like a fraternity road trip, his narrative of a Sand Hills elk hunt is a classic, revealing account of soldiering on the Plains. But it also demonstrates his eagerness for field service over the mundane routine of frontier garrison duty that the army endured most of its time.

The second part contains his cartographic record of the early weeks of the 1875 Jenney Expedition to the Black Hills. In this section, Foster's mapping skills became evident, with excellent detailed maps of the march. Skillfully drawn, they so impressed expedition commander Lt. Col. Richard Dodge, that he assigned Lieutenant Foster as one of two topographical officers mapping previously unexplored portions of the hills. In addition Foster included small watercolor paintings of scenery in the Black Hills which are some of the earliest artistic renditions of what had been, to Euro-Americans, an unknown and mysterious part of the west. Additionally, some of his other sketches of the expedition were published.

I first became acquainted with James Foster nearly forty years ago when researching the history of Fort Sidney, the military post once at my hometown of Sidney, Nebraska. This introduction was in the form of a detailed engraved view of Sidney done from the bluff just north of town in 1876. Created as an illustration for an Omaha newspaper, it pictured the close proximity of the post of Sidney Barracks, and the rough, frontier town of Sidney. The work was identified in the lower left corner of the engraving as "Sketch by Lieut. J. E. Foster U. S. A." In the course of subsequent research of the army in the west, I came across his name as one of the junior officers who served in the Third Cavalry. Upon further examination, his name turns up numerous times in both the recent studies and the classic works of Great Sioux War historiography and in compilations of biographies of officers involved in the war.

In 1992 one of my colleagues at the Historical Society sent me a page from an upcoming auction catalogue of western Americana. The particular page of interest listed a "Fascinating Nebraska Journal" kept by 2nd Lieut. J. E. H. Foster, of scouts in the region of Fort McPherson, Nebraska, and up to the Black Hills of South Dakota. The description also mentioned the journal contained "18 charming maps and watercolors." We agreed Foster's journal should be added to the State Archives collections and a bid was submitted. Unfortunately our bid amount was too low and the journal went into the hands of another dealer.

A short time later the journal was purchased from the second dealer by Clifton Hillegass, of Lincoln, the originator of the well-known *Cliff's Notes*. With an interest in art, he bought Foster's journal for the small watercolor paintings it contained, and presented it to the Museum of Nebraska Art at Kearney to add to its collections, where it is held today.

The journal itself is a standard composition book, bound in marbled cardboard covers, and contains 152 lined and numbered pages, each eight by ten inches in size. It was purchased from the firm of R. & J. Wilbur in Omaha, who were stationers, printers, and "Blank Book Manufacturers." Foster's Fort McPherson adventures were recorded on the first fifty-three pages. Over the next forty-four pages, certain sheets were deliberately left blank, and others were cut out, indicating that the paper was used for other purposes. His itineraries and maps of the 1875 Black Hills expedition, and watercolors of the scenery and incidents along the march, follow up to page 122; the last thirty pages remain unused. While some of his watercolors and maps were done directly on journal pages, others were possibly drawn and painted on the removed page sheets, then cut out and glued into the journal.

His journal is a great document of western history; it became the impetus to research his life and times. A search through period literature and civil and military records provided significant details to reconstruct his family life and military career. The resulting narrative put together with his interesting journal, paints a picture of both a "brave soldier and honest gentleman."

As is true with a project such as this, assistance is called on from a number of friends and associates, and from the staffs of various historical associations. First and foremost I would like to thank Michael Smith, Director and Chief Executive Officer of the Nebraska State Historical Society, and Ann Billesbach, my immediate supervisor and Associate Director of the Interpretation and Education Division, for their encouragement and support to write the lieutenant's story. As the work progressed, David Bristow, Associate Director of the Publications Division, was ready with suggestions to improve my efforts.

At the Museum of Nebraska Art in Kearney, Director Audrey S. Kauders was always an enthusiastic supporter of this project. My thanks also goes out to Jean Jacobson, Collections Coordinator, and Jill Wicht, former Director of Education at MONA, who initially spurred my interest in the Foster journal and to Jean for continued support throughout this project. And also to Richard and Marilyn Jussel, volunteers at MONA, who produced the initial transcripts of the journal.

Thomas A. Lindmier of Hulett, Wyoming loaned his microfilmed records from Fort Fetterman, which proved a boon to my research. Mark E. Miller of Laramie, Wyoming, provided a drawing of the Tongue River Heights fight from his collection. Deborah Harrison, Bel Air, Maryland, kindly provided information on the Foster family. Marc Abrams, Brooklyn, New York, sent newspaper information on Foster at the Rosebud and during the 1876 Sioux War. Michael Kraus, Curator, Soldiers and Sailors Hall, was my connection in Pittsburgh, answering questions relating to the Civil War and Duquesne Greys.

As always, my great friend and colleague, Robert E. Paul, manager of the Missouri Valley Special Collections of the Kansas City Public Library, answered the call, as did Jim Potter of the Society's Publications division. Equally, many thanks go out to long-time friends and leading Sioux War historians, Jerry Greene and Paul Hedren, who offered suggestions and advice. Gene Thomsen, Deputy State Surveyor, provided insights on nineteenth century surveying and mapping.

Staff members of the Carnegie Library of Pittsburgh and Pennsylvania State Archives in Harrisburg were quick to provide information. The Lawrenceville Historical Society provided important leads which aided my research. Closer to home, Historical Society staff readily provided information and assistance. At the NSHS Archives, Dell Darling, Linda Hein, Mary-Jo Miller, and Matt Piersol were always helpful. My thanks to Courtney Ziska for her excellent map work, to Nolan Johnson for his help on this project and others, and to Randy Kane of Crawford, Nebraska. John Schleicher, Head of Special Collections of the McGoogan Library of Medicine at the University of Nebraska Medical Center, furnished information on nineteenth century medical practices. And as usual, Sandra Lowry, librarian at Fort Laramie National Historic Site in Wyoming, was ready with suggestions and source materials.

CHAPTER I

Growing up in Pittsburgh

James Evans Heron Foster was born to a distinguished family that played a prominent role in Pittsburgh and Pennsylvania history. His great-great-grandfather was Alexander Foster, of Scotch-Irish descent, who came to America about 1725 as a fifteen-year-old emigrant from Londonderry, Ireland. After three years in New Jersey, Alexander moved to Lancaster County, Pennsylvania, where he was married about 1730 and obtained land. A prosperous farmer, he raised a large family of three sons and six daughters before his death in 1767.[1]

William Foster, the second of his three sons, was born in 1740. Inspired to preach the gospel, he was ordained a minister in the Presbyterian Church. Respected for his solid sense and unaffected piety, he became an inspiring patriotic orator during the Revolutionary War period. His sermons and speeches were so offensive to the British that Gen. William Howe ordered troops sent out for his capture. Foster managed to evade the British while he raised a family of four sons and four daughters. When walking home after a sermon one day in September 1780, he was caught in a driving rain and became seriously ill. He died shortly afterward.

James E. H. Foster's grandfather, Alexander W. Foster, was William's second son, born in 1771. An intelligent young man, Alexander studied law in Philadelphia and was admitted to the bar in 1793. In 1796 he and his family relocated to western Pennsylvania, where at Meadville and then Greensburg, he established large practices and enjoyed a reputation as "one of the ablest lawyers of his day."[2] Foster had the ability to expose fraud in testimony and reportedly excelled in his command of language and in organizing arguments. In 1802 Alexander married Jane T. Heron, the daughter of

VIEW OF
PITTSBURGH &
ALLEGHENY.
1861

Manchester

Birmingham

James H. Heron, a former captain in the Continental Army, who was once captured and held prisoner by the British. In and out of the courtroom Foster was an interesting character. Famous as a mentor to numerous students of the law, he once fought a duel, wounding his opponent. He also had greenhouses built to raise Spanish tobacco for his own cigars.[3]

Alexander William Jr., born in 1814 in Greensburg, followed his father in the legal profession. He was physically an "overgrown boy, being five feet eight inches in height," and like his father, very intelligent. At a young age he read *Blackstone's Commentaries* and wrote several political articles that were published in the Greensburg newspaper. When Alexander Jr. was fourteen years old, Alexander Sr. was confident enough in his abilities to make application for an appointment to the United States Military Academy as a cadet at large. Although his father lobbied for his appointment for several years, Foster Jr. was not selected to West Point. However, under his father's tutorage he began to read the law.[4]

About 1830 Alexander Sr. moved his family to Pittsburgh to establish a law practice there. Still maintaining his interest in the military, Alexander Jr. was quick to join the "Duquesne Greys," a new local military company

FIG. I.I. An 1861 view of Pittsburgh and its environs. By the 1860s the Foster family had moved from the lower city to the suburban areas shown in the upper right. *Under the Maltese Cross: Antietam to Appomattox*

ALEXANDER W. FOSTER,
ATTORNEY AT LAW,
City Solicitor, Notary Public, Commissioner for the States of Iowa, Missouri, Wisconsin, Michigan, Virginia, Tennessee, Louisiana, New Hampshire and Connecticut.

☞ Depositions taken for the several Courts of the United States, and for the Courts of the several States above named, and for Ohio, Rhode Island and Illinois.

☞ Titles to real-estate examined.

☞ Claims for Pensions, &c., prosecuted.

☞ Accounts, &c., certified for collection.

Office, 139 Fourth Street, above Smithfield.

FIG. I.2. Alexander Foster Jr. ad from the 1858 Pittsburgh directory.

composed of young men that was organized in 1831.[5] He was admitted to the Pittsburgh bar in 1833 at age nineteen and entered the law practice with his father. In December 1834, Alexander married Caroline C. Singer of Greensburg and began to raise his family; the first child, Pearson G., was born in 1835. Alexander Jr. and his father were civic minded and became involved with civil improvement projects to extend railroad lines to Pittsburgh and improve Allegheny River navigation. Although Alexander Jr. also became a prominent barrister, he had other personal and political interests. In 1838 young Foster served as secretary to the Democratic Young Men's State Convention, and during the 1840s was involved with the anti-slavery Pittsburgh Colonization Society, in addition to editorial work with his brother's newspaper.

His younger brother was J. Heron Foster, printer, editor, and publisher connected with the Pittsburgh press for thirty years. In 1846 he established the *Pittsburgh Dispatch*, for many years the city's leading newspaper. He made a trip to California to cover the gold rush for his paper, served several terms in the state legislature, and was one of the organizers of the "Washington Infantry," another of Pittsburgh's several antebellum military companies. J. Heron's daughter, Rachael Foster Avery, was a noted women's suffragist and close lieutenant of Susan B. Anthony. In 1882 she conducted the Nebraska amendment campaign, headquartered in Omaha.[6]

Alexander Sr. retired from the practice and moved to nearby Mercer, where he died in 1843. His first cousin was William Barclay Foster, the father of the famous American composer, Stephen C. Foster. Alexander Jr. and Stephen Foster were second cousins, making James a second cousin once removed.[7]

Alexander Jr. also became involved in Pittsburgh city government. In 1842 he served a short term as president of the city common council. From 1857 through 1859 he was the city solicitor, and in 1858 he codified the Pittsburgh ordinances. In between professional obligations and civic duties, his family grew. Following the eldest son Pearson, three sons and a daughter were born.

After marriage the Foster family resided in urban row housing, near the downtown business district. As his family grew, Alexander moved them into larger residences still in the main town. By the late 1840s the family lived in a row house at 164 Fourth Avenue, less than a block from Foster's office. It was probably there that the fifth son, James Evans Heron, was born on June 4, 1848.

Continuing the tradition of having large families, Alexander and Caroline Foster's family grew to five sons and three daughters. By 1860 the oldest son Pearson worked as a law clerk and still lived in the household. Sons George, who was a physician, and Alexander, a machinist and engineer, lived out on their own. Charles also worked as an attorney's clerk and resided at home. The three daughters were at home, and also son James, who attended school. The Foster family enjoyed an upper middle-class lifestyle, with property and a domestic to assist with household duties, and education for the children. James began his education in 1855, attending public schools in the Sixth Ward near the family residence.

By the 1850s, Pittsburgh residents who could afford it began to migrate to the suburbs. The crowded, sooty atmosphere of the city proper caused many well-to-do businessmen and manufacturers to move out to the new suburban areas of Oakland, Bellefield, and East Liberty. Additionally, the congestion and unsanitary conditions often found in the main city could be conducive to the spread of disease and sickness. In 1854, four hundred residents died in Pittsburgh's worst cholera epidemic. In 1859 the Foster family moved out of the city to the rural suburb of Oakland, then to Bellefield.

After the move, Foster attended the Minersville School in the Thirteenth Ward from mid-1859 through 1860. In January 1861 he entered the North Sewickley Academy, located thirty miles northwest of Pittsburgh in Beaver County. The academy was a private Presbyterian school, established in the 1840s to prepare both boys and girls for college. The rural site of North Sewickley attracted students from Pittsburgh and southern states. James was a student there until the early spring of 1862, when he returned home and enrolled at Western University of Pennsylvania. For the next several years he attended classes there.[8]

With its advantageous location on water and land routes of transport, Pittsburgh grew. By 1860 it was a major manufacturing center with nearly a thousand factories. While smelters turned out a steady stream of iron and steel, local shipyards, factories, and foundries built river vessels, railroad locomotives, stationary steam engines, girders, nails, and countless other items necessary of the industrial age. With a population of 49,200, Pittsburgh was well on the way to becoming a key player in American industry.

The Civil War

The outbreak of the Civil War in 1861 brought increased production of iron and armaments. The Fort Pitt Foundry alone produced 1,193 cannon (15 percent of the total U.S. wartime production) and almost 200,000 artillery projectiles. Pittsburgh foundries collectively manufactured 10 percent of the nation's total production of artillery shells. The Allegheny Arsenal was the army's main factory for accoutrements and horse furnishings and also produced fourteen million rifle cartridges a year. Four ironclad ships were built in Pittsburgh, and its rolling mills supplied the armor for New York and Philadelphia shipyards. By war's end, over half of the steel used in the war effort came from Pittsburgh.[9]

Pittsburgh also provided military manpower. During the war twenty-five thousand men of Allegheny County served in Union army or naval forces. While James was far underage for enlistment, his older brothers enlisted in Pennsylvania or local units. The eldest brother Pearson enlisted in the 100th Infantry, while George was a surgeon in the 13th Pennsylvania. Charles G. served as a sergeant in Nevin's Independent Battery in 1864–65, and Alexander III with the 15th Militia in 1861–62. Their uncle, J. Heron Foster, was a captain in the 102nd Infantry from 1861 to 1863, and Provost Marshal for the 22nd District, headquartered in Pittsburgh, from 1863 until the end of the war.[10]

Although only thirteen years old when war broke out, James thought he was "big enough" to be a soldier. Fearing he might run off and enlist, his parents brought him home from North Sewickley and enrolled him in Western University. Although at home and busy with college studies, young Foster's ambitions to join up continued.[11]

In the summer of 1863, the threat of direct attack by Confederate forces came briefly to Pittsburgh. In mid-June, fears that a rebel army would invade western Pennsylvania and target Pittsburgh led the War Department to create the Department of Monongahela, headquartered in Pittsburgh, to provide a military presence. A series of forts was quickly planned to control access to the city. Sensing alarm, businessmen and manufacturers sent their workers out to prepare earthworks. By June 26, some twelve thousand men were at work on thirty-two separate fortifications and connecting trench works. After receiving word that Gen. Jeb Stuart's cavalry was moving toward the city, the Pittsburgh militia and home guards prepared for attack.[12]

By July 4 the fortifications were all completed and manned. Fortunately, the Union victory at Gettysburg and the Confederate retreat south removed the present danger to Pittsburgh. The defensive works dug to repel Confederate attack ran right past Oakland, near where the Foster family resided. By this time young James had full opportunity to observe what was happening. He had seen the spectacle of war, at least for the time being. The next year James himself found a chance to serve in the war, not at Pittsburgh, but in the nation's capital.

Just after the outbreak of the war, a strong surrounding network of earthen fortifications and connecting trenches were constructed to protect Washington, DC By 1864, sixty forts and ninety-three batteries mounted 837 guns, with over twenty miles of rifle pits, all manned by 23,000 men to protect the city. For several years the defending soldiers faced only a monotonous daily schedule of drills and regular garrison duties. Surrounded with troops and cannon, and with the Army of the Potomac between them and Richmond, citizens of Washington became complacent to any thought of southern attack; with their substantial defenses, they believed the war would never come to the city. However, in the spring of 1864, their sense of security began to erode.[13]

Persistent attacks by Gen. Ulysses S. Grant on Robert E. Lee's vaunted Army of Northern Virginia led to mounting northern casualties. Grant drew from the troops assigned to defend the capital to replenish his army's depleted ranks. Most alarmingly, regiments transferred out of the trenches and forts included heavy artillery units, intended to man the big guns that provided Washington's shield.

To meet the troop shortage facing the capital's defense, Ohio and Pennsylvania governors provided troops for short-time service. National guard and "one-hundred day" units were formed and sent to defend the depleted forts and entrenchments surrounding Washington. Pennsylvania provided six infantry regiments, one battalion of cavalry, and, on special authority from the war department, one artillery battalion, all for one hundred days' service. The artillery battalion was to be raised and commanded by veteran artilleryman Capt. Joseph M. Knap.

FIG. I.3 Map of the Civil War defenses of Washington: Forts Meigs, Slocum, and Sumner, where Foster was stationed, are highlighted. *Battles and Leaders of the Civil War*

Knap, a native of New York, graduated from Rensselaer Polytechnic Institute in 1858 with a degree in civil engineering. He had been working in Pittsburgh when the war began and by October 1861 was a captain commanding a light artillery battery. Under his command, the battery, known simply as "Knap's Battery," served with distinction through eastern theater battles including the Peninsular Campaign, at Antietam, Chancellorsville, Gettysburg, and the Wilderness. In May 1864 Knap was ordered by Secretary of War Edwin M. Stanton to organize either a light or heavy artillery battalion at Pittsburgh for immediate service. With his experience in command of light artillery, Knap was promoted to major and quickly began to recruit four batteries; by May 19, the first battery was fully enlisted.[14]

A light artillery battery (or company) consisted of one hundred enlisted men commanded by three officers. Seeing an opportunity to go off to war, fifteen-year-old James Foster was one of the first enlistees in Capt. James Cooper's Battery A. Because he was so anxious to serve, and in a local unit not exactly headed to the front, his parents let him go. Although signed parental consent was required for a minor's enlistment, James told the recruiting officer he was eighteen years old. His battery was quickly sent off by rail to help man the Washington defenses. For the next one hundred days, James was off to the war.[15]

Two days after being mustered in, Foster's battery was assigned to garrison duty at Fort Meigs, a badly under-manned work on the eastern defense line. Located two miles east of Washington, Fort Meigs was the end of a line of fortifications on the long ridge that overlooked the Navy yard, the Washington Arsenal, and the Capitol Hill district. The fort also guarded the approach roads to the important Bennings Bridge crossing of the Anacostia River. A strong fort, it mounted nine heavy guns, several mortars, and seven pieces of light artillery. Within a week the three other batteries arrived from Pittsburgh and were sent both to Meigs and nearby Fort Mahan. Knap's men settled in for an unchanging routine of roll calls, fatigue parties, light artillery training, and infantry drill. Although enlisted as artillerymen, their basic role was mostly to serve as infantry for picket and guard duties.[16]

In an attempt to place its manpower in the best position to face any possible contingency, the department command continually shifted units between forts along the line. On June 14, Major Knap's command was moved seven miles northwest to Forts Slocum and Stevens, two of the most important works on the extreme northern point of the defense works. For several weeks Foster's battery garrisoned Fort Slocum, where their training and regular garrison duties resumed.

In July the normal, secure routine taken for granted by Washington

FIG. 1.4. Artillery troops man a typical Washington fort, armed with heavy and light artillery pieces and mortars. A bombproof magazine is visible to the left. Library of Congress

residents took a dramatic turn. While Grant was busy fighting Lee's army, a Confederate army moved down the Shenandoah Valley, in position to threaten Washington. Fully aware that his force was insufficient in size to capture and hold the federal capital, Gen. Jubal A. Early's 14,000-man Army of the Valley was to attack and break through the ill-defended lines. Such a raid would, in effect, demoralize northerners and cause Grant to divert manpower from the front to the capital entrenchments.

As the southern force neared Maryland, Knap's battalion was again shifted along the line. On July 4, Knap was ordered to move his companies to Forts Sumner, Mansfield, and Simmons on the far western end of the line. Batteries A and B took station at Fort Sumner, a powerful fort that overlooked the Potomac shoreline and guarded the river road, and the receiving reservoir for the municipal water system. While the Pittsburgh artillerymen established a tent camp and were deployed out on picket duty, the Department command scrambled to find enough manpower for trenches and works.

Over the next days Early's troops continued their advance on Washington. After defeating a smaller Union force commanded by Gen. Lew Wallace on the Monocacy River on July 9, the exhausted Confederate army arrived north of the city opposite Forts DeRussy, Stevens, and Slocum, within six miles of downtown. At that moment barely 9,500 Union troops awaited them on the defense line, a scratch force that included convalescent soldiers, civilian volunteers, and quartermaster employees.[17]

In the early morning of July 11, the shooting war began, and Foster was under fire for the first time. That morning he had been assigned duty on the picket line guarding the fronts of Forts Simmons and Mansfield, when the leading elements of Early's army appeared and opened fire. The pickets suddenly found themselves skirmishing with an advancing Confederate cavalry brigade. The outnumbered Federals were soon forced to retire to safety within the main lines. At Fort Sumner, Foster was plainly within earshot of rifle fire, and the Federal artillery as it shelled Confederate skirmishers moving on the forts just to the north. If his unit had not been transferred, he would have been right in the middle of the main attack at Fort Stevens. As heavy skirmishing took place throughout the day at the northern point of the line, reinforcing veteran troops arrived to bolster the northern line. Skirmishing continued the next day. But by nightfall Early broke off the engagement and began his return to the Shenandoah. The battle was over and blood had been shed. Outside of the British attack in 1814, this was the only time our nation's capital was under direct assault by an enemy military force in declared war.

After visiting his picket posts and the return of a cavalry scouting patrol he sent out, Major Knap confidently reported to headquarters on the thirteenth, "No enemy to be found."[18] With the excitement over, routine life in the forts returned. In addition to military duties, the troops manning the works spent large amounts of time repairing and improving their earthworks, which demanded frequent maintenance. Rain caused erosion damage, protective abatis needed replacement, parapets were sodded, and brush needed to be removed to provide clear fields of fire. Such work was continually necessary to keep the fortifications combat ready.

Foster spent his last days in the defense of Washington with the rest of his battalion, cutting the accumulated brush before Forts Sumner and Mansfield. By the last days of August his one hundred days were over. Battery A returned to Pittsburgh where on August 29 it was mustered out. His first service in the war completed, James received his discharge pay and went home. By September 12 the other batteries had all returned, and the First Battalion Pennsylvania Light Artillery was fully mustered out.

FIG. 1.5. Soldiers of the 155th Pennsylvania Infantry in Zouave uniform. *Under the Maltese Cross*

In the early spring of 1865 James was working in Pittsburgh as a printer and again decided to go off to war—this time in real harm's way. On March 21 he volunteered as a private in Company F, 155th Pennsylvania Infantry, for one year's service. As Foster was still a minor of sixteen years, his parents gave their consent and signed the enlistment form. His physical examination found him in good health and five feet eight inches in height, weighing 128 pounds, with grey eyes, light hair, and of fair complexion. Foster was enlisted by his uncle, Capt. J. Heron Foster, the Pittsburgh provost marshal. He was paid one-third of the $100 bounty, the balance due on discharge. Duly enlisted, he was quickly sent to join his regiment then in action on the front in Virginia.[19]

Organized in Pittsburgh in September 1862, the 155th earned the reputation of a fighting regiment. It fought well in major eastern theater engagements, which included Antietam, Fredericksburg, Gettysburg, Spottsylvania, the Wilderness, and was at the moment closing in on Lee's army in the waning days of the war. The 155th was a "Zouave" regiment, which wore a French-inspired uniform. Although most Zouave units discarded flamboyant dress early in the war, the 155th was allowed to adopt the style in January 1864 in recognition of brave service and excellence in drill. Foster was issued the distinctive uniform of the 155th, a short blue jacket with yellow trim and facings with matching wide blue knee-breeches, a yellow-trimmed red sash, and white canvas leggings, all topped with a red skull cap with dark blue tassel. The uniform was both comfortable and showy, and enjoyed immensely by the men.[20]

At the time Foster joined his company in Virginia, the 155th was in the midst of the Appomattox campaign. At the Battle of Five Forks the regiment captured more prisoners than men in its ranks. Four days later it was at Amelia Court House, continuing the Fifth Corps' relentless pursuit of the Army of Northern Virginia. Day after day the northern forces doggedly attempted to get in position to block the retreat of the tattered yet defiant men of Lee's army. In the early morning hours of April 9, the hard-marching Pennsylvanians were on the skirmish line at Appomattox Court House, where, for the last time, they came under fire. As the final fight with Lee's army began, the regiment suffered possibly the last combat death incurred by the Army of the Potomac. Immediately before the firing ceased, a young private on the line, a Pittsburgh boy not much older than Foster, received what proved a mortal wound. Suddenly by 9:00 a.m., the firing ceased—the war was over for the Army of the Potomac.[21]

Three days after Lee signed the surrender, his battle-weary troops turned over their arms. Maj. Gen. Joshua L. Chamberlain drew up his division with the 155th Pennsylvania ordered off the picket line and placed in line opposite of where the Confederate soldiers were to stack their muskets, cartridge boxes, and battle flags. Standing in the Federal ranks, James Foster was a close witness to the daylong process.[22]

Several weeks later the Union army began the march to Washington for disbandment. On May 6 Foster's regiment passed through Petersburg, then Richmond on its way to the capital. Six days later the Fifth Corps went into permanent camp near Arlington Heights, where they awaited muster-out and made preparations to participate in the two-day Grand Review of the victorious armies of Grant and Sherman. On May 23 it took most of the day for the Army of the Potomac to pass down Pennsylvania Avenue; an hour and a half for the Fifth Corps alone. An observing correspondent remarked, "... the steadfast blue of the infantry, the gay, dashing yellow of the cavalry, and the showy uniforms of the zouaves gave variety to the scene."[23]

Another witness to the passing of the 155th regiment recalled, "No Roman legion returned from conquest of foreign lands ever received more enthusiastic applause then did this regiment of Pittsburgh zouaves."[24] At

FIG. 1.6. Troops of the Grand Review marching down Pennsylvania Avenue.
Library of Congress

that moment James Foster was an acknowledged part of the triumph of the Union.

On the second day, Gen. William T. Sherman's triumphant armies of the Tennessee and Georgia passed in six and one-half hours. During those two days, 145,000 men, "with their battle-torn flags and the panoply of war," marched past the reviewing stand and back to civilian life.[25] After their part in the review, the regiments of the Fifth Corps returned to their camps to wait while muster out rolls were prepared in multi-copy and certified.

On June 1 the 155th Pennsylvania was ordered to Camp Reynolds at Pittsburgh for discharge and final pay. Unfortunately, this movement did not involve the new recruits or soldiers recently transferred in. Orders from the war department specified that troops with terms of service to expire before September 30 were to be immediately mustered out. Those with more time left in service were to be transferred to other organizations.[26]

As his regiment left Washington on June 2, Foster marched to the camp of the 191st Pennsylvania Infantry and was assigned to Company G. Faced with an uncertain future and disappointment about not going home with his regiment, he settled in with the others to further camp life and waiting. Fortunately for them, the war department decided to avoid the expense of maintaining the large Federal army, and accelerated its discharge policy. After three weeks idling in camp, James was discharged by special order on June 23 (five days before the rest of the regiment) and returned to civilian life.[27]

Just as Alexander Sr. had tried to get his son into West Point, Alexander Jr. now sought a commission in the regular army for his son. After reading that 299 second lieutenants were to be appointed, he wrote Secretary of War Edwin M. Stanton in late November asking a commission for seventeen-year-old James. Alexander listed his son's service in the war and added that he was "healthy and of good habits." Stanton informed Foster that his son's name would be placed on the list of applicants, and that was the end of it. Foster Sr. probably did not realize there already were more than enough former officers of volunteers to fill the openings. Nevertheless, he was proud of his son's service in the war. He later wrote to a former officer and friend, "a young fellow who went into the service while so very young shows possession of the right stamina."[28]

The Civil War was undoubtedly the defining moment in Foster's life. In 1863 he had seen the preparations for war from his house in Pittsburgh. In 1864 he first came under fire and heard the sounds of war during Jubal Early's attack on Washington. In 1865 he had his "cup of blood" in the last combats of the war.

As an impressionable youth, he did not see the power of the Federal government through the judicial system as did his father and grandfather. He saw the power and glory of the Union in 1865, when Lee's once formidable army stacked its arms at Appomattox, and while marching in the triumphant Washington grand review. These experiences bore a powerful influence on his subsequent decision to pursue a career in the United States Army.

1   The early history of the Foster family is from Stephen Collins Foster & Morrison Foster, *Biography, Songs, and Musical Compositions of Stephen C. Foster* (Pittsburgh: Percy F. Smith, 1896), 3–4; George Dallas Albert (ed.), *History of the County of Westmoreland, Pennsylvania* (Philadelphia: L. H. Everts & Co., 1882), 324–25.

2   John N. Boucher, *History of Westmoreland County Pennsylvania* (New York: The Lewis Publishing Co., 1906), 38–39.

3   Letter, A. W. Foster, Jr. to the President, Jan. 21, 1851, Pearson G. Foster File, "U. S. Military Academy Application Papers, 1805–1866," RG 94, Records of the Adjutant General, National Archives & Records Administration; Boucher, *History of Westmoreland County*, 39.

4   Letter, A. W. Foster Sr. to Secretary of War, Dec. 3, 1828, Alexander W. Foster, Jr. File, "U. S. Military Academy Application Papers, 1805–1866," RG 94, NARA.

5   Col. Edward Martin, *The Twenty-eighth Division, Pennsylvania's National Guard in the World War* (Pittsburgh: 28th Division Publishing Co., 1924), 261.

6   Personal correspondence dated Dec. 28, 2010, from Deb Harrison, Bel Air, Maryland; Frances E. Willard & Mary A Livermore, ed., *A Woman of the Century* (New York: Charles Wells Moulton, 1893), 37–38.

7   Albert, *History of the County*, 326; Deb Harrison, Dec. 25, 2010.

8   All information concerning Foster's education is from his "Brief Sketch of my life" submitted to the senior officer of his examining board, Sept. 17, 1873, Appointments, Commissions, Personal File (ACP 1873), RG 94, NARA.

9   Miriam Meislik and Ed Galloway, "History of Pittsburgh," Society of American Archivists Annual Conference, Pittsburgh, 1999.

10 Registers of Pennsylvania Volunteers, 1861–1865, RG 19, Records of the Department of Military and Veterans' Affairs, Pennsylvania State Archives, Harrisburg.

11 Letter, A. W. Foster to James S. Negley, Dec. 12, 1872, ACP 1873.

12 Pittsburgh Timeline, *Historic Pittsburgh Project*.

13 For a thorough discussion of Washington's wartime defenses, see *A Historic Resources Study: The Civil War Defenses of Washington, Part I* (Chevy Chase, MD: CEHP Incorporated, n.d.).

14 *The National Cyclopedia of American Biography, Vol. X* (New York: James T. White & Co., 1900), 352; War Department, *The War of the Rebellion: A Compilation of the Official Records of the Union and Confederate Armies, Series I, Vol. 37, Parts 1 & 2* (Washington, DC: Government Printing Office, 1891), 458; RG 94, Records of Enlistments, First Battalion Pennsylvania Light Artillery, NARA.

15   Letter, Foster to Negley, Dec. 12, 1872, ACP 1873; James E. Heron Foster Muster Card, RG 94, Register of Enlistments, First Battalion Pennsylvania Light Artillery, NARA.

16   Benjamin F. Cooling & Walter H. Owens, *Mr. Lincoln's Forts: A Guide to the Civil War Defenses of Washington* (Shippensburg, PA: White Mane Publishing Co., 1988), 194.

17   *Mr. Lincoln's Forts*, 14–15; Margaret Leech, *Reveille in Washington, 1860–1865* (New York: Harper & Bros., 1941), 329–44.

18   *War of the Rebellion, Series I, Vol. 37 (Part II)*, 882.

19   RG 94, Records of Enlistments, 155th Pennsylvania Infantry, NARA.

20   Adjutant General's Office, *Official Army Register of the Volunteer Force of the United States Army, Part III* (Washington, DC: Adjutant General's Office, 1865), 994–95; The 155th Regimental Assn., *Under the Maltese Cross, Antietam to Appomattox* (Pittsburgh: 1910), 224–26.

21   The young soldier was Pvt. William Montgomery, who died of his wounds on April 28. *Under the Maltese Cross*, 615.

22   *Under the Maltese Cross*, 367–68. For the sequence of events of the last days of the Appomattox Campaign, see pages 347–62.

23   *Army and Navy Journal* (ANJ), May 27, 1865.

24   *Under the Maltese Cross*, 381.

25   Edwin M. Coffman, *The Old Army: A Portrait of the American Army in Peacetime, 1784–1898* (New York, NY: Oxford University Press, 1986), 215.

26   ANJ, May 27, 1865.

27   War Department, Adjutant General's Office, Special Orders No. 323, June 22, 1865, RG 94, NARA.

28   A. W. Foster to Stanton, Nov. 21, 1865, ACP 1873; Foster to Negley, Dec. 12, 1872, ACP 1873.

CHAPTER 2

Commission in the Regular Army

In the years immediately following the war, Foster resided at home and worked in Pittsburgh. With the establishment of the highly successful *Pittsburgh Dispatch*, his uncle and father had long been connected with the city press. Consequently, James was involved with newspaper work for five years, and became a well-known local journalist. The paper changed hands after his uncle's death, and by the early 1870s Foster was employed as a clerk in a Pittsburgh savings bank. Like his father and grandfather, he was intelligent with "scholarly attainments and character."[1] By this time he had no interest in following in the legal profession, but heard a military calling.

Foster became interested in the army at a young age, some of this through a family tradition that dated from the Revolutionary War. He was not the only family member to have entertained thoughts of a career in the United States Army. Years before, applications had been made for his father, and then older brother Pearson, to receive appointments at large to West Point. Additionally, his brothers and other relatives saw service during the Civil War. In late August 1870, he signed an oath to become a first lieutenant in Company A, Pittsburgh Light Guards.[2] By enlisting in a local militia unit, Foster could hone the skills he had learned in the army, and gain more of a military background while remaining at home.

In 1871, Congress authorized the replacement of the old militia system by a trained national guard. Although provisional battalions of militia units were reorganized into regimental organizations, the names of some traditional Pittsburgh units were maintained. As a consequence, one new regiment was designated the "Eighteenth Regiment (Duquesne Greys) National Guard of Pennsylvania." Foster resigned his commission in company A and became the regimental quartermaster of the Eighteenth Regiment, the lineal descendant of the old Greys, the long-standing Pittsburgh militia in which his father once served.[3]

The "Duquesne Greys of Pittsburgh" was organized on August 5, 1831, to train educated, high-level young men for military service in case duty called. The unit adapted the gray uniform, reminiscent of that once worn by regular army rifle regiments and currently by West Point cadets. Members met for drill, assisted in local emergencies, made martial appearances at patriotic celebrations, and marched in parades. Although militia units were commonly seen as social organizations, they did serve when called. During the Mexican War the Greys were part of the First Pennsylvania Volunteers, where they saw major action. They also suffered considerable casualties: thirteen of the members died at the siege of Puebla alone. After the war it reorganized back into the Duquesne Greys, and continued to prepare men for military service.

Although during the Civil War, the Duquesne Greys served as a unit for only a short period in 1861, sixty-nine officers for the Union army eventually came from its ranks. After the war, service in the Greys grew in popularity. In addition to an increase of new enlistees, many men from Foster's old regiment, the 155th Pennsylvania Infantry, who had served in the Greys, rejoined it after the war. With this boost to enrollment, the unit was expanded into a three, then five-company battalion assigned to the Eighteenth Division of the state militia. In December 1871 the battalion was further increased to a regiment of eight companies and designated the Eighteenth Infantry.[4]

At the time Foster was in the Greys, its members were required to buy their own uniforms, an expensive ensemble that cost as much as $55. The state of Pennsylvania furnished the troops with arms, accoutrements, and camping and field equipment. The Greys fitted up the old city hall in downtown to serve as their armory. Foster apparently did his homework, and became knowledgeable enough in military drill and procedures to be appointed to the Eighteenth Infantry staff as regimental adjutant.[5]

As regimental adjutant, Foster was responsible in a large part for the management of his regiment. Adjutants handled correspondence, issued orders pertaining to the command, and kept the staff informed on regimental affairs. During his tenure as adjutant, a major logistical operation for the Eighteenth Infantry took place in March 1873, when five companies of the Greys, averaging seventy men per company, went to Washington to march in President Ulysses Grant's second inaugural parade. Guardsmen also made occasional trips to Latrobe, Pennsylvania, for training encampments. Foster proved an efficient and popular officer while serving in positions of

R. H. CLINE, PHOTO   MAYVILLE, N. Y.

CAMP SCOTT DUQUESNE GREYS, Co B.
MAYVILLE, N. Y. JULY 18, 1875.
PLATE No. 16

FIG. 2.1. Guardsmen of the Duquesne Greys relax while at summer encampment near Mayville, New York, in the mid-1870s. Historical Society of Western Pennsylvania

responsibility. Additionally, through performance of guard administrative duties, he gained practical experience that would be of later value.

With his father's full support, in the late months of 1872 James began the process of applying for a regular army commission. During the nineteenth century, it was possible for a civilian like Foster to receive a commission. Applicants were required to be between twenty and thirty years of age; Foster was twenty-three. He was a well-qualified candidate, both physically and mentally fit, and had prior military service. In addition to those personal qualifications, Foster had the full endorsement of the hierarchy of the National Guard of Pennsylvania. Moreover, his father knew influential friends, an important benefit in any highly selective process.

In the years following the Civil War, regular army officers received their commissions in one of three ways: graduation from West Point; direct promotion as qualified non-commissioned officers within the enlisted ranks; and via direct appointment from civilian life (with preference to former volunteer officers). During the first several years, forty-two per cent of those commissioned were former volunteer officers. After the army was reduced in size, only 2,105 officers remained in service by 1871. Over the next twenty-seven years, this number did not vary by more than one hundred. The officer corps of the regular army was indeed a select group.[6]

As Congress reduced its manpower, however, the army gradually culled out ineffective officers. Throughout the rest of the century and until the Spanish-American War in 1898, West Point graduates filled seventy-five per cent of the vacancies, civilian appointees about fourteen percent, and promotions from the ranks filled the remainder. Because fewer openings remained for civilian candidates, obtaining a commission became a very competitive process.[7]

On December 12, Alexander Foster wrote to Congressman James S. Negley asking his assistance obtaining a commission for his son. Negley, a personal friend and a major general during the war, replied that James "will make a splendid officer," and that his favorable recommendation was passed on to Secretary of War William W. Belknap. Several days later Belknap forwarded the application to the Adjutant General and the wheels were in motion.[8]

In early January, James sent his personal letter of application to Secretary Belknap, along with letters of support from the Pittsburgh mayor and other city officials, as well as from Alfred L. Pearson, major general of the Pennsylvania National Guard. During the war Pearson commanded the 155th Infantry, in which Foster had served. The general gave James a glowing recommendation: "I know there is not a more competent officer in this state," and closed with, "His appointment will be a gratifying recognition of the soldiers of this country, and will gratify, especially the National Guards of this division." On the first day of February, his application was reviewed and approved by General of the Army William T. Sherman. After considering Foster's endorsements and recommendations, Belknap ordered his name placed on the list of applicants.[9]

Meanwhile, James was eager to receive an army appointment. He wrote Congressman Negley that he was more than willing to serve in any regiment that was on frontier service, and confidently added, "If appointed [I] would remain in the service for life & do my duty, in whatever station might be assigned." At the same time that he applied, scores of other candidates were filing applications for the limited number of commissions available that year.[10]

According to established protocol, each year's officer openings were to be filled first by graduates of the U. S. Military Academy. Consequently, the graduating class of 1873 would automatically fill forty-five of the fifty-three second lieutenant vacancies projected for June 15. Foster and the other non-academy applicants were subjected to an intense selection process where all the unqualified were weeded out. For all candidates, the next several months saw anxious waiting while the applicant list was narrowed down.

For the year 1873, the war department received nearly four hundred applications for commissions. Out of that number, President Ulysses S. Grant eventually approved forty-five suitable appointees to appear before the army examining board. In mid-August the list was released. This short list included sons of active duty and retired army and naval officers, former military academy cadets, government civil servants, active duty enlisted men, and regular civilians, all of whom sought commissions to enter the officer ranks. The names included William A. Carson, the son of famed frontiersman Kit Carson, who did not make it. Second to last on the published list was James E. H. Foster, of Pennsylvania.[11]

On August 18 orders were issued for a board of four officers to convene in Washington on September 15 to examine each candidate for a presidential appointment. Two days later Foster received his official notification to appear before the board. He immediately sent an acknowledgment of notification, replying "I shall hold myself in readiness to report . . . at the time and place designated." He additionally provided a statement of his wartime service, which was checked against his record in the Adjutant General's Office.[12]

Army regulations called for officer examining boards to interview applicants to determine overall fitness for command, moral character, academic attainments, and physical soundness for duty. The rules for examination were established by general order issued through the adjutant general's office. When appearing before the board, each candidate was extensively examined and graded on command of grammar, mathematical skill, history and geography "particularly in reference to the northern continent of America," as well as knowledge of government and constitutional rights. Board members received specific guidelines in regard to the weight of subject grades awarded to determine an overall score that represented the candidate's mastery of the required topics. In addition, a medical officer gave each applicant a physical exam to determine his fitness to "endure the exposure of the service."[13]

Foster was so confident he would pass the board, that on August 28 he submitted his resignation as officer and adjutant in the Duquesne Greys to accept an appointment as a commissioned officer in the regulars.[14] But at this stage, receiving a commission was still subject to examination and recommendation of the board of officers.

On September 17, Foster appeared before the board, presided over by Lt. Col. William H. French, Second Artillery. After presenting his notification letter, he received a physical examination by Maj. Basil Norris, the board surgeon, who certified that he was "physically qualified to perform the active duties of a commissioned officer." Foster and the other candidates each submitted a written sketch providing his educational, military service, and career backgrounds, and all were interviewed. The written examination consisted of forty-four questions from the five prescribed subject areas. Grammar questions related to correct spelling and orthography, while the arithmetic section required the solving of complex computations and practical applications. Geography dealt with identification of physical features, states and countries (including the capital of West Virginia). A question on constitutional and international law asked about the legality of pursuing hostile Indians into Mexico. Foster did very well on the exam, scoring an average of 7.8 out of an 8.8 maximum score.[15]

Foster was then asked to list in order the regiments in which he would most desire to serve. His first three choices were cavalry regiments—the Fifth, Third, Eighth—followed by four selected infantry regiments. With his work before the board completed, Foster returned to Pittsburgh to await the results. On October 13 the war department issued an order listing the candidates who had passed the boards for 1873. Of the twenty-six men who successfully completed the examination process, James Foster received the highest marks. Two days later, he was notified of his appointment and signed his oath of office as a second lieutenant in the U. S. Army (fig 2.4).[16]

The order of the thirteenth stated that his commission by the President was to date from October first and also listed the assignments of the new lieutenants to line army regiments. While six of the junior officers were sent to the cavalry, the remainder went to the infantry. Because there were no available openings in the Fifth Cavalry, Foster was assigned to his second choice, the Third Cavalry. Even though the new lieutenants had been appointed by the President, his action still required the formal advice and consent of the Senate for full confirmation, a formality that would take months. Still, the new officers immediately prepared for active service after they received commission notification from army headquarters.

The twenty-five officers commissioned with Foster proved a typical cross-section of the men who entered the officer corps. Five of the appointees, including Foster, had seen Civil War service. By 1880, two had been dismissed and three resigned from the service. Twenty years of military

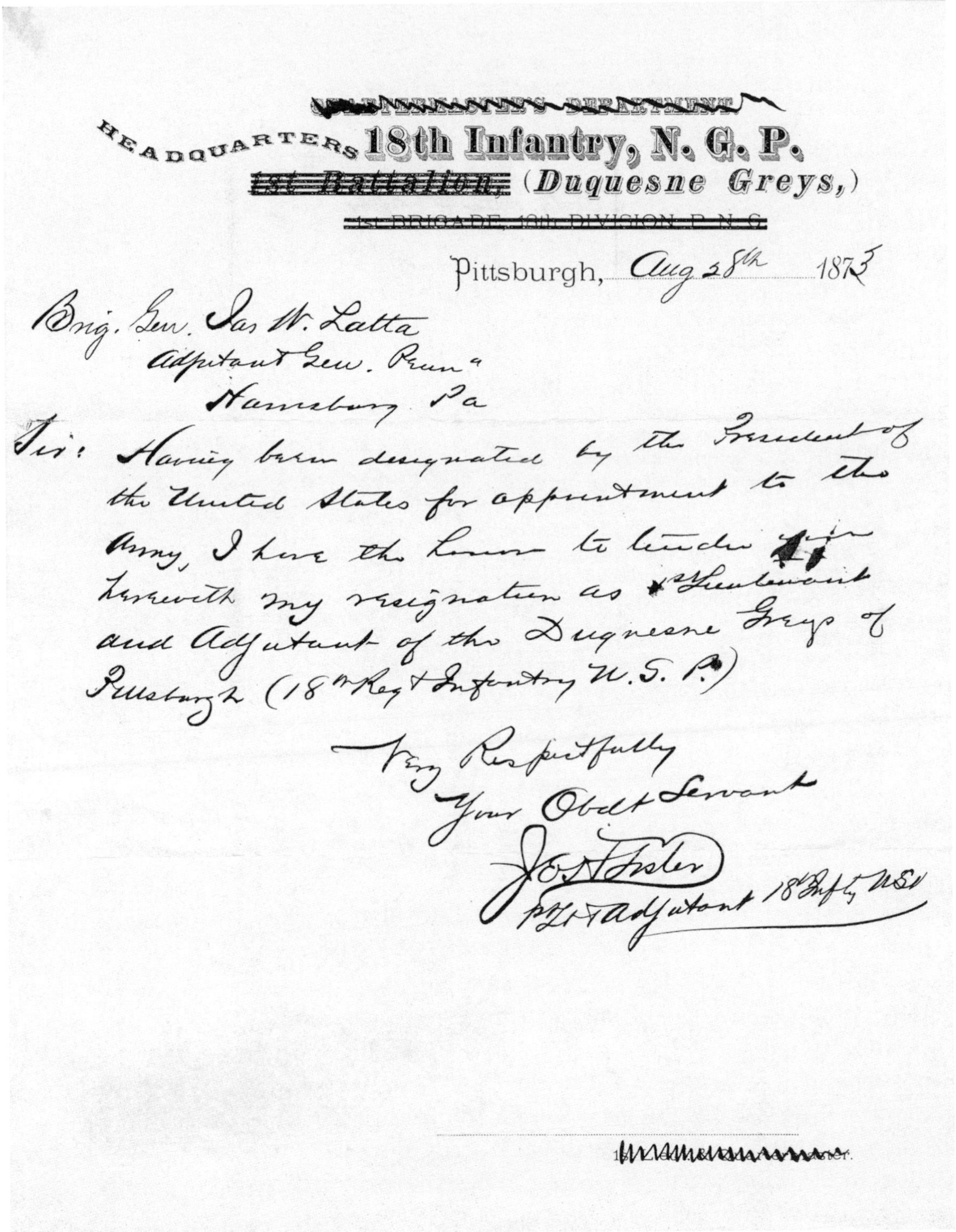

HEADQUARTERS 18th Infantry, N. G. P.
1st Battalion, (Duquesne Greys,)
1st BRIGADE, 19th DIVISION P. N. G.

Pittsburgh, *Aug 28th* 1873

Brig. Gen. Jas W. Latta
Adjutant Gen. Penn^a
Harrisburg Pa

Sir: Having been designated by the President of
the United States for appointment to the
Army, I have the honor to tender
herewith my resignation as 1st Lieutenant
and Adjutant of the Duquesne Greys of
Pittsburgh (18th Reg't Infantry N. G. P.)

Very Respectfully
Your Obdt Servant

Jos. T. Foster
1st Lt & Adjutant 18th Inf'y N.G.P.

FIG. 2.2. Foster's letter of resignation as a commissioned officer and adjutant of the Duquesne Greys. Pennsylvania State Archives

WAR DEPARTMENT, ADJUTANT-GENERAL'S OFFICE, }
WASHINGTON, October 18, 1873. }

LIST of candidates who having passed the required examination, under War Department, General Order of August 1, 1873, have been appointed second lieutenants in the regiments opposite their respective names.

Frank A. Edwards, First Cavalry.
James E. H. Foster, Third Cavalry.
Henry H. Bellas, Fourth Cavalry.
Henry G. Carleton, Eighth Cavalry.
Charles W. Merrett, Ninth Cavalay.
H. J. Gasmann, Tenth Cavalry.
Frederick Thies, Third Infantry.
Frank S. Hinkle, Fifth Infantry.
William H. C. Long, Seventh Infantry.
Fred F. Kislingbury, Eleventh Infantry.
F. Von Schrader, Twelfth Infantry.
W. W. Wotherspoon, Twelfth Infantry.
John H. H. Peshine, Thirteenth Infantry.
G. K. McGunnegle, Fifteenth Infantry.
Theodore Smith, Fifteenth Infantry.
George H. Kinzie, Fifteenth Infantry.
William Lassiter, Sixteenth Infantry.
George H. Roach, Seventeenth Infantry.
Oliver B. Warwick, Eighteenth Infantry.
J. Granville Gates, Twentieth Infantry.
Joseph W. Duncan, Twenty-first Infantry.
George Geddes Smith, Twenty-third Infantry.
Charles H. Heyl, Twenty-third Infantry.
James B. Lockwood, Twenty-third Infantry.
Frank H. Mills, Twenty-fourth Infantry.
James C. Ord, Twenty-fifth Infantry.

FIG. 2.3. Official appointment list of second lieutenants for 1873 published in the *Army and Navy Journal,* October 18, 1873.

service saw further attrition of 1873 appointees. By the turn of the century, eight had died while on active service, three had retired, and in 1899 one was killed in action in the Philippine Insurrection. Nine remained on active duty, providing the army with one colonel, one lieutenant colonel, and seven majors.[17]

The composition of the United States Army in 1873 consisted of five regiments of artillery, ten of cavalry, and twenty-five of infantry, in addition to officers and enlisted men required for the ten bureaus and staff departments that provided necessary support services. At the time Foster became a commissioned officer, the authorized strength of the army was 25,000 enlisted men commanded by an officer corps of 2,150, which included 450 junior lieutenants. After accepting his commission, he prepared to set out on his new career as an officer in the Third United States Cavalry.[18]

The Second and Third cavalry regiments were the two mounted regiments assigned to the Department of the Platte. Under the command of Col. Joseph J. Reynolds, the Third regiment spent the post-Civil War years serving in the southwest in Arizona and New Mexico. In 1871, the Third was transferred for duty in the sprawling Department of the Platte, which consisted of the states of Iowa, Nebraska, Wyoming, and northern Utah. By November 1873, companies of the Third regiment were stationed at Fort McPherson, Sidney Barracks, and North Platte Station in western Nebraska, and at Forts D. A. Russell, Fetterman, and Sanders in Wyoming Territory.[19]

A cavalry regiment was composed of twelve companies (troops), each commanded by a captain, assisted by a first and a second lieutenant. The enlisted component of a company consisted of a first sergeant, five duty sergeants, four corporals, two trumpeters, and fifty or sixty privates, making a total not to exceed seventy-eight men. While the term of enlistment for the regular soldier was five years, an officer was commissioned to serve until eligible for retirement, unless he chose to resign his commission.[20]

As a second lieutenant of cavalry, Foster would receive pay of $1,500 a year, one hundred dollars higher than an infantry lieutenant. The reason for the discrepancy was that mounted officers had to bear the expense of providing their own horses. All soldiers received pay monthly, but department paymasters only made their rounds every two months. Consequently the troops were paid only six times a year. Commissioned officers were also entitled to thirty days of paid leave per year, and received a 10 percent increase in pay for each five years of service completed.[21]

Size of officer living quarters on army posts was allotted by rank. According to regulation, as a junior lieutenant, Foster could expect to have one room for quarters and a kitchen for his living accommodations, with a corresponding allowance of cordwood for heating. Depending on the availability of on post housing, he might also receive more living space. As a cavalry officer he would be issued forage for two private mounts, and because daily rations were not issued to officers, he was allowed to purchase foodstuffs and other supplies from the post commissary on credit and at cost prices.[22]

From 1865 to 1890, the primary purpose of the army was to provide protection to the continuing flow of settlers entering western regions. This meant control of the various Indian tribes who resisted white encroachment, and often resulted in violence. The nature of warfare with Plains tribesmen saw few pitched battles, but rather numerous skirmishes and small combats, coupled with a seemingly ceaseless progression of scouting patrols and fruitless pursuits. Into this oft-time thankless job, frequently criticized by citizens demanding military protection, Foster began his army career.

Officers appointed from civil life were to report to their first duty stations within thirty days of appointment. The business of receiving Senate consent and confirmation could come weeks later. Lieutenant Foster bade farewell to family and friends at Pittsburgh and boarded a train for the long trip to western Nebraska, to join his regiment at Fort McPherson for service on the Plains.

1   *Pittsburgh Dispatch*, May 9, 1883; Letter, A. L. Pearson to William Belknap, Jan. 3, 1873, ACP 1873.

2   Oath of office signed by Foster, Aug. 30, 1870, RG 19, Pennsylvania Army National Guard, Pennsylvania State Archives, Harrisburg, PA (hereafter PANG).

3   George E. Kelly, ed., *Allegheny County: A Sesqui-Centennial Review, 1788–1938* (Pittsburgh: Allegheny County Sesqui-Centennial Committee, 1938), 297; Oath of office signed by Foster, Oct. 24, 1872, PANG.

4   Historical information on the Duquesne Greys is from Martin, *The Twenty-Eighth Division*, 261–66. The Duquesne Greys exist today as the 165th Artillery of the Pennsylvania National Guard.

5   Martin, *The Twenty-Eighth Division*, 266; ANJ, May 19, 1883.

6   Don Rickey, *Forty Miles a Day on Beans and Hay* (Norman, OK: University of Oklahoma Press, 1963), 71–72; Coffman, *The Old Army*, 222.

7   Coffman, *The Old Army*, 222–23.

8   J. S. Negley to Alexander Foster, Dec. 23, 1872, ACP 1873.

9   Pearson to Sec. of War, Jan.3, 1873, "Memorandum of papers in case of 1 Lieut. James E. H. Foster 3rd Cavalry," ACP 1873.

10 James Foster to J. S. Negley, Jan. 17, 1873, ACP 1873.

11 ANJ, Aug. 16, 1873.

12 James Foster to AGO, Aug. 20, 1873, ACP 1873.

13 ANJ, Aug. 16, 1873.

14 Foster to Gen. Latta, Aug. 28, 1873, PANG.

15 "Memorandum of Papers"; Foster's examination paper, ACP 1873.

16 ANJ, Oct. 18, 1873; Foster to AGO, Oct. 15, 1873, ACP 1873.

17 Individual entries from Francis B. Heitman, *Historical Register and Dictionary of the United States Army, Vol. I* (Urbana, IL: University of Illinois Press, 1965).

18 Heitman, *Historical Register, Vol. II*, 610–11.

19 "Returns from Regular Army Cavalry Regiments, Third Cavalry," RG 94 Records of the Adjutant General, NARA.

20 Secretary of War, *Regulations of the Army of the United States and General Orders in Force on the 17th of February, 1881* (Washington, DC: Government Printing Office, 1881), 290.

21 Sec. of War, *Regulations*, 316–17.

22 Sec. of War, *Regulations*, 207, 210, 240.

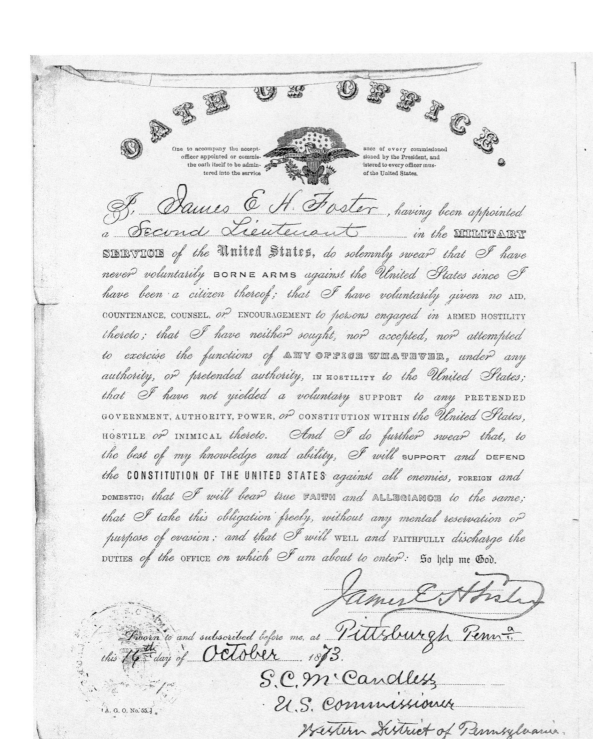

OATH OF OFFICE.

One to accompany the acceptance of every commissioned
officer appointed or commissioned by the President, and
the oath itself to be administered to every officer mustered into the service of the United States.

I, *James E. H. Foster*, having been appointed a *Second Lieutenant* in the **MILITARY SERVICE** of the **United States**, do solemnly swear that I have never voluntarily BORNE ARMS against the United States since I have been a citizen thereof; that I have voluntarily given no AID, COUNTENANCE, COUNSEL, or ENCOURAGEMENT to persons engaged in ARMED HOSTILITY thereto; that I have neither sought, nor accepted, nor attempted to exercise the functions of ANY OFFICE WHATEVER, under any authority, or pretended authority, IN HOSTILITY to the United States; that I have not yielded a voluntary SUPPORT to any PRETENDED GOVERNMENT, AUTHORITY, POWER, or CONSTITUTION WITHIN the United States, HOSTILE or INIMICAL thereto. And I do further swear that, to the best of my knowledge and ability, I will SUPPORT and DEFEND the CONSTITUTION OF THE UNITED STATES against all enemies, FOREIGN and DOMESTIC; that I will bear true FAITH and ALLEGIANCE to the same; that I take this obligation freely, without any mental reservation or purpose of evasion: and that I will WELL and FAITHFULLY discharge the DUTIES of the OFFICE on which I am about to enter: So help me God.

James E H Foster

Sworn to and subscribed before me, at *Pittsburgh Penn* this 16th day of *October* 18*73*.

S. C. McCandless
U.S. Commissioner
Western District of Pennsylvania.

[A. G. O. No. 55.]

FIG. 2.4.

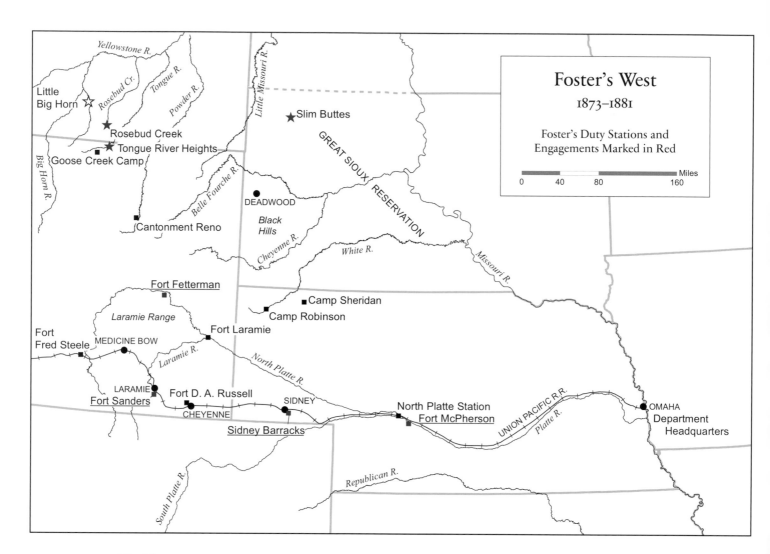

Yellowstone R.

Rosebud Cr.

Tongue R.

Powder R.

Little
Big Horn ☆

Big Horn R.

★ Rosebud Creek
■ ★ Tongue River Heights
Goose Creek Camp

Little Missouri R.

★ Slim Buttes

GREAT SIOUX RESERVATION

Belle Fourche R.

● DEADWOOD

Black
Hills

Cheyenne R.

■ Cantonment Reno

White R.

Missouri R.

Foster's West

1873–1881

Foster's Duty Stations and
Engagements Marked in Red

			Miles
0	40	80	160

Fort Fetterman
■

Laramie Range

■ Camp Sheridan
● Camp Robinson

Fort
Fred Steele   MEDICINE BOW
■   ●

Fort Laramie
■

Laramie R.

North Platte R.

LARAMIE ●
Fort Sanders   Fort D. A. Russell

CHEYENNE

SIDNEY
■
Sidney Barracks

North Platte Station
■ Fort McPherson

UNION PACIFIC R.R.

Platte R.

● OMAHA
Department
Headquarters

South Platte R.

Republican R.

FIG. 3.I.

CHAPTER THREE

First Posting—Fort McPherson, Nebraska

After crossing the Missouri River into Nebraska, Foster traveled west aboard a Union Pacific passenger train for nearly three hundred miles to McPherson Station, located thirteen miles east of North Platte City. Fort McPherson was five miles southeast of the station, across the often turbulent south and north channels of the Platte River. With road ranches and military post on the south side of the river, and the railroad on the north, enterprising locals built wooden bridges to ease the crossing. Fort McPherson was a typical western post, with cedar log and lumber buildings surrounding a parade ground 844 by 560 feet in size (fig. 3.2). The officers' quarters were built on the north side and enlisted barracks along the south. To the rear of the barracks row were cavalry stables, shops and storehouses. The west end was enclosed with a guardhouse and post headquarters building. A large flagpole stood in the middle of the parade.[1]

The post was situated on a short plateau about one-half mile from the river. Behind the building area, there rapidly rose a series of loess hills, spotted with cedar trees and broken by rugged ravines and canyons of drainages that entered the valley from the south. The post was established on September 27, 1863, near Cottonwood Springs, to protect travel on the Overland Road. Regimental headquarters for the Third Cavalry, it housed the regiment's field staff, band, and five companies, which averaged nine officers and 260 enlisted men in garrison.[2]

Immediately after Foster arrived at post, he reported for duty to Colonel Reynolds. He was assigned to Company I, to fill the vacancy created when the company's second lieutenant, Edgar Steever, left on October 1 for two years detached service in Palestine. After this, Foster then went to

Lt. Frederick Schwatka, to receive his housing assignment on officers' row. During the next two days he met the other officers on post, and familiarized himself with his first duty station.[3]

On November 15 he fell into a situation challenging enough to face any rookie cavalry lieutenant. When he arrived at post two days before, Foster was actually the only Company I commissioned officer present. With his company captain and first lieutenant both absent, he soon found himself in command of the company. As the only company officer at post, he was suddenly responsible for command, a role he was expected to accept and perform without question. The troop commander, Capt. James Curtis, had gone on sick leave on October 3. While on leave he was promoted to major in the Tenth Cavalry in May 1875, and left the regiment. He was never at Fort McPherson while Foster was there. The company first lieutenant, Albert D. King, was also absent, in command of a detachment sent out hunting for the garrison. Foster commanded the company until King returned five days later and assumed command. Lieutenant Foster was with Company I for nearly two years before he even saw his company captain. During this time the two subalterns were totally responsible for company administration and command.[4]

For the rest of the month Foster found his place in the daily routine of post and company activities, standing roll calls and retreat ceremonies, supervising stable call and fatigue parties, inspections, drill, and guard duty. Early in December, however, he found a chance for his first field service.

FIG. 3.2. View of Fort McPherson looking north, 1875. The Platte River and the Sandhills are in the background. NSHS RG951-03

With Lakota and Cheyenne bands still roaming the area, detachments from Fort McPherson were regularly sent out on scouting patrols. Although scouting was the main purpose of these details, the troops also had opportunity to hunt game to supplement barracks mess halls. During the winter months, hunting deer and elk actually became the primary mission of those patrols. On December 4, thirty enlisted men of Company F under command of 1st Lt. Alexander D. B. Smead,[5] assisted by 2nd Lt. Bainbridge Reynolds,[6] were ordered to make a routine scout north of Fort McPherson into the Dismal and Loup River country. 1st Lt. John B. Johnson,[7] Third Cavalry regimental adjutant, went along for the ride.[8]

A report filed of a similar scout made in late October informed that the Loup country had recently been devastated by prairie fires, and that signs of recent Indian hunting parties had been observed. The officer in charge of the scout recommended that hay forage be taken along for mounts and transportation animals.[9] Taking that into consideration, Smead's small column included several wagons of long forage. Additionally, Lieutenant Foster was allowed to accompany the patrol to get a taste of winter field service. Eager to prove himself, Foster jumped at the opportunity. Desiring to record his adventures, he took along a standard journal to keep a record of his first field service in the west. In the following transcriptions, Foster's spelling and punctuation have been retained to preserve the flavor of his journal. His story of the "Dismal River Scout" is followed by several shorter sketches, where he described scouts and events observed in the winter and spring months of 1874.

Dismal River Scout

Dec. 4–19 — 1873

DEC. 4

Marched at 11.am with four wagons and thirty men of "F" Co. 1st Lt. A D B Smead comdg—Lt. Jno B Johnson Adjutant 3d Cavalry and 2d Lieut Bainbridge Reynolds 3d Cavalry also accompanied the detachment Wagons moved about an hour ahead of the column as they had to pass the South Platte by Burckes Bridge[10] owing to the condition of the River at the ford. Crossed South Platte with the column Ice just strong enough <u>not</u> to support a horse and Trooper and the result was that the passage of the stream was not unaccompanied with difficulty. Came up with the Wagons at the South end of North Platte Bridge and after they had passed that wonderful example of the ingenuity of man, the Column moved over on foot leading horses.

After crossing the Union Pacific Railway track at McPherson Station[11] we turned to the left and marched until we reached a point midway between Station and North Platte, where we recrossed the railway and went into camp on the bank of the River.

Immediately after establishing our Camp Reynolds and I started off in search of "Food and adventure", he with a Remington Single Barreled Breach Loading Shot Gun and I with a Sharps Carbine. We crossed the North Platte on the ice and after getting on the island Palliday[12] and Johnson who had joined us, left us. Shortly after Reynolds and I became separated soon afterward. As I moved along carelessly, having given up all hope of seeing any game, two White-tail Deer arose about 100 yards in my front—I fired three shots as they ran but without producing any other effect than accelerating the speed of the animals and making a little noise and smoke. Rejoined Reynolds soon after, and neither of us having distinguished ourselves particularly we returned to camp.

At night we all—Johnson, Smead Reynolds, myself and Palliday our Guide Philosopher and friend gathered in one of the wall tents—The weather was growing colder and Palliday confidently predicted a snowstorm apropos of the cold weather. Johnson called up a reminiscence of the past in the shape of a pleasant little fable about a trip that "Buffalo Bill"[13] made from North Platte to the Post one winter night. William started from "The Platte" in a wagon and had wrapped himself up in Buffalo robes and laid himself down in the bottom of the wagon among the straw. Unfortunately for the great guides comfort he had deposited

FIG. 3.3. First page of Foster's journal.

Dismal River Scout
Dec. 4 – 19 – 1873.

Dec. 4 – Marched at 11. AM with four wagons and thirty men of "F" Co. 1st. A & B Snead cavalry – Lt. Jno B Johnson Adjutant 3d Cavalry and 2d Lieut Bainbridge Reynolds 3d Cavalry also accompanied the detachment Wagons moved about an hour ahead of the Column as they had to pass the South Platte by Bundles Bridge owing to the condition of the River at the ford. Crossed South Platte with the Column Ice just strong enough not to support a horse and Troopie and the result was that the passage of the stream was not unaccompanied with difficulty. Came up with the Wagons at the South End of North Platte Bridge and after they had passed that wonderful Example of the ingenuity of man, the Column moved over on foot, leading horses.

his whiskey flask at his feet and it was actually so cold that he could not muster courage to come out from his covering and reach for it and did not take a solitary drink during the 18 mile ride.

The story was recd with a doubting grunt by all hands.

Palliday—in order to give us pleasant anticipation of our trip related how an Officer of the 2d Cavalry with a body of troops was caught in a snow storm in the Sand hills and marched all night in a Circle in his effort to reach the Platte.[14]

DEC. 5TH

Palliday's prediction as to weather proved correct this morning—Cloudy Snowing and blowing—all idea of starting for the South Loup today given up. Kett,[15] our cook, a very old soldier with a very bald head and Tuetonic accent announced "Den ve dont start. Den ve Vant more vood" Ketts "vants" we supplied by sending a party who brought in some cottonwood logs bearing a peculiar likeness to railway ties.

Absorbed all the reading matter in camp except a copy of "Middlemarch"[16] Well have to suffer even more acutely from ennui[17] before I can concentrate myself sufficiently to wade thro its prosy pages

DEC. 6

Still snowing. What shall we do? Johnson is suddenly struck with an idea. Opening his liquor case he removes the parts of newspapers that have been used to wrap around the bottles so as to hold them tight in their places and distributes them among those of us who are of a literary turn of mind. We read the fragments carefully and with much enjoyment.

Johnson, Reynolds and I hold a Council of war and find that We have woefully mis calculated the quantity of "Genuine Pate"[18] necessary for the campaign. Result—Johnson and I conclude to ride to North Platte and replenish. After a ride of 8 miles we reach the Railway bridge over the North Platte, which is covered with Snow and ice—We get over at last—in fact our horses slid over and are soon in the "City". Leave our canteens at Otto Uligs[19] and proceed to the Post—Call on Col. Mills & wife Lt Paul[20] & wife also

When we called at Lt Pauls house little Reunie Paul came to the door and at the same moment Somebody from the head of the stairs called

"Who is there?"

We made no reply and Johnson cautioned Reunie to keep quiet

"What do you want?" came from the head of the stairs, and then

"Do you want to see the Lieutenant?" still we said nothing, but waited events.

FIG. 3.4. The Post of North Platte Station (L to R): guardhouse, storehouse, officers' quarters, duplex officers' quarters occupied by Lt. Paul and family. Union Pacific Railroad Museum

"They are two soldiers" whereupon we laughed, in perhaps an unseemly manner

"And they are <u>Drunk</u>" continued the voice as though addressing someone up stairs Johnson & I started down to Schwatkas quarters laughing so hard at the idea of being taken not only for Common Soldiers but drunken ones at that that we could hardly Keep on the narrow path But it was not much wonder that the mistake was made as we wore nothing about us denoting rank In fact we were dressed for a Scout and officers and men looking very much alike in such occasions — as for as dress is concerned. We had hardly finished relating to Schwatka our little adventure when Paul came rushing in full of apoligies for the occurrance, which we laughed at and told him that we had not the most distant idea of feeling offended

Started back to Camp and night overtook us before we rode half way to our destination — Crossed a trail made by Wolves or Coyotes and succeeded in getting off our own trail which we at last rejoined. Got into Camp at last and Kett dished us up Something warm to re-enforce the inner man

DEC. 7

Storm still continues, and we remain in Camp, which we now call "Dissapointment." Being reduced to a state bordering on desperation I really began to read "Middlemarch" It was a hard fate, but of such is a soldiers life

DEC 8

We rise this morning and see the Sun once more. One wagon with several men who are used up by the Cold weather is sent back to the Post and the balance of our party commence the march at 8:30am pursuing a northerly direction, which after entering the Sandhills is changed a little to the Westward. Halted several times to allow the wagons to come in sight. They were having a hard time of it as the Snow was on the ground in quantities and in some places had drifted until quite deep—The column broke the way as well as possible however. At about noon I was directed to take four men and proceed back on our trail until I found the wagons. Did so and struck them about four miles back. Corporal Berger[21] who was in charge of the Wagon guard reported everything all right except that one of the mules showed signs of giving out. Directed him to throw off as much hay as would enable him to reach camp before sunset and to double the teams at any bad hills. Rejoined the Column about 2 pm. At 4.30 we struck a lake near the head of the South Branch of Loup were we dismounted, unsaddled and prepared for the arrival of the wagons. We had seen immense herds of antelope during the day, but unfortunately they were too timid to approach within range

The weather grew rapidly colder after sunset and the wagons not having arrived we endeavored to keep warm by making fires of dried Sun flower stalks, reeds &c &c. Found that although a good blaze was given but little warmth came from it. Indeed the fire melted the snow and made the feet wet which added still more to our discomfort.

On reaching the lake or pond on the banks of which we Encamped—or hoped to encamp if the wagons came up—we found it to be out of the question to break the thick ice in order to water the horses. All the axes had been left with the wagons, and it was all the more necessary to water as the horses had not drank but little before starting, the weather being so cold. I took my carbine from the boot on my saddle and by firing four shots in the same place drove a hole through the ice, which being enlarged by the knives of a number of the men whom I called made an aperture about as large as a horse-bucket. A number of these were made in the same manner and the horses were soon relieved from their thirst, which they had been trying to overcome by Eating Snow.

Palliday estimates the distance marched by the column today at 34 miles and confesses that we traveled at least 6 miles out of our proper route. As my ride back to the wagons & return to the column was at least 8 miles I estimate the distance traveled by myself at 42 miles. Being the longest days march I have ever yet had.

Finding it impossible to keep warm we concluded to try the expedient that the men had adapted—Tramping up and down on the ice. We found this to work admirably but the moment we halted the cold air would go thro overcoat, 3 woolen shirts clear to the very marrow of the backbone. We had no Thermometer, but the general idea was that the Thermometer must register about 20 or 25 below fahrenheit

The Tramping up and down on the ice was dismal work indeed, but each of us endeavored to scout such an idea by telling all the stories that he knew and singing all the songs that he thought he knew. Stories and songs have an end however and as we marched up and down together in dead silence Reynolds suddenly threw an apple of discord among us by proposing a conundrum—"What shall we name this camp?" three answers followed at once. Then dispute produced heat—caloric was very much needed indeed—but finally ended in adapting Smeads suggestion, which was to call the place Camp Caena, in deference to Dante's wintry hell.[22] Fears were now entertained that the wagons had missed the Trail in the darkness, and in order to guide them to our camp an immense fire was built of Dry Grass, Reeds and Sunflower stalks and a number of volleys were fired from the carbines of a dozen men detailed for that purpose. No answer came to our signals and we concluded that we were in for "a night of it". Palliday joined us some time after this and said that he had gone back two miles and had heard no sounds or seen no signs of the wagons

Things were looking serious. No wood No food and nothing to drink but the water of the Pond which was far from being tasteless—Johnsons moustache had frozen to his beard & Reynolds and Smead had retired within themselves in despair when the quick sharp challenges of a sentry aroused us all to attention. "Who goes there?" "Corporal Berger" A shout went up from the men who had as yet shown no signs of discontent although all of us had been without food since break of day. In a few moments the Corporal reported to Lieut Smead stating that he had left the wagons four miles back—The mules very nearly played out and things in a demoralized condition generally. He had ridden on to find where we were in order to know whether it was possible for the mules to come up with us, heavily laden as they were within half an hour after the arrival of the Corporal we heard the peculiar noise made by wagon wheels as the[y] grind through snow—Joy, no doubt lightens every countenances but it was too dark to see it.

Soon the complainings of that much abused and but little understood animal the government mule was heard in the distance, thus establishing on a firm basis our hopes for relief. We all broke forth in a song of Thanksgiving, adapting the good old doxology beginning "Praise God from whom all blessings flow" and although a majority had not yet experienced what the Preachers call a "change of heart" neither had we been "born again" I really believe that every man of us felt a devout thankfulness when we heard the cheery tones of "Limber Jim"[23] cursing his mules for all, and perhaps more than they were worth.

Jim was a scientific rotary of profanity. He could swear more in the same breath than any living man west of the Missouri and it is fair to presume could beat the world in that line.

"Our Army in Flanders"[24] were innocent sucklings compared to our "Boss" Teamster.

We knew when Jim vociferously consigned the several souls of his six-mule team to the everlasting torment of the Lake that burnith for ever and ever, that James meant business clear up to the handle, and that he would come into camp with ears wagging if not colors flying if it resulted in the complete destruction of that portion of his inner man which at some period after driving contains the food of humanity—In other and more vulgar terms "if he bust a gut"

At 9.45 PM the wagons came in. Fires were at once built. Tents pitched and cooking commenced. At 10.30 we eat our dinner. Having fasted since 7 that morning.

An interview with the "Blue Box"[25] finished the days proceedings and we all turned in, thankful that we had gotten off as well as we had. Reynolds and I occupied one wall tent and Johnson and Smead the other.

DEC. 9

Broke camp and moved at 9 am. Two men found to have had their feet frozen so badly that it was found necessary to send them back to North Platte

Dick Seymour or "Red Dick"[26] joined us at one oclock this morning mounted on an Indian Poney which he had lassoed on his ride from the Platte. He reported one great toe severely frozen. The march today was unattended by any adventure or items of interest. The country passed through was one succession of Sand hills, rising with monotonous regularity one after the other. From a high point they looked like a vast ocean that had been instantaneously paralyzed in the midst of a mighty storm. Nothing more monotonous can be imagined than a march through these Sandhills. No variety of scenery whatever, the eye wearied by dwelling constantly on the snow clad hills. The only variety being when the head of the column went plunging suddenly into a drift breast high

During one of the halts that were made every hour, I heard Sergeant Warfield[27] congratulate himself on the fact that he had "hardtack" in his saddle bag—"Will be trumps tonight! They will be worth just one dollar a piece in Camp, for I'll just give these wagons four upsets before they get to the bottom of that last hill; they're obleeged to do it"

"Well" said another "I don't want a hand in such another game of 'freeze-out' as we had last night" "Freeze out" be it remembered, is a branch of the Great American Game of Draw Poker and is played in this wise. A certain number of "Chips"—usually gunwads—are distributed to each player and then a regular game of Draw Poker begins with one chip ante—the first player "broke" is in the language of the game, "frozen out" and is obliged to pay for such refreshment as the others may order.

At last we caught sight of the Timber that fringes the banks of the Dismal River. Smead Johnson and Palliday had ridden ahead some hours before under the impression that we were much nearer our destination than we really were, and as the Column approached the stream we saw Smead on the north bank of the River, which at this point is about thirty feet wide, four feet deep and very rapid.

From this point a Courier was sent back to the wagons with orders to unload all the grain but barely sufficient for the evenings feed, and for them to push on to camp as rapidly as possible This was about 4.30 pm.

We crossed the river, some of the horses proving somewhat fractious and requiring persuasion in the shape of a lariat hitched to the lower jaw and two or three men pulling at the other end before they could be induced to cross. Poor "Red Dick" had to dismount and wade over while his Poney was dragged across ignominiously by the same means.

I rode on to the point selected for the camp, and found Johnson hard at work adding fuel to an already large fire. We felt absolutely wealthy as we looked at the great plentitude of fuel all around us—Just across the river was a splendid grove of trees, whilst on our side were thickets and trees all around amply sufficient to break the force of the fierce winds that sometimes prevail here and are known by the name of "Nebraska Zephyrs" Becoming very thirsty, I determined to get a drink of fresh water from the [river] and having no cup or similar utensil with me, I unbuckled my canteen from the saddle and proceeded to the river bank. On the way I discovered a Beaver House that rose in a conical form 6 or 7 feet above the marsh in which it was built—It had no means of entrance above water, but the ice was broken in different places all around it showing plainly where its trowel-tailed denizens passed in and out. On reaching the river I found that the ice remained bordering the shore about three feet in width, and by personal experience discovered that it was not strong enough to support me Cutting a sapling about six feet in length & secured the canteen firmly to its end and actually fished up the water in this way—It was splendid water too, and tasted especially good, as I had an immense "Dry" on.

On returning to camp found that the Column had come up, dismounted unsaddled and built fires. Reynolds had been sent back to the ford with a detachment for the purpose of helping the wagons to pass the stream. He found help unnecessary, for at about 8 oclock or after the familiar voice of Limber Jim was heard issuing from the Sand hills on the other side of the river as he brought his team down the steep hill at a run and plunging crossed the water so rapidly that the detachment who had their lariats all ready to pull him over had to run out of his way. The other teams came over without accident although not with Limber Jim's style and dash. No living mule driver that ever swore could hope to equal <u>that</u>.

It was just 8.45 pm when the wagons reached the camp, and being speedily unloaded, tents were pitched and the mysteries of the Cuisine were seen in progress. The Blue Box was brought forth and Johnson, Reynolds and myself each reinforced our almost frozen innards by transferring thereto a certain quantity of the liquid yclept[28] "Genuine Pate"

And here let it be recorded that on the Ninth Day of December, Anno Domini One Thousand Eight hundred and Seventy Three, on the Dismal river in the State of Nebraska at or about the hour of nine o'clock in the night, Mr Smead of the Third United States Horse absolutely, unreservedly and without mental reservation water or Sugar, did take a glass of <u>Gin</u> !!!

None of us fainted, but after an examination of the box we concluded not to encourage him to go any further on that day.

At about ten o'ck we sat down to Dinner and enjoyed it hugely. Palliday had reconnoitered the country below, and informed us that he had discov- a herd of Elk on the river bottom about 3 miles from camp. We turned in with the determination to dine on "Buck-Elk" next day.[29]

DEC. 10
After breakfast Johnson Smead, Palliday and myself together with three of the [enlisted men] started after the Elk, Reynolds preferring to remain in camp.

We struck into the Sand-hills north of the river and after a long detour came in sight of the place where the Elk had been seen the night before only to find that they had had business elsewhere & had evidently gone to attend to it.

Palliday, by some occult reasoning of his own, concluded that they must have moved down stream; so continuing in the hills we moved in that direction, Palliday occasionally examing the country from a hill top with my field glass. At last our patience was rewarded by a sight of the game about three miles away & on the other side of the river.

Again resuming the march, we followed Canons as much as possible, occasionally being compelled to put our horses along the side of frightful looking places where a misstep would infallibly hurl horse and rider hundreds of feet below. But we had no missteps. The horses planted their feet carefully and firmly in the sand—The snow having almost departed—Thus gaining a foothold from which it would have been more difficult to loosen him than it appeared. At last we struck the river some little distance below the Elk, and having crossed it, we moved up stream being completely hidden from the band by intervening hills. Having dismounted we pushed up a very steep hill, from the crest of which we saw the Elk, about 400 yards away—lying down. There were ten of them in all, and all Bucks. Not allowing ourselves to be seen—we were all right as to sent or sound as we "had the wind on them"—we made a circuit and approached under cover within 150 yards.

"Get ready!" said Palliday

We crawled to the crest of the hill, and kneeling so as to just expose enough of the head to aim at the prey, we each of us—I know I did—shook a little and awaited the Signal.

"Now!!" said Palliday

"Ban—n—n—g!!!" Said we. Up leaped the Elk—leaving one of their number dead on the field

"Bang! Bang! Bang!" went the carbines, whilst the Bucks stood bewildered for a moment and then tossing their immense antlers in the air started at a gallop away from us. Three of them we could see were wounded, one of them left the balance of the band and started down the hill on three legs in the direction of the river .

We gave chase at once, and began to fire at him whilst he was yet in the marsh that bordered the river, but our nerves being shaken perhaps by the sharp run we had just had, none of hit him. Gaining the river the noble animal plunged in and struck out gallantly for the other shore whilst all the while the bullets fairly churned the water around him. He

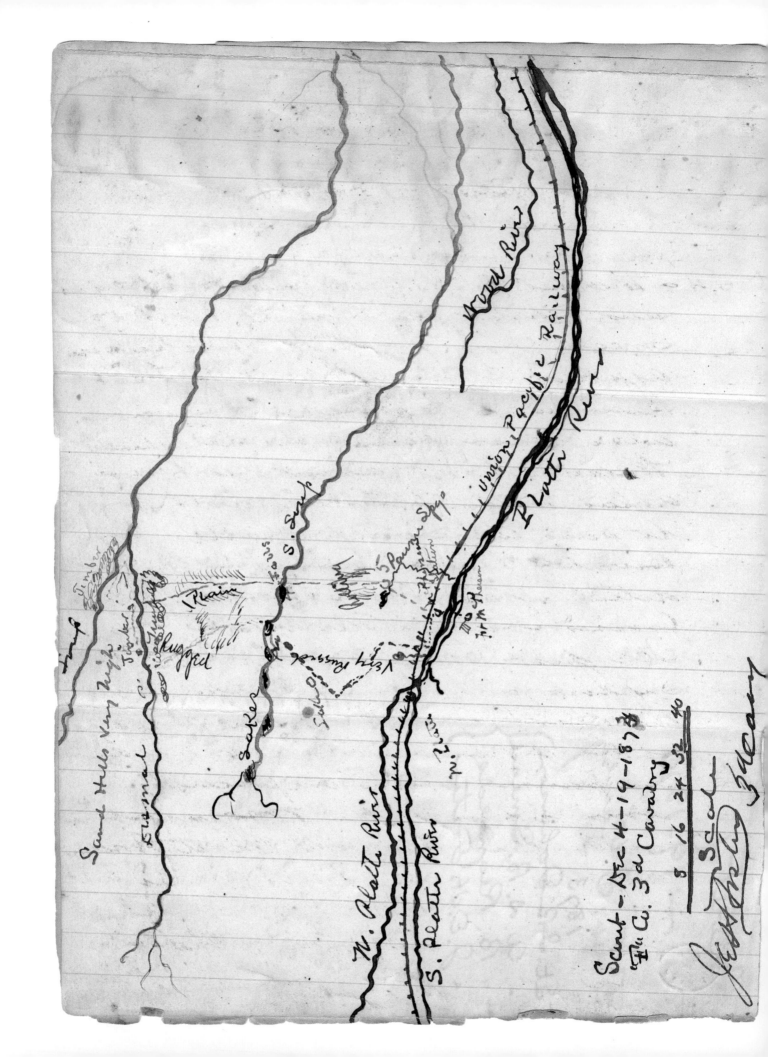

was upwards of 300 yards away, but just as he was coming out a ball struck him in the back. He stopped, and then with one mighty effort, was high and dry on the shore. Another shot hit him when he sank on his knees but again regaining his feet was making for the bushes when I sent a bullet through his neck about two inches back of the ear and on line with them. That shot settled the matter—He dropped and never kicked again.

Our horses having been brought up, we all mounted and away we went after the main body. And just here the fun came in. The first half mile was up a Canon in which fell our third Elk, a victim to the prowess of Mr Smead, who kept sending lead into that animal and asking us not to shoot with a persistency truly admirable. Leaving Smead to finish the bloody deed in which he had become interested Johnson, myself & the men pushed on—Palliday having gone ahead—About a mile or two farther on we found Palliday in a canon standing beside the body of an Elk. His horse was dead lame, and all our horses were covered with foam We had had an exciting ride if galloping down hills that ordinarily would be descended very carefully at a walk, and coming suddenly upon deep fissures and leaping them as you rode, can be described as exciting. I know that I never had so much real enjoyment crowded into so short a time as I had from the time we pulled trigger on the Elk until we came up with Palliday on the run.

It was concluded after mature consideration that this Elk should be cut up on the spot and packed into camp on our saddles, which was accordingly done, Palliday dissecting the subject. Reaching camp a little after 4 o'ck I procured a fresh horse (Sergeant Hacketts)[30] and with two fresh men started to find the other three Elk in order that they might be disemboweled so that the Coyotes would let them alone and the meat remain in good order until next day Johnson could send for them.

A peculiarity about Elk meat is worth noting: Of all animals their flesh will spoil the quickest and unless disemboweled promptly it is said they will be utterly unfit to eat after being killed 12 hours, even during the coldest weather. The reason given for this is that the heat of the entrails being retained within the body brings on mortification inwardly.

Being desirous of getting through as soon as possible I endeavored to strike the Elk that I had killed by going in a direct a line as possible. The result was that we had to pass some frightful places, much worse than any we had seen earlier in the day.

The Elk was somewhat farther down the river than was anticipated, and it was about dusk before we reached him. Found that he had in his last struggles rolled partly into the water, and had a great deal of trouble

FIG. 3.5.

getting him out. He was a very large splendid looking animal with fine antlers — The head & antlers I then and there determined to save and present to the Duquesne Greys.

Leaving Elk No. 1 after it was quite dark we pushed on down the river to find a crossing. Found a place where I determined to try it and knowing that Quick sands prevailed in the streams in Nebraska, ordered the men to remain on the bank until I had crossed and if anything serious occurred to throw me a lariat. I then urged the horse in, the swift current forcing him a little down stream. When I came within a short distance down he went into a hole. He came out of it as suddenly as though a case of Nitro Glycerin had been exploded under him Another bound carried us safely on the bank. I ordered the men to cross one at a time, and directing them to come out of the stream below where I did, they both got over without accident.

We managed to get on the Trail at last, but found afterwards that we had struck it beyond the point where the first Elk was killed. This lead us to suppose when we found the Elk killed by Smead that it was the one killed by Johnson at the first fire — an error that came very nearly compelling us to spend the night in the Sand hills. Acting under our misapprehension, we followed the Trail on into the hills, until it diverted and finally we lost it entirely. I was now certain that a blunder had been made and determined to get back to the Elk just butchered. This however was much easier said than done, for I found that we were undoubtedly <u>lost</u> <u>in</u> <u>the</u> <u>Sand</u> <u>hills</u>. The bare idea of such a fate on such a night was sufficient to unhinge most men, and especially was this the case now, for heavy clouds were massing on the horizon and a snow storm appeared to be eminent. The trip had appeared to be such a simple task that no compass had been brought with us. I pushed back on the direction we had come as near as I could judge. The wind was rising slightly when I detected a peculiar oder in the air. I recognized it at once as the peculiar perfume arising from Elk meat, and following it about two hundred yards found the carcass of the Buck that had been disemboweled last. Again we searched for the missing Elk, until Lynch[31] the butcher of "F" Company assuring me that the meat would not spoil on so cold a might and seeing that <u>clouds</u> were growing more and more threatening every moment I determined to push for camp as I knew we had a ride of ten or twelve miles before us. When we reached the Elk I happened to recollect a remark that somebody in our party had made to the effect that the dipper at this season lay directly north and looking for it, soon found that heavenly utensil with its handle pointing at a planet that shone "like a diamond in the sky" and which I concluded was the North Star; an institution gotten up expressly for the purpose of guiding lost folks out of the Wilderness. I turned our direction to the westward, keeping the dipper on my route and started for camp. I knew that if I kept this direction long enough I would most certainly strike the trail made by us when returning from where Palliday had killed the Elk. A Bee line is one of the most difficult thinks [things] in the world to pursue in the Sand hills; Many a time I just checked my horse in time to save him from going plunging over a precipice, whilst at others he would go sliding down a Steep hill "on his hunkers" as we used to say.

About half a hour before we come on the trail I overheard one of the men say to the other in a lugubrious Tone not intended for me to hear, "Wall we're in for it!"

"Yes" said the other "Gone up."

I smiled all to myself, and when we struck the trail broke into a trot which brought us safely to Camp in due time. Tonight I tasted for the first time, the flesh of the Elk. I confess I was dissapointed . It was tough and by no means agreeable to the taste. The fun in going after Elk, I concluded, was <u>all</u> in the hunting & killing.

DEC 12

We had had glory enough for one day yesterday, but another had dawned upon us. Again we sallied forth in search of the bounding Bucks. This time going up stream, as the six Elk that escaped us yesterday had taken that direction. Plenty of deer appeared but they were treated with a lofty contempt only to be attempted by the mightiest of hunters. <u>We</u> were after <u>Elk</u> and Elk we <u>would</u> have. We didn't want any contemptible white tails in ours! Oh no! Besides a single shot fired at a deer would alarm the vast bands of Elk that were supposed to be feeding in the vicinity. For this reason we let a fine specimen of the Lynx which came along on the other side of the river, go free and unmolested. We rode about 12 miles up the river and did not see even the track of an Elk. A change of tactics was demanded by the occasion, and it was agreed that now we <u>would </u>shoot deer. But the deer found it out somehow and refused to come out and be shot with wonderful perversity.

At last we raised one. He ran out and stopped just on the brow of a Sandhill. I dismounted as quick as possible but before I could get the carbine on him he had started home. I fired but the bullet arrived an instant too late. Just clipping the dust where he had been a moment before.

Remembering that there is more joy in camp over one deer brought in than forty and five that escape, we kept a sharp look out for venison on the hoof.

An hour after I missed the buck we started up quite a drove of Black-tails but they had too much transportation for us, and got away. As they ran off in the direction of our camp we concluded that they were going there in order to save us the trouble of packing them in on our saddles, but through some cause or other, perhaps their ignorance in leaving the trail, they failed to reach their destination.

On arriving in Camp we found that Red Dick had killed a deer and that Elk that we did not find last night had spoiled

DEC 12

Remain in camp today, concluding that a little rest would be about the thing. Sergeants Warfield and Keech[32] each take out a party and each succeed in killing a deer.

We have called this Camp Paradise on account of the vast degree of enjoyment found here as compared to our camp on the South Loup.

DEC 13

Broke camp at 9. am and marched 10 miles down the river to "Camp Boss" so named because it is the "Boss" camp as got struck. Column arrived at 11 o'clock, wagons half an hour later. We found the march easier than we had expected, as we followed canons almost all the way thus avoiding the hills.

This is the place where the Earl of Dunraven[33] and Lord Parker encamped. We found a govt Picket rope, old wagon tongue and Log chain that had evidently been left by the Dunraven party These articles were seized in the name of the United States in part liquidation of the Consequential damages. On the way down Smead and I left the column for a hunt. Saw plenty of prairie chickens but having no fowling pieces, they went their way unmolested. Saw one deer. Reynolds reported 12 in sight of the column

Had Beaver-tail soup today at dinner. It is one of the luxuries of life.

DEC.14.

In camp. Weather beautiful today and fires found superfluous.

DEC.15.

Marched 45 miles today. Left Camp at 7.45 am. Struck north by northeast until we reached the main Loup about 7 miles above the mouth of the Dismal—Proceeded down the Loup to mouth of Dismal and then up the Dismal to Camp. Marched very rapidly and only halted for water once. Reached camp at 5.05 pm My horse came in prancing.

DEC 16

In camp <u>just</u> a little used up from yesterday's ride. The "Little Trumpeter" Waldering,[34] and Corporal Bessie both see the same herd of quadrapeds. Bessie says they are Elk, which L.T. reports that he saw them quite near and that they are deer.

Private Rowe[35] killed a fine black tail Buck today about a mile from camp and brought him in on his shoulders

Party went out this after noon to investigate the query, Deer or Elk? raised by the Corporal and the Small Trumpeter. They found the trail to be that made by Elk, and follow it 12 miles south of the river, where finding that the Elk were going directly for the South Loup they gave it up and returned to Camp.

DEC 17.

Marched to the Falls of the Loup[36] — 24 miles — today. Hills not so high on This route as on the upper one — There is also a level plain of about 10 miles in extent to be passed over The grass was all burned off and the country presented a very dreary aspect indeed

DEC 18

Left Loup Falls — 18 inches high — at 7.30 A.M. marched 30 miles to Pawnee Creek,[37] arriving at 3. P.M. When within about 5 miles of Pawnee Creek, Palliday who was fully a mile in advance of the Column sighted a drove of Antelope. On leaving the Column he thought he <u>might</u> possibly see game and took with him Springfield Rifle, but concluding after all that it was doubtful he did not take any ammunition. The only means he had of getting any of the herd was in the four loads left in his revolver. With these he succeeded in wounding 3 of the animals, one of which ran toward the Column and laid down about 400 yards from its right flank.

Corporal Freeland[38] with two men left the column to dispatch & bring in the game and I followed to see the fun. When we approached within about 50 yards it arose suddenly and away it went at a pace that was surprising. The Corporal and myself started in hot pursuit, giving our horses their heads and using the spur. I lost sight of the pursued whilst endeavoring to free my pistol from its holster, and the Corporal lost sight of it in putting a charge in his carbine — I thought the Corporal had the beast in sight and the Corporal thought the very same thing of me We had ridden neck-and-neck for almost two miles at a dead run when I called to the Corporal

"Do you see him yet?"

"No Sir!"

I pulled up as did also the Corporal "Where did you lose sight of him?"
"Away back Sir, while I was loading my carbine."

I appreciated the perfectly ridiculous position of affairs then, but still more when I returned to the Column and found that while we were charging our fire-arms the Antelope and turned to the right out of our course. Palliday saw it, and having no ammunition ran it down, dismounted and cut its throat with his hunting knife.

On reaching Pawnee Springs[39] Johnson and Palliday left us and rode into the Post, whilst we went into camp on the North side of the creek, the south side being burned off

DEC.19.

Left Pawnee Creek at 8.am And reached the Post at 10.30. It felt <u>good</u> to get back, and I experienced the same sensations as those felt on returning home (the one in Pennsylvania) after a long absence.

I had made my first trip, killed an Elk and ridden 291 miles; besides learning a great many things that will be of use to me hereafter

* * *

For the next two months, Foster remained with his company at post performing regular garrison duty; evidently nothing of interest occurred to be written down. In February, Foster again took up his journal, briefly noting detached service to the North Platte subpost. While there, he watched enviously as other troop units passed through on the railroad, to join the major expedition massing at Fort D. A. Russell to march on the northern Nebraska agencies. With their purpose to restore order and provide protection to the agencies, two new army posts, Camps Sheridan and Robinson, were established.

In the last of March, Foster recorded an intriguing episode of the darker side of military life: the probable homicide of one soldier by two companions.

1874

FEBY 11

On returning from retreat roll-call this evening, met King,[40] who confirmed that Mills had been ordered to march for Ogallala tomorrow morning early, owing to reports of hostile Indians in that vicinity, and that we were to take Post at North Platte[41] and await his return, or join him if necessary

Marched to North Platte with sixty men. Lt King commanding

Mix's and Spaulding's[42] companies of the 2d Cavalry arrived and disembarked to feed and rest their horses. They are enroute to Cheyenne to join the Sioux Expedition[43] Gregg, Peale, Ceale, La Point and Dr Tower[44] are with them

Meinhold[45] passed up yesterday enroute to the same point

Mills returned about noon and we returned to Fort McPherson

Accompanied Paymaster Simon Smith[46] to North Platte "by request" His request. Left Post 9.45 P.M. Escort 6 men of "M" Company accompanied us Overtook two or three parties of men evidently on the way to Oumets or Boyers to get rid of the pay drawn today

Found the Chief Paymaster of the Department of the Platte a very pleasant old gentleman—Saw him safely on board the Western bound train, with his greenbacks, & then "turned in" at Browns hotel

Mch 27 Returned from North Platte accompanied by Schwatka

WAS IT A MURDER?

On the morning of March 27 1874 the body of Trumpeter Maellie[47] "I" Company 3d Cavalry was found about midway between Fred Oumets Saloon and Boyers Store—west of Fort McPherson Nebraska—near the arroyo at the head of Burkes Slough and between the road and old John Burks grave.[48]

When found the body was stripped to the waist, the removed clothing being found under and around it. The ground near by bore evident marks of a struggle and two buttons were found which had been torn from the overcoat of deceased.

A post-mortem was held by Dr Flint[49]—who stated to me after the Corners Inquest, that he would have made a more thorough examination if he had known that there was to be an inquest.—which resulted in absolutely nothing. Scratches, evidently made by the deceased himself—were found on the breast, and abrasions on the elbow; but no mark internal or external sufficient to cause death

The following facts chiefly elicited after the Inquest may be of interest:

1st Phillip Socier,[50] a clerk at Boyers Store states that Maellie was there on the night of the 26th and left a little after nine ock in company with Privates Agett[51] and Gray[52] both of I Company.

2ᵈ Just before leaving Maellie was sober enough to lie down on his back, place a glass of whiskey on his fore-head & rise up with it without spilling a drop.

3ᵈ Deceased had "some words" with Gray and Agett who desired to maltreat a man who was too drunk to take care of himself

4ᵗʰ Lt King interrogated Agett and Gray as to whether they had been with Meallie on the night in question—They denied seeing him after leaving Boyers. Both men were confined but released after the Corners Jury had rendered a verdict of "Cause of death unknown. They were subsequently re-arrested on charges preferred by Lt King based on information gotten after the Inquest.

5ᵗʰ Private Frank Mooney[53] of "I" Co. was on Post at the guard house on the morning of the re-arrest. After being relieved he was in the main room of the Guard-house when Agett said "What am I confined for?"

"Don't you know?" said Mooney, "You are in for murder."

"Hell" said Agett "Fred Oumet must have 'tumbled to it'" meaning told all about it.

6ᵗʰ Fred.Oumet, keeper of a low saloon just west of the reservation line, states that about 9.30 on the night of the 26ᵗʰ of March he heard sounds as though of quarreling between his ranche and Boyers and distinguished the words "Don't hurt me" "go for him" "Damn him, throw him in the Ditch." These sounds came from about the spot where the body was subsequently found

7ᵗʰ Agett and Gray came to Oumets a few minutes afterward. Agett was bleeding at the ear and Gray was scratched on the face

8ᵗʰ Deceased recd an express package by way of North Platte the day before his death. Not known what it contained

9ᵗʰ Before Guardmount[54] on the morning of March 27ᵗʰ Gray sent a Postal money order for $25.00 East and expressed a desire to the P.O. Clerk (Mr Feay) that nothing should be
said about it.

10ᵗʰ Both of the prisoners possess villainous countenances and bad reputations. They have been in the company long before this affair occurred.

At this date (April 19) this is as far as Is known about the affair. Tomorrow the General Court Martial will convene to try them, the charge being "Conduct prejudicial to good order & military discipline in violation of the 99ᵗʰ Article of war"
Specifications: "Absence from quarters Without authority," and, "Engaging in a fight which resulted in the death of Trumpeter Meallie."

JUNE 8

Agett sentenced this evening at Undress Parade[55]

"To forfit to the United States all pay and allowances now due or which may hereafter become due, and undergo confinement in a Penitentiary to be designated by the proper authority for two years"

Madison Penitentiary designated

JUNE 9TH 1874.

Am Officer of the day. Recd orders to release Agett in pursuance to a War Department order which directs his release and discharge[56]

* * *

In the next section of his journal, Foster records a quick raid where horses were run off a ranch east of Fort McPherson. At that moment he was with the company at weekly target practice scoring hits. During the 1870s soldiers were allowed to fire only ten practice rounds per month: two shots one week, three the next, then two, then three, to total ten shots in all. In an attempt to pursue the raiders, Company F rode east to see if they traveled to cross the Platte River. Company I quickly moved south then east across the canyons entering from the south to check if the trail went in that direction. The soldier pursuit was unsuccessful, as happened more times than not. Fortunately, in this case the horses returned on their own.

THE FIRST JUMP OF '74

On the 3d April about noon, news was bro't by Erickson[57]—a rancheman living west of the Post—that the Indians had "Jumped" the horses at Jesters[58] ranche about 4 miles from here, and had struck south with them, into the Sand-hills.

We had just finished Target practice at the time and 1st Sergt Allen,[59] Company Clerk Bahr[60] and myself were examining the 300 yard target. As soon as the news reached us we ran in and soon the Company were mounted and marching up Cottonwood Canon whilst (F) Moores[61] company marched to Jesters in order to strike the trail and follow it. At 12.10 P.M. we moved out Cottonwood Canon, diverging to the left up a branch canon about two miles from the Post and taking a south-easterly direction. Continuing until 6 miles from the Post we moved Eastward crossing Snells and Conroys Canons and finally reaching Gillmores[62] by which route we again reached the Platte Valley

We reached Ericksons ranche about sundown and halted to water at a hole between the ranche and the river. This hole we soon found was about 20 feet deep & about thirty yards across each way. I had watered my horse as had also most of the men when a soldier named Slickert[63] got off his horse into the deepest part and not knowing how to manage him under such circumstances pulled on the reins which brought the animals nose under water. The horse after struggling fearfully freed himself from his rider and got ashore whilst poor Stickert encumbered as he was with a Carbine, Cartridge belt overcoat &c &c was just keeping above water and shouting for help. The men appeared paralyzed for the moment and I determined to make an effort to save the man although I had never swam a horse in my life.

I spurred Diamond off the bank into the water and had him swimming gallantly for the drowning man, when he became frightened at Stickert (who was throwing his arms about wildly in his efforts to save himself) and turned toward the shore on the right. I attempted to turn him again but this only resulted in putting his nose under water and knowing that my only safety lay in my horse as I had on a heavy overcoat boots & revolver. I let him have his own way. After two efforts he got out on the bank—which was very steep at this place—& King and myself had just gotten off our arms & coats & were pulling our boots with the intention of making a final attempt when Private W Chymann, the bunkmate[64] of Stickert plunged in and caught the cape of his overcoat just as he was making a final go of it and brought him safely to shore, where he was duly brought back to life.

a short time afterward we were in the Post and found that two hours after we had left the horses had returned lead my [by] Standing Bull, a fine stallion once owned and ridden by Buffalo Bill. The Indians finding that they were likely to be intercepted had abandoned their plunder and next morning are said to have recrossed the Platte River.

started 12.10

returned 7.45 distance 30 miles

* * *

In early April the War Department issued General Orders No. 27, announcing its bi-annual list of army promotions and appointments. Six months earlier Foster had been appointed by the President as a second lieutenant, pending confirmation in the Senate. While he was out chasing Elk on the Dismal, the process of Senatorial approval was underway. As required by law, all presidential appointments, including postmasters, district judges, collectors of customs, and army officers, were brought on a steady basis before the Senate for its proforma approval. On December 10, the list of

FIG. 3.6. Although this map was drawn by his company clerk and was not his own creation, Foster inserted it in his journal.

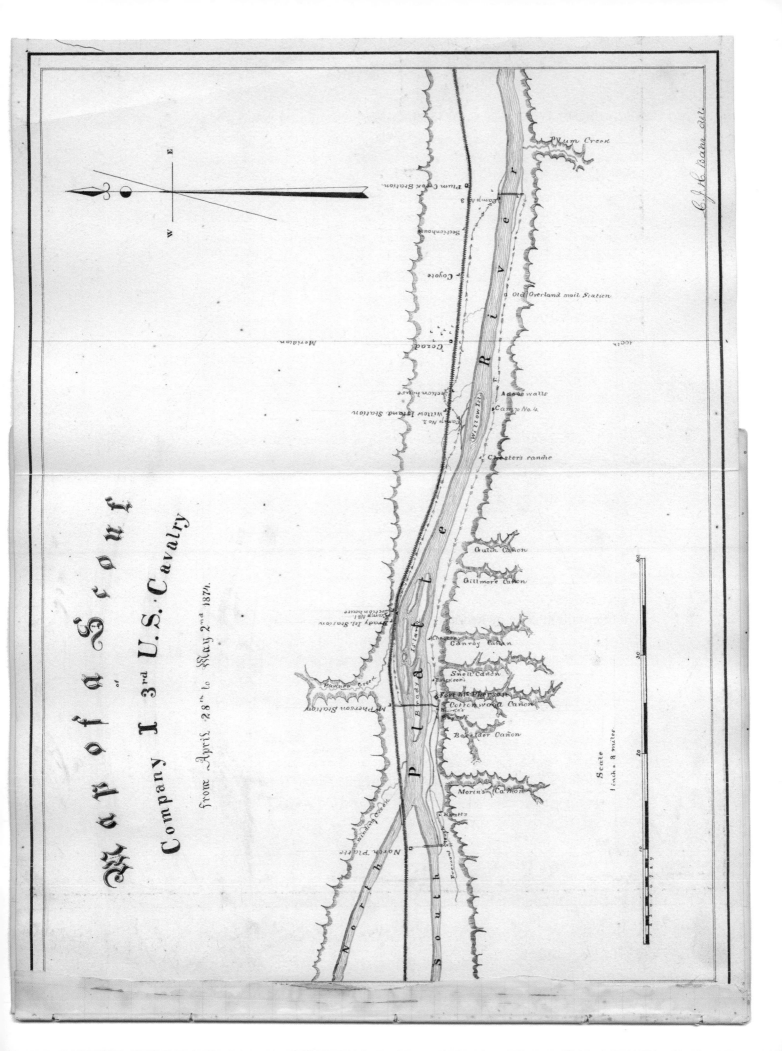

Map of a Scout
of
Company I 3rd U.S. Cavalry
from April 28th to May 2nd 1874.

Scale
1 inch = 8 miles

twenty-six new lieutenants, Foster included, appeared and was referred to the Committee on Military Affairs for review. The committee rubber-stamped its endorsement, and passed the names back before the Senate, which, on December 19, agreed to, and gave its full advice and consent to Grant's appointments for commissions. Orders 27, dated April 1, 1874, announced that Foster was a second lieutenant to date from October 1, 1873. The last formality completed, he was officially an officer in the United States Army.[65]

On April 28, Foster's company was ordered out to hunt for an Indian band reported to have committed depredations in the vicinity of Brady Island Station. Hoping to find and then follow their trail, Company I searched north of the Union Pacific tracks down river for fifty miles. Foster expresses the typical frustration of officers leading men on hard scouts based on false rumor. After finding no signs of the purported raiding party, the weary command returned to post. In this entry, Foster records interesting comments regarding soldiers, events, including the recovery of a badly-mired wagon, and local landmarks passed in the course of the four-day scout (fig 3.6).[66]

PLUM CREEK SCOUT
April 28 — May 2 1874
1st Lt. A. D. King 3rd Cavalry
2d " J. E. H. Foster 3rd Cavalry
47 Enlisted Men 3rd Cavalry
3 Wagons
Distance Traveled — 118 miles
<u>April 28</u>

Lt King left the Post at 11.30 am with a portion of the Command, leaving orders for me to follow him with the wagons & 18 men and join him at or near Brady's Island Station[67] where he was leave written instructions for me

Left Post at 12.15 P.M. McHugh[68] who at the beginning of the late War was 1st Sergeant of the Comp'y & marched it out of the rebel lines when the Company Officers went over to the Confederacy, was so drunk that I was compelled to dismount him and put him in one of the wagons. An old soldier can do some things with comparative im-punity that another would be punished for with promptness and severity.

In crossing Burks Bridge over South Platte one of the mules broke thro' and for a moment things looked a little serious. The beast was gotten out all right, however, and the column moved on.[69]

Went on to McPherson Station. The Agent there had heard no news about Indians. Crossed Railway track & moved down north side—Had a little trouble in crossing Pawnee Creek which at the point of passage is a miry ditch. Reaching Brady Island Station Recd the following note from King:

Union Pacific R.R. Company
Agents Office
Brady Station April 28 1874
Lieut. Foster:
     The trail bears S.E. from this point. Keep this side of the River with the wagons until you catch me. In all probability I will camp a short distance East of this station on this side of the River
     A. D. King
     1st Lt 3d

Crossed to South side of the Railway & pushed on. Saw "Men in the hills" & on examination found them to be Lt. King & Bahr the Company Clerk and "Shorty" Pushed on as directed and soon came up with the Troop when Sergt Allen informed me that a trail had been found & that the Lieutenant had got the stick & white rag mentioned in Hendersens (the station agent Brady's) letter.

King soon joined us and after moving a little further we went into Camp. King & "Shorty" both agree that the pony trail is old with the exception of a few fresh marks. As to the solitary Moccasin track how easy a matter is it for a white man to draw his boot & make a first rate one with his stocking feet. King is of the opinion that the whole story about Indians being here is a deliberate lie gotten up by the R. R. agent We afterwards learned that this scoundrel had cattle toward the South Loup & was afraid to go after them although herders had lived there in absolute safety all winter & hadn't seen even the sign of an Indian.

APRIL 29
Broke Camp at 7.30. King "Shorty" & two men left column & went into the hills to try and see an Antelope.

Struck a bad slough (Pro. Slue) & every thing got over excepting the Rear wagon—The driver pulled out of the track followed by the others & stuck fast—his mules sinking into the mud up to their bellies. Seeing the trouble, rode back & had the mules taken out. Then got the Picket line, doubled it & attached one end to the Wagon Pole & the other to 8 mules—The Rope parted. Then had every thing taken out of the mired wagon and the Line attached to the hind axle—the wagon being much nearer the west side of the Bog—and succeeded in restoring it to Terra ferma—The mules were now placed in their proper position and being incited by the liberal application of three Blacksnake whips "made the riffle" at a run. The wagon was unloaded & Lieut King rejoining us it was decided to go into camp about 2 miles further on.

APRIL 30

100 in the Shade! Passed through the Great Growing City of Cozad[70] which consists now of 17 and ¾ houses and all brand new—Their Hotel Building is really one of the best looking structures that I have seen west of Omaha—The town is not much more than six weeks old and bids fair to amount to Something, as its founder is very wealthy & famous as a builder up of cities The greatest institution that they have in the town is the 100th Meridian—They have a hugh sign board announcing that astonishing fact planted in a prominent position.[71]

Went into Camp at the North End of the Plum Creek Bridge over the Platte river[72]

So far we have not seen a solitary man woman or child who knows any thing about Indians being in the country except this fellow Henderson It is a pity that we cannot tie the fellow up for a few hours just to teach him that it is a serious matter to spread false alarms of this nature.

This being the last day of the month the Company was mustered.[73]

MAY 1ST

Marched 2 miles West of Adobe Walls—which same are the Ruins of an old Overland Stage Station[74] Frightfully Hot and no breeze stirring we suffer much more than yesterday. A mule played out today. Wind blew our tent down tonight

MAY 2ND

Marched into the Post today Raining and cold. Thermometer at the Post registering 45° above—Got in about 4 o'ck Cold & wet.

* * *

Between detached services in the field, Foster assisted Lieutenant King with regular company duties. In addition, commissioned officers were usually required to perform other duties necessary for supply and operation of the post. In June he was appointed to serve as post quartermaster (AAQM) and commissary officer (ACS). In this combined position, he

FIG. 3.7

North Platte

North Platte

U.P. R R

South Platte

North Platte

41 Parallel

Map of a Scout
detachment of
"M" Co 3d Cavalry
May 26 - June 6th 1874
J. Ed Foster
2d Lt. 3d Cav.

Scale
6 Miles = 1 inch

Eagles nest

5th pm Camp

Medicine Creek

South Medicine Creek

Strawberry Butte

4th Camp
3d Camp

Red Willow

Stinking Water

Whitemans

Crazy Woman
Red Camp

Meridian

Blacks Wood Cr.

Beaver Cr.

Red Willow Cr.

Frenchmans Fork

Red Willow

Republican River

69

became responsible for equipment, clothing, forage, transportation, fuel, buildings and provisions needed at the post. The job of post AAQM & ACS was demanding and time consuming but necessary, and it provided good training for junior officers, who frequently received the assignment.[75]

Several weeks later Foster had an opportunity to familiarize himself with the country south of the Platte. On May 25, he rode to the Post of North Platte Station to join a small detachment commanded by Lieutenant Schwatka, sent out to scout the country to the small settlement of Red Willow on the Republican River. Ten days and 398 miles later, the detachment returned and reported no roaming Indian bands sighted. The next day Foster returned to Fort McPherson. Although he did not write about all his scouts in the journal, he did record it in another way. After Foster returned from scouts, he began to draw detailed maps that included the line of march, campsites, and physical features. Collectively, his maps recorded information, possibly for future reference, that also demonstrated his improving skills as a topographer.[76]

An incident in the summer of 1874 brought major excitement to the North Platte vicinity. In mid-July, thousands of buffalo suddenly "charged down from the hills and canons [canyons] and filled all the Platte Valley."[77] For several days the herd, variously estimated from ten to fifty thousand animals in size, grazed on the south side of the river near North Platte. Many local citizens and soldiers took advantage of the situation and went out to hunt; Foster was undoubtedly among them. The heading on an otherwise blank page of the journal after the Plum Creek scout simply states "My First Buffalo Hunt." Unfortunately he did not describe this adventure.

That summer, war with the southern tribes broke out in Kansas, Oklahoma, and the Panhandle of Texas. Disillusioned with reservation life, Cheyenne, Comanche, and Kiowa tribesmen began a series of raids and attacks on white settlers. Although subsequent field operations involved troops from the Department of Missouri, Foster's company was ordered to take station at Grinnell, Kansas, positioned to guard along the Kansas & Pacific Railroad. On July 31 Lieutenant King and the troop left the post, but Foster did not ride with them.[78]

With two of its companies absent on expedition into Wyoming, and one sent to Kansas, only three officers were left on duty at Fort McPherson. Instead of the potential excitement of field duty, Foster, also recently assigned as acting post adjutant, had to remain behind to assist with post administration. With a depleted number of garrison officers available, those left at post could find themselves encumbered with additional duties. In August Foster was relieved as acting adjutant, but continued as

FIG. 3.8 Map, scout of Sept. 12–20, 1873

Scout
"K" Company 3ᴰ Cavalry
Sept 12 – 20th 1874
289 miles

Left Ft McPh. 4.30 P.m. reached
Brady's 8. P.m. Bivouced.
Left 4.50 a.m, marched to N.42. on
trail. Heavy rain Set in at 9. P.m

SAND HILLS
Dismal river
Very High
Loup river
South Loup Fork
North Platte river
N. Platte 8#
South Platte river
P. R. R.
Platte river
Fort McPherson

quartermaster and commissary officer, in addition to post treasurer and signal officer assignments. Although he would have preferred the challenge of field service, he gained professional experience by remaining behind.[79]

September gave Foster his chance to ride after a confirmed raiding party. On the twelfth word was received at post that a band of Sioux had killed a man near Brady Island and ran off stock from the station. Company K of the Third, under command of Capt. Gerald Russell, was dispatched in quick pursuit. Lieutenant Foster was temporarily detached from his post duties to accompany the troop as second officer. The detachment picked up the trail and followed it from Brady Station to Pawnee Springs, then northwest into the Sand Hills. However, owing to a heavy rainfall that obliterated the track, the trail was lost on the third day.[80]

In an attempt to relocate the trail, Russell led his company down to the North Platte River, then west and up Birdwood Creek. After several days of searching north and toward the east, the soldiers reached the Dismal on the seventeenth and made camp. There the officers decided further search was useless, and the weary command returned to Fort McPherson. In what proved a fruitless chase, Russell's company covered 289 miles in nine days. After his return, Foster again drew up a map of the march and added it in his journal (fig 3.8).

Later that fall, Foster had applied for and was granted his first sick leave, a routine procedure that proved an ominous harbinger of things to come. Regardless of any threat to personal safety or health, Foster willingly jumped at every opportunity for field service. While on the spring scouts months before, he had contracted laryngitis, and never fully recovered from its effects. His laryngitis was aggravated by his desire for field service and eventually became the cause for his needed leave. His affliction might have been additional reason why Foster was not deployed with his company to Kansas.

In late September orders arrived at Fort McPherson that relieved Foster of the duties of post quartermaster and commissary officer, and directed him to join his company at Grinnell. To avoid further risk to his health active field service might bring, Post Surgeon Charles L. Heizmann[81] advised James to apply for sick leave and take care of his nagging illness. While on authorized sick leave, army officers were entitled to their full pay and could receive permission to leave the department for milder regions to aid in their recovery.[82]

Foster had spent most of October finishing up his work as post quartermaster. On October 26 he applied for an absence of six months on a surgeon's certificate of disability. The certificate Heizmann prepared stated he had been suffering from Chronic Laryngitis for the past six months and was presently unfit for duty. Surgeon Heizmann also recommended a leave of six months and added "A change of climate is absolutely necessary for his recovery." Foster's paperwork was quickly passed through department headquarters and was forwarded to the Department of the Missouri for notification (Foster's company was at the time assigned to Fort Dodge in western Kansas).[83]

On November 2 James was granted a one month's leave; twelve days later he left Fort McPherson and traveled to St. Augustine, Florida, to convalesce. While on leave he could be granted additional leave time in thirty-day increments on a surgeon's certificate, to total six months. At that time it was thought the mild climate of the Florida coast was beneficial to the sickly, particularly to consumptives. According to the army surgeon at St. Augustine, several hundred health seekers spent the winter months there. However, at the same time St. Augustine as a health resort was "overrated," with the climate there seen by others as being "damp and enervating."[84]

In order to continue on sick leave, convalescent officers were required to get renewal certified every thirty days from the post surgeon at the nearest military post, in Foster's case, the post of St. Francis Barracks. Acquired by the United States in 1821, the main building at the post was a former Franciscan monastery built in the eighteenth century. Several other more recent frame structures completed the complex. In 1874 the post was garrisoned by two artillery companies. While in St. Augustine James went to the barracks each month for a medical check-up from Post Surgeon Alfred A. Delany.[85]

Evidently, the sick leave time Foster spent at St. Augustine improved his physical condition. Surgeon Delany's certificates, duly filed to continue his leave time, counted down the months until it was determined he was capable to return to duty.

1   Surgeon General's Office, *A Report on the Hygiene of the United States Army, With Descriptions of Military Posts* (New York: Sol Lewis, 1974), 358. Reprint of 1875 edition.

2   Robert W. Frazer, *Forts of the West: Military Forts and Presidios and Posts Commonly Called Forts West of the Mississippi River to 1898* (Norman, OK: University of Oklahoma Press, 1965), 88; Returns from Regular Army Cavalry Regiments, Third Cavalry, Oct.-Dec. 1873, RG 94, Records of the Adjutant General, NARA.

3   Post Returns, Fort McPherson, Oct.–Dec. 1873, RG 94, NARA.

4   Ibid.

5   Alexander Dallas Bache Smead, from Pennsylvania, was a civilian appointee to the Third Cavalry in 1868. He was promoted to first lieutenant in 1871 and resigned in 1880. He briefly served as a captain in the Signal Corps during the Spanish-American War. Heitman, *Historical Register*, 893.

6 Second Lt. Bainbridge Reynolds, son of regimental Colonel Joseph Reynolds, graduated from the USMA in 1873 and was assigned to Co. F. He resigned as captain with the Third in 1891, and died in 1901. He received a brevet as first lieutenant for his actions at the Rosebud in 1876. Heitman, *Historical Register*, 824.

7 John B. Johnson, from Massachusetts, served as an officer with black infantry during the Civil War. Assigned to the Third Cavalry in 1870, he was promoted to captain in 1878, and died in 1896. Heitman, *Historical Register*, 576.

8 Post Returns, Fort McPherson, Dec. 1873.

9 Report of Capt. Alexander Moore, Oct. 24, 1873.

10 The bridge, built by trail entrepreneur John Burke with the arrival of the Union Pacific Railroad, crossed the Platte River south of McPherson Station.

11 Established by the railroad in 1867, the name was changed to Maxwell in 1882. Elton A. Perkey, *Perkey's Nebraska Place Names* (Lincoln: Nebraska State Historical Society, 1982), 128.

12 Born in Missouri in 1831, Leon Francois Pallardie, "the Wolf," was a well-known frontiersman in western Nebraska. Living and trading in the region since 1849, he served as scout and interpreter at Fort McPherson since 1864.

13 William F. Cody served as a buffalo hunter for the railroad and later as a scout for the army at Fort McPherson. By the time Foster was at the post, Cody was back East on the theatrical stage.

14 Refers to the plight of Co. M, Second Cavalry, commanded by Capt. John Mix, which was caught in a winter storm south of the Platte River in 1868.

15 Henry Kett, from Naussau, Germany, enlisted in 1868 at New York and was assigned to the Third Cavalry. He died in 1880 while serving with the Mounted Service at Jefferson Barracks, Mo., the recruit depot for the cavalry arm. Unless otherwise noted, all information on enlisted men's service is from "Register of Enlistments in the U. S. Army, 1778–1914," NARA.

16 *Middlemarch: a Study of Provincial Life* was an English novel by George Eliot, which appeared in serial form in 1871–72. Although not to Foster's tastes, it was nevertheless a popular work.

17 A French term for boredom resulting from inactivity or lack of interest.

18 Although an expensive spread made from goose liver, "Genuine Pate" was the facetious term the officers used when referring to their liquor supply.

19 Originally from Prussia, Otto Uhlig, was a well-established grocer in North Platte.

20 Augustus C. Paul was the first lieutenant of Mills's company. He was brevetted a lieutenant colonel for his actions at Spotsylvania Court House in the Civil War, and resigned in 1881. Heitman, *Historical Register*, 776.

21 George Berger from Pennsylvania enlisted in 1869. He was discharged ranked as a corporal at Fort McPherson in October 1874.

22 From Dante's *Divine Comedy*, Caina was one of the nine circles of Hell where traitors to kindred are immersed in ice up to their faces to suffer.

23 Although Foster did not know his proper name, "Limber Jim" had been in the Fort McPherson vicinity since the 1860s. In 1873 he was one of ten civilian teamsters hired by the post quartermaster.

24 Originating from the eighteenth century English expression, "Our army swore terribly in Flanders," the shorter version was commonly used to describe another's use of strong language.

25 An obvious reference to Johnson's liquor case.

26 A minor frontier figure, Richard Seymour made his appearance in western Nebraska during the early 1870s. Reportedly the son of British aristocracy, he took on the self-styled nickname of "Red Dick" or "Bloody Dick."

27 John C. A. Warfield enlisted in 1873 and was assigned to Co. F. He was discharged as a sergeant at Fort McPherson, and discharged a private at the end of his second enlistment at Fort Laramie.

28 Yclept is an archaic term for "called" or "named."

29 Native to the western Plains, elk herds once freely roamed throughout the state. As the elk population increased in recent years, limited hunting seasons were held in northwestern Nebraska in 1986 and 1987 and continuously since 1995. Today the population in the Sand Hills is returning.

30 A career N.C.O., Sgt. Thomas Hackett first enlisted in 1868 and retired as a first sergeant of the Third Cavalry in 1891, after serving six enlistments.

31 Pvt. Richard Lynch, from Ireland, initially enlisted in 1869. The company butcher, he retired in 1892, still ranked as a private.

32 Sgt. George Keech also enlisted in 1869. He was discharged at Fort McPherson in October 1874 by expiration of service, character listed as "excellent."

33 Windham Thomas Quinn (1841–1926), Fourth Earl of Dunraven, spent his leisure time hunting. In 1872 he hunted in the west, guided by John B. "Texas Jack" Omohundro, who led the earl's party on buffalo and elk hunts in the region.

34 Trumpeter Francis Woltering enlisted in 1872. His listed height was 5 feet, 3 inches, leading to his nickname "the Short Trumpeter." He was discharged in December 1877 at the subpost of Hat Creek, Wyoming Territory.

35 Foster means Pvt. Gilbert Roe, who surrendered from desertion and was transferred to Co. F, 3rd Cavalry in November 1873. He was killed in battle at Rosebud Creek, June 17, 1876.

36 He refers to a minute falls then on the South Loup River, located near present-day Gandy in Logan County.

37 Pawnee Creek flows south and southeast out of the Sandhills and enters the Platte River near present-day Brady.

38 Corp. George H. Freeland, from New Jersey, enlisted in 1869 and was discharged from Co. F in August as a private.

39 The headwaters of Pawnee Creek, the springs are six miles north and two mile east of Maxwell.

40 Albert D. King served as a private in the Second Cavalry, 1864–66. He was commissioned into the Third Cavalry in 1866 and promoted to captain in 1881. He retired in 1891 and died in 1900. Heitman, *Historical Register*, 594.

41 For more on North Platte Station, see Thomas R. Buecker, "The Post of North Platte Station, 1867–1878" *Nebraska History* 63 (Fall 1982): 381.

42 Capt. Edward J. Spaulding, Co. C, Second Cav.

43 For more on the 1874 Sioux Expedition, see Thomas R. Buecker, *Fort Robinson and the American West, 1874–1899* (Lincoln, NE: Nebraska State Historical Society, 1999), 1–42.

44 First Lt. Thomas J. Gregg, Co. C; 1st Lt. James T. Peal, Co. M; 2nd Lt. John H. Coale, Co. C; 2nd Lt. Henry C. LePoint, Co. M; George W. Tower, Acting Assistant Surgeon (civilian contract surgeon) at Omaha Barracks.

45 Capt. Charles Meinhold, Co. B, Third Cav.

46 Maj. Simon Smith, from New York, became an army paymaster, in August 1861. He retired in 1879 and died in 1884. Heitman, *Historical Register*, 903.

47 James Mealie, from Cork, Ireland, enlisted Feb. 13, 1874, at Fort McPherson. As his previous occupation was as a musician, he became duty trumpeter. He is buried at Fort McPherson National Cemetery.

48 After high waters washed out several spans of his bridge, John Burke drowned in June 1872, while rafting supplies across the rampaging Platte.

49 A. J. Flint was the Acting Assistant Surgeon at Fort McPherson.

50 On the 1870 census Phil Saucier was reported as a "clerk in store." He was also a day laborer for Boyer.

51 William H. Agett, from upstate New York, enlisted January 26, 1874, in New York City. Twenty-five years old, he was a stage driver in civilian life.

52 Armor Gray, from Tyrone, Ireland, enlisted March 30, 1872, also in New York City. At the time he was a twenty-six-year-old teamster. Both Agett and Gray were placed in confinement on April 24.

53 Pvt. Frank Mooney, from Ireland, enlisted in 1871 and was discharged in March 1876 at Sidney Barracks, Nebraska.

54 Guard Mount was the formal ceremony held at every army post each morning at 9:00, when the old guard went off post and was replaced by the new guard.

55 A formation held at army posts at the end of each day when troops assigned to the post were accounted for, and general orders, including findings of court-martials, were published (read) before the assembled command.

56 Agett was discharged June 7 per General Court-Martial Orders 30, Department of the Platte. His purported accomplice Armor Gray was later discharged on June 29, per GCM Order 34.

57 Erie Erickson from Sweden, was listed on the 1870 census as a contractor. His ranch was actually located several miles east of Fort McPherson.

58 Albert Jester, a cattle dealer from Maine, ranched east of Erickson's place.

59 William W. Allen, 1st First Sgt., Co. I, was serving his fifth enlistment. He was killed in battle at the Rosebud on June 17, 1876, as a private. For more information, see Chapter 5.

60 Christian J. H. Bahr joined Co. I in 1871 and became company clerk. During his second enlistment he transferred to the Medical Department and became a hospital steward, and deserted at Omaha in September 1876. Although he surrendered from desertion, Bahr was discharged without honor in 1881.

61 Alexander Moore, from Ireland, served as an aide-de-camp during the Civil War. He received several brevets, including colonel for gallantry and meritorious service in the battle of Gettysburg. He was assigned as a captain, Third Cavalry, in December 1870 and resigned in 1879. Heitman, *Historical Register*, 721.

62 The mouth of Gillmore Canyon was about fourteen miles east of Fort McPherson.

63 Fritz Strikert, born in Prussia, enlisted in January 1874 and was assigned to Co. I. He was discharged in January 1879 at Fort Fetterman, character "excellent."

64 New recruits were paired with older soldiers, who shared blankets and shelter-halves in the field, field cooking, or teamed in combat situations. As a result, one's so called "Bunky," tended to be a best friend or confidant. Rickey, *Forty Miles a Day*, 57.

65 Adjutant General's Office, *Index of General Orders, Adjutant General's Office, 1874* (Washington, D.C: G.P.O., 1875), G.O. 27; Senate, *Journal of the Executive Proceedings of the Senate, Vol. XIX* (Washington, DC: G.P.O., 1901), 179, 182, 197.

66 Post Returns, Fort McPherson, April, May 1874, RG 94, NARA.

67 Brady Island Station was nine miles east of McPherson Station. Its name was changed to Brady in 1894. Perkey, *Nebraska Place Names*, 127.

68 Thomas McHugh, from Ireland, enlisted in the Regiment of Mounted Riflemen (the predecessor of the Third Cavalry) in 1858. He served as a N.C.O. with Co. I until he deserted in May 1872. He surrendered from desertion in April 1873, and was discharged after finishing his term as a private at Fort McPherson in July 1874.

69 Evidently John Burke's bridge was no engineering work of art. After crossing the bridge in 1869, Mary Carr, wife of Maj. Eugene A. Carr, recalled the bridge as "a most unsafe and awful looking structure, and why we did not fall through it was simply from good luck." James T. King, ed., "Fort McPherson in 1870," *Nebraska History* 45 (March 1964): 104.

70 The town of Cozad was founded in 1873 by John J. Cozad from Ohio. His son was the noted artist Robert Henri. Perkey, *Nebraska Place Names*, 56.

71 The Union Pacific Railroad originally marked the meridian with a sign in 1866. Cozad has been long remembered as the 100th Meridian City.

72 Present-day Lexington was originally known as Plum Creek. Perkey, *Nebraska Place Names*, 57. The bridge over the Platte south of town was actually four miles west of where the creek with that name flowed into the river.

73 For the army's bimonthly pay purposes and accountability, company units were mustered the last day of each month.

74 Probably the remains of the Miller and Penniston ranche.

75 Post Returns, Fort McPherson, June 1874.

76 Ibid., May–June 1874.

77 *North Platte Enterprise*, July 15, 1874.

78 Ibid., Aug. 7, 1874; Post Returns, Fort McPherson, July 1874.

79 Post Returns, Fort McPherson, July 1874.

80 Ibid., Sept. 1874; *North Platte Enterprise*, Sept. 19, 1874.

81 Charles L. Heizmann, from Pennsylvania, became an assistant surgeon in 1867. He was promoted to surgeon (major) in 1886 and became an assistant surgeon general (colonel) in 1902. Heitman, *Historical Register*, 521.

82 GO 139, Dept. Platte, ACP 1873; Sec. of War, *Army Regulations*, 17–18.

83 Endorsements to letter of Oct. 26, 1874; "Certificate of Disability," Oct. 26, 1874, both ACP 1873.

84 Surgeon General, *A Report on Hygiene*, 174–75.

85 Post Returns, St. Francis Barracks, Dec. 1874–May 1875. Today St. Francis Barracks is the headquarters for the Florida National Guard. Alfred Delany served as a surgeon during the Civil War and was commissioned as Assistant Surgeon on October 1867. He died in February 1876. Heitman, *Historical Register*, 365.

CHAPTER 4

The 1875 Jenney Expedition

In the early spring of 1875 preparations were underway for a major exploration of the Black Hills in Dakota Territory. Foster returned from leave in time to play a key role in a significant event of western history. As a result, his service on the expedition enhanced his growing reputation as an efficient and capable army officer.

To whites entering the West, the Black Hills had always been a region said to be of importance to the Plains Indian, but also rumored to contain untold mineral wealth. During the years prior to the Civil War, two army explorations neared the Hills—but did not explore its interior. The first was in 1857 when a party led by topographical engineer Lt. Gouverneur K. Warren approached the Hills from the south. Near Inyan Kara Mountain, he was warned by a large band of angered Lakotas not to enter the Hills. Heeding their warnings, Warren retreated south, and then turned through the southern hills and along the eastern side north to the Belle Fourche River. He then departed for Fort Randall on the Missouri River.[1]

Two years later, a small expedition under the command of Capt. William F. Raynolds explored the region from Fort Pierre into the Yellowstone country. Moving westward from the Missouri River, Raynolds merely skirted the Hills on the north side. Still, the interior remained largely unknown to the army—that is until the summer of 1874. That summer a major expedition into the Black Hills was led by Lt. Col. George A. Custer, Seventh U. S. Cavalry. Custer's large expeditionary force left from Fort Abraham Lincoln on the Missouri River in present-day North Dakota, supplied for sixty days in the field. Because of the long distance traveling to and returning from the Hills, Custer was only able to spend three weeks exploring and mapping its interior. But, he reported the discovery of gold.[2]

With the subsequent public clamor to allow entry into the Hills (as part of the Treaty of 1868 the Black Hills was on the Great Sioux Reservation and whites were prohibited from going there), the government examined the possibility of negotiations with the Indians about its purchase. If there was to be a cession of the Hills to the whites, Secretary of State Columbus Delano authorized the formation of a geological surveying party to provide a more thorough examination of the region to determine its mineral potential.[3]

On March 26, Edward P. Smith, commissioner of Indian affairs, appointed Walter P. Jenney, of the Columbia School of Mines in New York City, to survey the Hills "for the purpose of ascertaining the extent and value of the gold deposits there." The desired end result was to establish a fair value for purchase. Professor Jenney was assisted by Henry Newton, assistant expedition geologist, and astronomer Capt. Horace P. Tuttle. The expedition engineering and topographical officer was Dr. Valentine T. McGillycuddy, late of the Lake and Northern Boundary Surveys. The geological survey party was aided by a small corps of assistants, miners, and laborers. Later the expedition was joined by official photographer Albert E. Guerin of St. Louis.[4]

Although the Black Hills were actually in Dakota Territory, and under the jurisdiction of the Department of Dakota, escort troops for the expedition and logistical support came from the Department of the Platte. With troops stationed much nearer the Hills and a major railroad route running through the Platte which would aid supply, department commander Brig. Gen. George Crook quickly selected Lt. Col. Richard I. Dodge as his commander in the field. Dodge, then on garrison duty with his regiment at Omaha Barracks, was an excellent choice for command. An 1858 graduate of West Point, he was a seasoned soldier, with administrative competence and the ability to lead. He also was an avid outdoorsman.[5]

The army command had no idea of what the attitude of Plains tribesmen might be toward a second penetration of their sacred Black Hills; as Crook's aide-de-camp 2nd Lt. John G. Bourke put it, ". . . prudence commands vigilance and thorough preparedness."[6] Consequently, a large military force was marshaled at Fort Laramie to protect the expedition. The mounted portion consisted of two companies of the Second and four of the Third Cavalry regiments, totaling 363 men and 376 horses. Two companies of the Ninth Infantry provided nearly one hundred men for supply train escorts and guards. To provide additional firepower, the troops took along a twelve-pounder Howitzer and a Gatling gun, both manned by infantrymen. Seventy-one wagons, four ambulances, and four hundred mules plus the requisite number of civilian teamsters and packers, were furnished for transportation needs. Finally, three herders to drive 134 head of beef cattle, and one butcher for beef slaughter, handled the livestock necessary for daily ration issue.[7]

During April and May of 1875 men and supplies for the expedition were readied at Fort Laramie. On March 30, Company I was assigned to the expedition, and was ordered to change station from Fort McPherson to Fort Laramie. Foster evidently had heard of the upcoming expedition while at St. Augustine. Dr. Delany approved his early departure from his sick leave to join his troop.[8]

Foster returned to Fort McPherson on April 29. Four days later Lieutenants King and Foster, with forty-five men and sixty-three horses, rode to McPherson Station to board a westbound Union Pacific train for Fort D. A. Russell at Cheyenne. Three days later Company I marched overland the near-ninety miles to Fort Laramie, where it joined other units assigned to protect the Jenney expedition. While in camp, the cavalry companies and quartermaster teamsters groomed and rubbed down long lines of horses and mules, while infantry soldiers were exercised in company drill. Tons of commissary and quartermaster supplies were checked and packed for wagon transport.[9]

Whenever the army sent troops into a new region, officers were required to map the routes taken and record itineraries of the march. Information on road difficulties, campsites, and the availability of water, wood, and grass, were recorded for future reference. Lieutenant Bourke was assigned Engineer Officer, to map routes to and through the Black Hills for military purposes. Many officers, including Colonel Dodge, felt that military maps would be more practical than the more intricate, artistic maps that were created by cartographers of the Geological Survey. For the duration of the expedition, Dodge's engineer officers worked in full cooperation with Dr. McGillycuddy, surveying and mapping a very rugged region.[10]

On May 24, Dodge issued orders for the arrangement of the column on the march. The cavalry companies were rotated daily through positions in the troop column. The leading company served as 'pioneer troops,' preparing the way for wagons to cross draws and creek bottoms. Immediately behind the leading company, the pioneer wagon contained axes, shovels, spades, nails, rope, and other items necessary to temporarily improve the road. As the column advanced across the Wyoming plains and through the Black Hills, the pioneer companies were continually occupied building temporary bridging, cutting down edges of draws and ravines, and constructing corduroy roads.[11]

FIG. 4.1. An overall map of the Black Hills, showing much of the interior blank, which Foster drew in his journal to record his travels while on the expedition. He copied an 1874 map of Nebraska and Wyoming prepared by the department engineer prior to the Custer expedition. On it Foster located Camp Jenney and the new route he helped pioneer to Camp Harney.

The Blackhills of Dakota

104. Hd. Ho.
104
103.36

44°30"
104°
103°30"
Belle Fourche
30

Bear Creek

Peak

Box Elder cr
44
Rapid cr

44°30"
44°
00

Camp Jenney
43.49.25 W.
104.21 N

French Cr
Harney's Peak
Spring Creek

Beaver Cr

43°30"
Big Cheyenne
43.30

104
5   10   15   20
103 36
30

Next came the headquarters and scientific wagons, followed by the cavalry force, company wagons, and supply wagons, the latter guarded by the infantry. At the end of the column was the beef herd, followed up by the rear guard. The lead company one day served as the rear guard the next, as the other companies rotated through the marching order. Each day the column broke camp early, about six o'clock, and went into camp early, usually before two or three in the afternoon.[12]

During the early weeks of the expedition, Lt. Foster was involved mainly with regular troop duty on the march and in camp. Soldiers and animals were inspected, company areas were laid out and maintained, guards placed, and other duties that normally fell to junior subalterns. But, Foster was also interested in recording his part in the expedition. He regularly drew sketch maps and recorded itineraries of each day's march. He also wrote down short observations on the landscape and incidents of the march. At 6:00 a.m. on May 25, the Jenney Expedition broke camp on the North Platte River, and made its way north to the Black Hills. Foster's notes and maps on the march to the Hills form the next section of his journal:

Black Hills Expedition

MAY 25th 1875
Broke Camp at 6. am. Marching due magnetic north
In 17+ miles struck summit of Sand Bluffs
Buttes on left of road of no great height
Road very sandy all day.   Much Cactus
crossed Branch of Rawhide Creek   (Nopal Cucius)
Camped on Rawhide Creek
"C" Troop 2d Cav advance guard
Thunderstorm this Pm for 2 hours

The cactus was identified by Bourke as the nopal or "tuna cactus," which grew in great tracts in the region. Both Bourke and Dodge described how it could be used to clean and settle alkaline water[13]

MAY 26th 1875
Marched at 6.am. Dug patch for wagons to cross Rawhide.
Banks steep. Creek 10 ft wide by 1 ft deep. Marched
N.W. 2 miles through canon deep with loose white Sand.
couldn't get through and returned. Camping on
Rawhide.

FIG. 4.2

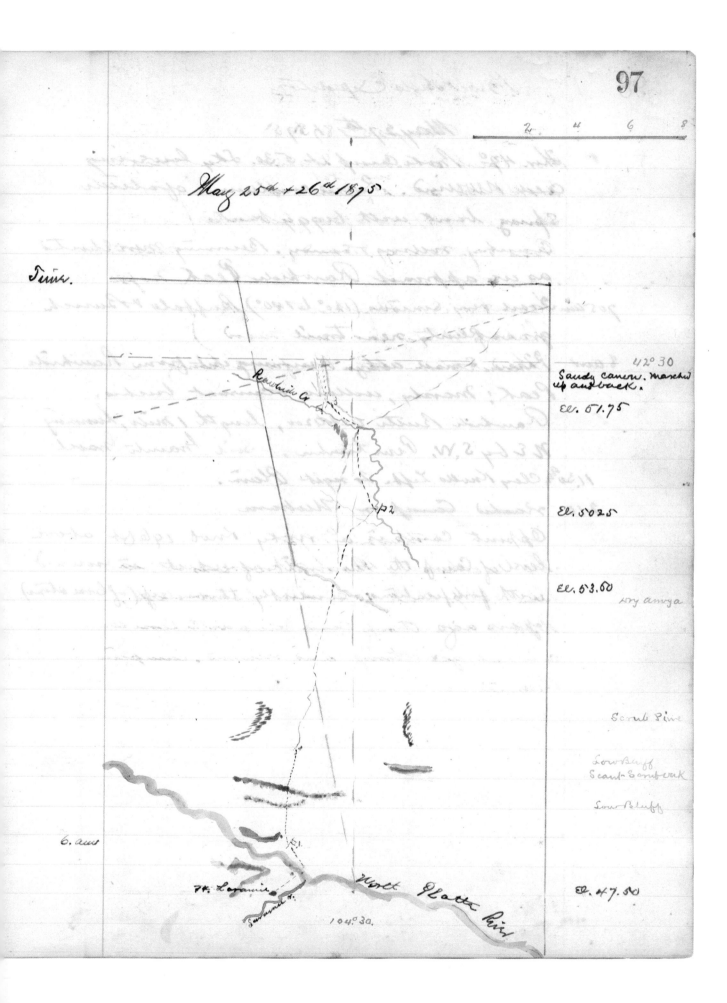

May 25ᵗʰ + 26ᵈ 1875

2   4   6   8

Time.

42° 30

Rawhide Cr

Sandy canon. marched
up and back.

El. 51.75

P2

El. 5025

El. 53.50

Dry arroya

Scrub Pine

Low Bluff
Scant Sanbank

Low Bluff

6. aus

El. 47. 50

Ft. Laramie

Laramie R.

North Platte River

104° 30.

Dodge had hired Joe Merivale, a longtime resident of the Fort Laramie vicinity as expedition guide. He had served the army before, and was said to be knowledgeable about the route to the Black Hills. On the second day out, Joe led the troops up a wrong fork of the Rawhide. Consequently the expedition only made seven and one-half miles that day. After that misadventure, Dodge wrote in his journal, "My faith in Merivale is gone, & I must myself play guide."[14] After that day he performed no further service as guide, but was retained as an interpreter.

MAY 27th 1875
Ther. 49 Broke camp at 5.30. Sky lowering
Cold NW wind. Passed confluence of a little
Spring bank with boggy banks
Country rolling & sandy. Becoming more Elevated
as we approach Rawhide Peak

705 am	Trail very sinuous (120 to 140) Buffalo & Bunch grass plenty near trail
8.am	Passed small arroyo running out from Rawhide Peak; Marshy, willows & currant bushes Rawhide Butte alt 6200, length 1 mile, running N E by S.W. Pine lumber. Soil Granite Gravel
11.30 am	Clay Knolls Left. To right Plains.
210	reached Camp on Niobrara Opposite Camp is a rocky Knob 196 ft above level of Camp the summit of which is covered with fortifications evidently thrown up (of loose stone) years ago.

Dodge recorded it had been very cold all day and towards evening it got worse. Reveille call for the expedition was at 4 a.m. That morning Bourke reported the whole camp turned out "uniformly equipped" in army over-coats and "frozen noses." The next morning it was even colder.[15]
Of "Fortification Butte," Bourke wrote in his diary:

In front of camp was a butte (196 ft high) of granite . . . Persons who climbed to the summit told me of some Indian fortifications there found; from their descriptions, these structures of rude piles of stone not over 3 feet high, probably served once as rifle pits or trenches to defend the Crow Indians, originally possessors of this region, against the Dacotahs or Sioux, the present occupants. The summit has no

FIG. 4.3

May 27 1875

Niobrara river

4.9

Rawhide Peak
El. 6200

Rawhide Creek

10.30

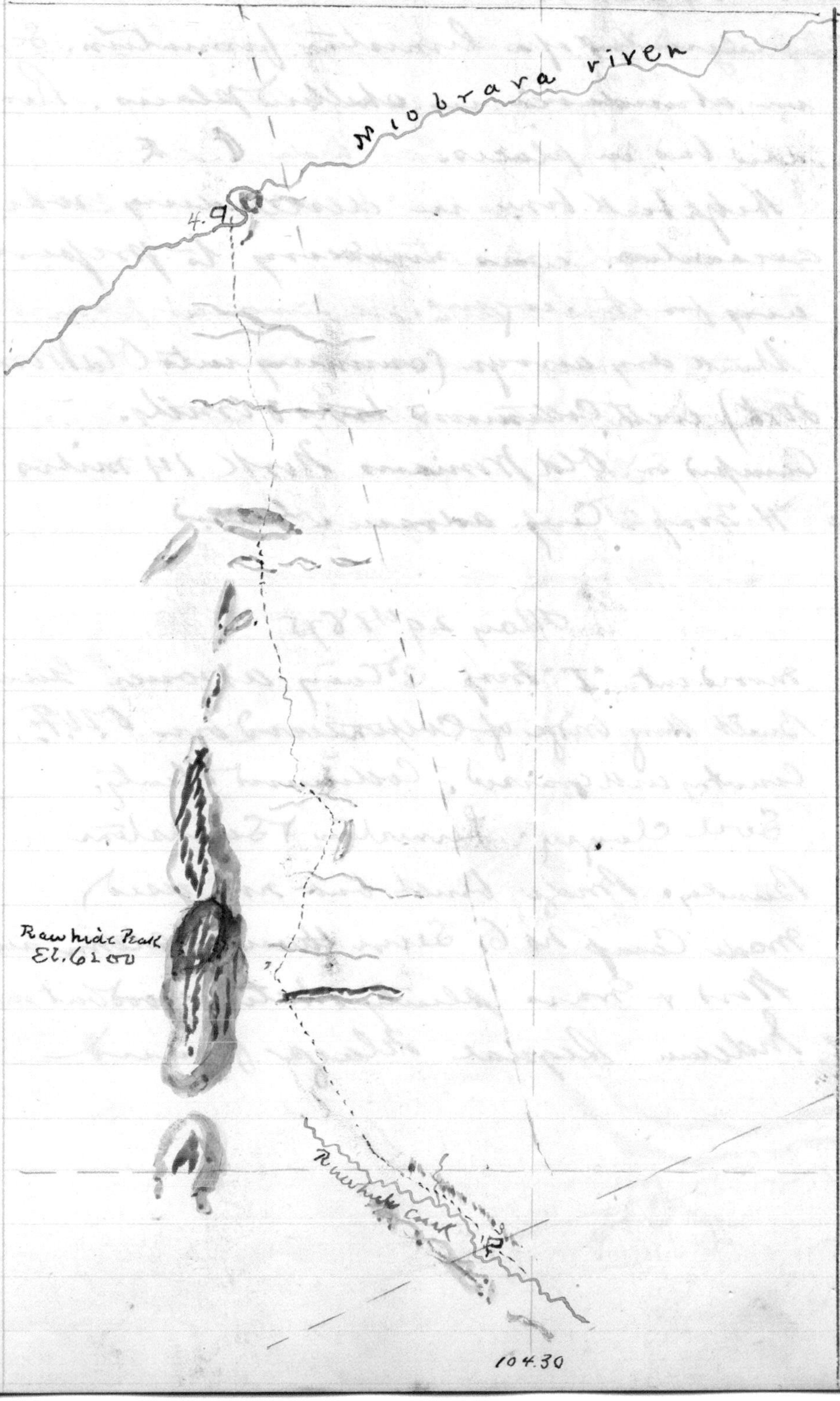

Fortification Butte 5496
El. 5300

El 5400
Red Feldspar Knob
Clay Knobs
5575
5500

5350

El 5450

El. 5350
arroyo. with trees

(42.30. N)
El. 5400

El. 5175

positive evidence to sustain it, and neither the fortifications nor the conjuncture were deserving of further attention.[16]

MAY 28th 1875
Last night quite cold. Heavy frost   31 5.am
Broke camp 5.30.am
7.28am.   Day changed to warm & cloudless
815   Country of a limestone formation. Scrub Pine
           in abundance in sheltered places. Road rocky
           and bad in places.
           High back bone in descending which
           excavation was necessary to prepare a
           way for the wagons.
1020   Struck dry arroyo (running into Old Womans
           Fork) with cottonwood trees & brush.
1235   Camped on Old Womans Fork 14 miles
           H Troop 3d Cavy advance guard

As the expedition moved north, they reached the top of the high land above the drainage of Old Woman's Creek, the western margins of the vaunted Pine Ridge. From here they had their first view of the still-distant Black Hills. The descent down into the valley was an arduous task. Colonel Dodge admitted in his diary that "The route was most difficult and it required no little Engineering skill to get down," but then added, "My pioneering and [1st Lt. John F.] Trout's wagon management finally got us down without accident or delay."[17]

MAY 29th 1875
610   Moved out. "I" Troop 3d Cavy advance guard
           Built strong bridge of cottonwood over O.W.F.
730   Country well grassed. Cottonwood Plenty.
           Soil clayey. Limestone & Sandstone
205   Bunkey Bridge built but now used
235   Made Camp No. 6 Severe thunder storm and wind
           Wood & grass plenty. Water good but muddy
           Indian signal flags found

This was a rough day for Foster's company serving on pioneer duty. Progress was slow with great labor: two stretches of corduroy, one brush bridge built, and a good log bridge (the bunkey bridge) were built. Because the   FIG. 4.4

May 28th + 29th 1875

Bunkye Bridge

42.56 W Lat

4400 El

4700 El

4725 El
5100 El
5350 El

5180

5875

Knau
196

4

road work caused a long series of rests, it was an easy day for the other men and horses of the command. Although a hard day for the pioneer troops, the column managed to cover fifteen miles. Bourke noted that Old Woman Creek was crossed eight times that day.[18]

What was identified as a medicine rag or flag was found that afternoon by Lieutenant King as he was posting pickets. The white cotton flag was 14x23 inches, emblazoned on one side with seventy-five horse shoes, and on the other with a profile of a human head. Camp was made across the creek and south of Old Woman's Butte. According to Lieutenant Bourke, the butte, "called the Old Woman's Mountain, upon whose summit at night the spirit of some mysterious old Indian hag enjoys the recreation of tripping the light fantastic."[19]

MAY 30th 1875

am 5.10	Broke Camp. "K" 3d Cavy in advance
am 550	Hill with fossil shells
Pm 115	Passed on Corduroy (50 yds) OW.F. horses mired
	Sandy Soil. Hills barren with large amounts
	of Sandstone
Pm 310	Reached Cheyenne river at big bend. 30 feet wide
	8 in deep. Current moderate. Banks mirey.
	Lined with timber & bushes
	Water muddy & slightly Alkaline
P.m. 3 20	Crossed & went into camp. Wells dug and good
	Water found at 6 feet. (No. 7) 17 ½ miles
	Alarm tonight. Loose horses. Sentry fired.

Marine fossils are abundant in this part of Wyoming. Bourke noted, "Throughout this section are to be found the same fossil bivalves (brachyopods I think they are) of which we observed such great quantities yesterday and the day before."[20]

A corduroy road was built of logs laid side by side transversely, usually in low or swampy places. The corduroy mentioned by Foster took three hours to build.

Although signs of Indians were sighted all along the route so far, none were actually seen. Believing that Indians were raiding the picket line, a nervous infantry guard fired his rifle, alarming the camp. Dodge commented in his journal, "There was nothing the matter a "Doboy" recruit having got scared at a loose horse, & fired to give the alarm." The shot

FIG. 4.5

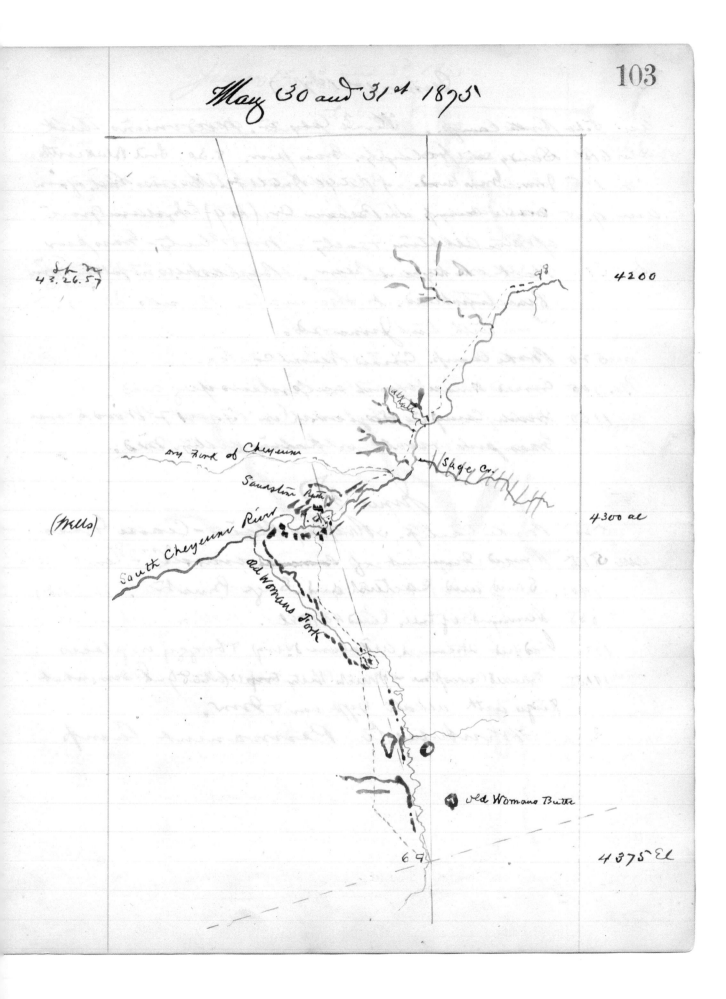

May 30 and 31st 1875

43.26.57

4200

98

Dry Fork of Cheyenne

Sage Cr.

Sandstone Butte

(Wells)

South Cheyenne River

4300 al

Old Womans Fork

Old Womans Butte

69

4375 El

alerted Lieutenant Trout, the expedition quartermaster, who established that a single shot be fired if there was trouble with his beef herd.[21]

MAY 31st 1875

am 5.25	Broke Camp. Crossed river. "C" 2d Cavy advance
740	Crossed Dry Fork of Cheyenne. 100 ft wide. Muddy Sandy Bottom. Miry banks. Bottom rich alluvial Good farming land. Timbered
11.35	Made Cap on N. Bk. Cheyenne (No. 8) Wood, Grass & water
3.Pm	rain. Storm during night

As the expedition moved further toward the foot of the Hills, stream water draining out of its eroded anticline formations gradually became more milky and alkaline. By this point the soldiers dug shallow wells to obtain a palatable source of water. Dodge recorded good water was obtained by digging in the bed of a side arroyo at this camp.[22]

JUNE 1st 1875

5.20	Broke camp. Level plain. Wild onions thick
615	Sandy soil & clayey. Grass poor. 830. Soil Black with Iron. Grass good. Black knolls Silecious Carb. of iron
am 9.25	Made camp on Beaver Cr (No. 9) Indian grave Water Alkaline & salty—Wood Plenty—Grass poor 4 Elk one deer 1 Bear. Black hills in plain view Pine timbered

Beaver Creek was fringed with a scanty growth of cottonwood, the larger of which occasionally contained Indian burials. Colonel Dodge was critical of the looting of one tree burial near the camp by the several medical doctors of the expedition.[23]

That day the hunters of Lieutenant Hall's company of the Second Cavalry killed four elk, Lieutenant King shot a black-tailed deer, and a party of Captain Burt's infantry company killed and brought to camp a "cinnamon" bear. Of the successful hunts that day, Lieutenant Bourke noted, "the fresh beef of the Elk was a very savory and toothsome morsel which claimed and received our fullest attention."[24]

JUNE 2D

| 520 | Broke Camp. Crossed Beaver C. |

FIG. 4.6

June 1st 2d and 3d 1875

43.49.40
St. 43. 50. 12 N
49.40
Long 104. 19. W

Sage & Sand
Cactus

Camp Jenney
Alt. 4250

4200

4150

4000

3900

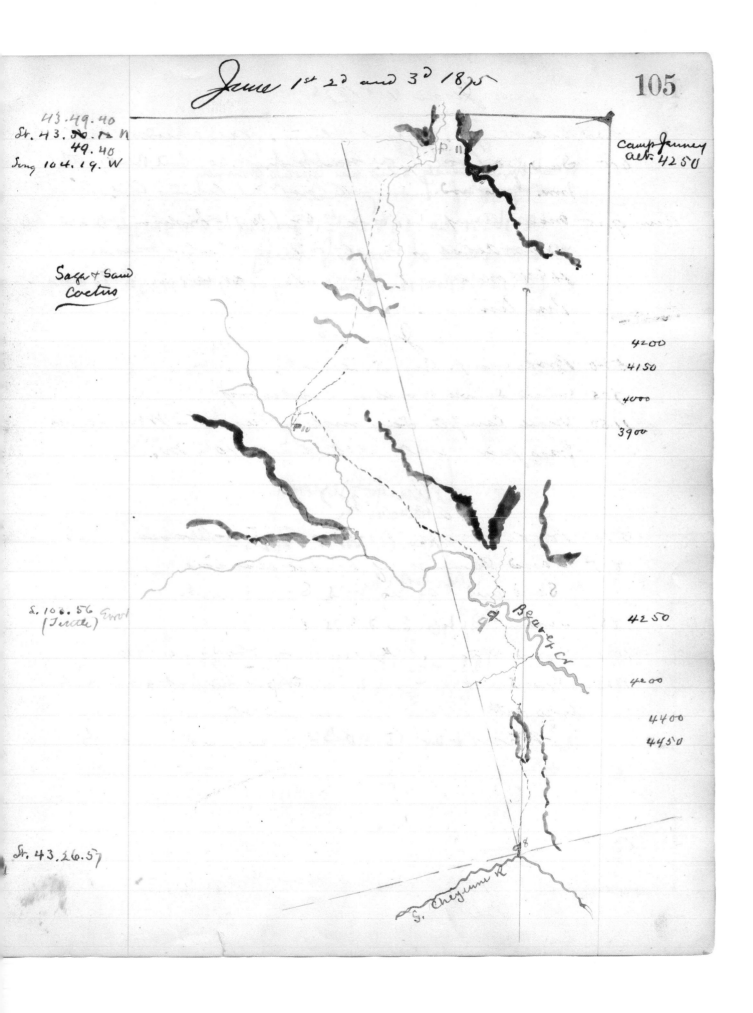

S. 103. 56 Snd
(Turtle)

Beaver Cr

4250

4200

4400

4450

St. 43. 26. 57

S. Cheyenne R.

"Red Butte" -
From Camp Jenney. June 18th 1875.

| 705 | Crossed small branch on Corduroy |
| 1150 | Made Camp in Sage brush on Beaver—Wood scarce Grass poor & water alkaline. 10 ½ M. |

In the words of Colonel Dodge, this day's march and camp were both "horrible." Camp No. 10, located on a dreary alkaline plain, was one of the last campsites of the expedition before they entered the Hills.[25]

JUNE 3D

520	Broke Camp. Rolling Plain—Coarse Grass
815	Passed summit of small divide Sand and Cactus and Sage Brush
855	Summit of table land 4375 El
1020	Crossed stream. Alkaline (very) & boggy in places.
1025	Crossed another—Much better water but somewhat tinged with alkali Gypsum & Iron Went into Permanent Camp (*Note: this was Foster's last entry in his journal record of the march to the* Black Hills)

After a fourteen-mile march, the expedition arrived at a "very beautiful camp" under the shadow of the Black Hills. Here, nine days and 138 miles out of Fort Laramie, Dodge established the first of eight camps or bases for supplies and operations. Located on a branch of Beaver Creek (named Spaulding Creek in honor of Capt. Edward J. Spaulding, who commanded C Company, Second Cavalry) the first camp was christened "Camp Jenney."

Dodge had planned to establish a series of "permanent" camps, each to serve as a supply base for scientific parties sent out to map and explore specific areas. When the work in one area was finished, the expedition would move forward to the next location. Dodge thought the Spaulding Creek site was an ideal location, with abundant wood, water, and grass. Work details began to build a large log storehouse and two defensive redoubts, one a small palisade work atop a hill that commanded the immediate area.[26]

While the expedition was at Camp Jenney, the regular routine for exploration by the scientific corps was set in motion. Each day Professor Jenney and the miners were to examine mineral deposits; Newton, Tuttle, and Dr. McGillycuddy, were in charge of topographical and geological studies. Escorted by cavalry detachments, the scientific parties set out to explore and map specified regions. Likewise, the accompanying military force broke into daily details for road building, guard duty, mapmaking, and other necessary

FIG. 4.7. Camp Jenney, view to the east with Red Butte toward the northeast. On the hill above the camp was the redoubt Bourke described as "a little palisade work on the crest of a little hill . . . from which our artillery can be enabled to play with deadly effect on any party of Indians that may have the temerity to attack us."

functions. Lieutenant Bourke, the army topographic engineer, had several tasks besides mapping streams and trends of ranges, namely determining the best line for wagon roads and potential sites for military posts.[27]

After the storehouse was completed and filled, a wagon train escorted by the infantry companies was sent back to Fort Laramie to replenish depleted supplies. Unfortunately, it was found that the deceptively "clean, cold water" of Spauldings Creek was highly alkaline and began to affect the command.[28] It was quickly decided to get the expedition into the Hills and locate a new base near a pure water supply. On June 9, Colonel Dodge led the scientific corps and three cavalry companies north up Spaulding Creek valley, searching an easy entry route into the Black Hills. While the main portion of the expedition advanced into the interior, Companies A, I (Foster's company) and K of the Third Cavalry, under command of Capt. William Hawley, remained to guard the supplies coming up from Laramie. When a new base camp was established, the soldiers and the supplies at Camp Jenney were to be moved there.

Several days after the main expedition left Camp Jenney, they entered the interior of the Hills via Custer's Floral Valley route. On June 14, a new base camp was located on French Creek just south of Harney Peak, and aptly named Camp Harney. Back at Camp Jenney, Foster had time after completion of his daily duties to work on a series of colored ink and watercolor maps. Five maps were redrawn in his journal from his daily sketch maps, which detailed line of march from Fort Laramie, topography, and elevations. Opposite each map, he re-copied its corresponding daily itinerary. Additionally in the journal, he painted several watercolors that illustrated scenes along the route and at the camp. Done for his own entertainment and to make his record of the expedition, they demonstrated Foster's interest and skills in watercolor painting and in cartography.

On June 17, Colonel Dodge sent Captain Spaulding and Lieutenant Trout with empty wagons back to Camp Jenney to pick up the supplies and move everything to Camp Harney. Spaulding was to locate a shorter, cut-off route that led to the Beaver, and then north to Jenney. He failed to find a southern passage, but did locate a more direct wagon road than the one Dodge had used to enter the Hills. When Spaulding arrived at Camp Jenney on June 19, he found Captain Hawley's command in bad condition, with many sick from the alkaline water. Additionally, all the grass in the vicinity had been destroyed by large swarms of grasshoppers.[29]

On the 21st Camp Jenney was abandoned, and on the 22nd the troops and supplies started for Camp Harney. On the return trip, the train used the new route pioneered by Spaulding and Trout, which was only forty-three

FIG. 4.8

2 4/10 inch to the Inch

Camp Jenney to Coldspring Valley
21 miles.
June 22d 1875

J. H. Foster
2d Lt. 3d Cavalry

Coldspring Valley.
Dry rocky Bed of Creek

Fosters Butte — Bald
Butte East of Camp.

Calamity Gap. Dangerous
long and rapid descent
into Cold spring valley

Backbone — Elevated view
Right mountains with Gap, in
the distance. High Wooded
ranges.

9.38. Low Ridge with Pine
Beginning of main ascent
onto backbone

7.10 am Sutlers Gulch
Valley — Grassy but with
Steep sides — Difficult
ascent and descent
Sutlers Wagon Stalled
East side in Gulch

7.30 a.m. Out of camp onto
broad Mesa. Water Hole
in mills to right

out of Canyon. Rocky. Bad
foot hold into Canyon
again
7.30 am
Through Canyon —
Left saw Red Bluffs
Right Rocky hills
Sparsely timbered with
Scrub Pines

Spring about 380 Fah.

View West from Fosters Butte June 22, 5 pm

N 17° Var East
15° 40' 40" East

S.W.

N.W.

Calamity Gap

Coldspring Ca.

Fosters Butte

Saw Buttes with Pines timber

Saw Bluffs with Pine timber

Low Red Bluffs

Pilot Head

Kings Spring

Mill to left and right

Red Butte

Camp Jenney

Low Red Bluffs

Scale

Grades
1 2 3 Ascending x Heavy
3 2 1 Descending x Very Heavy
1 0 Level

Vidette - On Old Womans Fork - May 29. 1875
Camp no. 6 and Old Womans Butte in the distance.

California Joe - June 27th 1875

miles in length, nearly thirty miles shorter than the northern route. On the 23rd Lieutenant Foster was sent ahead to inform Dodge the train was coming in. Later that evening, the wagons arrived, carrying supplies and photographer Guerin, who had been delayed by illness. On that same day, Lieutenant Bourke, the topographical officer, received orders to return to Department Headquarters. Dodge reluctantly gave him up and appointed 2nd Lt. Charles Morton of Company A as his replacement.[30]

After he arrived at Camp Harney, Foster settled in to the regular routine of escort and camp duty. While he was off-duty and on his own time, he drew up a detailed map of the new route from Camp Jenney, showing topography, landmarks, stream valleys, and grades incurred (fig 4.8). Like his other works, this map was done in ink and watercolors, and drawn to scale. He added several small paintings of landforms along the route, even labeling one unnamed butte "Foster's Butte," in his own honor.[31]

Other scenes were made as separate illustrations in his journal, which included mountain ranges, an overall map of the Black Hills, a view of "Castle Rocks," just north of the encampment, and a portrait of "California Joe," the famous frontiersman who accompanied the expedition and eventually became its guide (figs. 4.9–4.12).[32] On June 28 Foster and Capt. Henry W. Wessells of Company K, made a short excursion north to scale a near-vertical peak he christened "Headstone Peak." They managed to reach the summit of the slick granite mount after leaving their weapons behind and climbing in their stocking feet (fig. 4.11).

Colonel Dodge decided that more ground could be covered if he had an additional topographical officer in the field. While he sent Lieutenant Morton out on more out-lying assignments, Dodge himself mapped the area immediately around Camp Harney. About this time, it was brought to his attention that Lieutenant Foster had drawn credible maps of the expedition's march to the Hills. Consequently, on July 4 Dodge put Foster on detail as an additional topographical officer, and the next day sent him off to map the route west to Camp Jenney.[33] The expedition's military topographers were more interested in travel routes. Although their mission was to study topography, their mapping emphasis was separate from that of the geological surveying parties. For the next several months, mapping the Hills became Foster's full-time preoccupation on the expedition. He became part of the first effort to map the entire Black Hills; map making was official business, and he no longer drew them for his journal record.

The mandate for army field topographers came straight out of regulations. In 1873 a circular from Army Headquarters was added to Article LXVII, "Itineraries of March—Maps." It instructed that commanding officers of

FIG. 4.9. "Vidette" is a variant spelling of *vedette*, a mounted sentinel in advance of an army or troop movement. This watercolor was probably painted at Camp Jenney.

Of Joe, another expedition participant later recalled, "After entering the Black Hills, California Joe traveled entirely on foot . . . wearing an old cavalry overcoat, cavalry pants tucked in his boots, his gun in hand and on his head an old black, broad brimmed slouch hat." Harry Young, *Hard Knocks* (Chicago, IL: Laird & Lee, Inc., 1913): 166.

Headstone Peak — Climbed June 26th 1875 by Capt Henry W.
Wessels Jr + Lt J E H Field 3d Cavy — What was
believed to Rawhide Peak run 17° west of south
1 H + 20 m in climbing, rock on top 225 ft high
Had to reach summit by climbing in stocking
feet, leaving arms behind.

View — E. S. E. S. and S. W. Mountain ranges undulating
in succession until they ceased and
were merged in the Plain beyond — West
Mountain ranges as far as the eye could reach

N. W. N C + North — View cut-off by range of Bald mountains
quite near (

Camp Harney alt. 5600.

10.20. Took angle on Peak supposed to be Harneys Peak (35° East) found to be
Mistaken.

Water in springs to left of mouth of Gulch descending into Pleasant Valley — Water
in stream at crossing where road turns to N.E from South — Trail leading N E by E. from mouth of
Gulch is a cut off but is more difficult to get through
Dodges Park — Surrounded by mountain ranges to all appearances on all
sides — Beautiful cone-shaped Hillocks crowned with Pine trees scattered here
and there throughout, which winding through it is a creek bed, but where we
passed it, it was dry. Park ends (South) at Point marked &.am. which is the
beginning of another slight ridge — From this on to Pleasant Valley
the timber is larger and plenty of it (Pine)

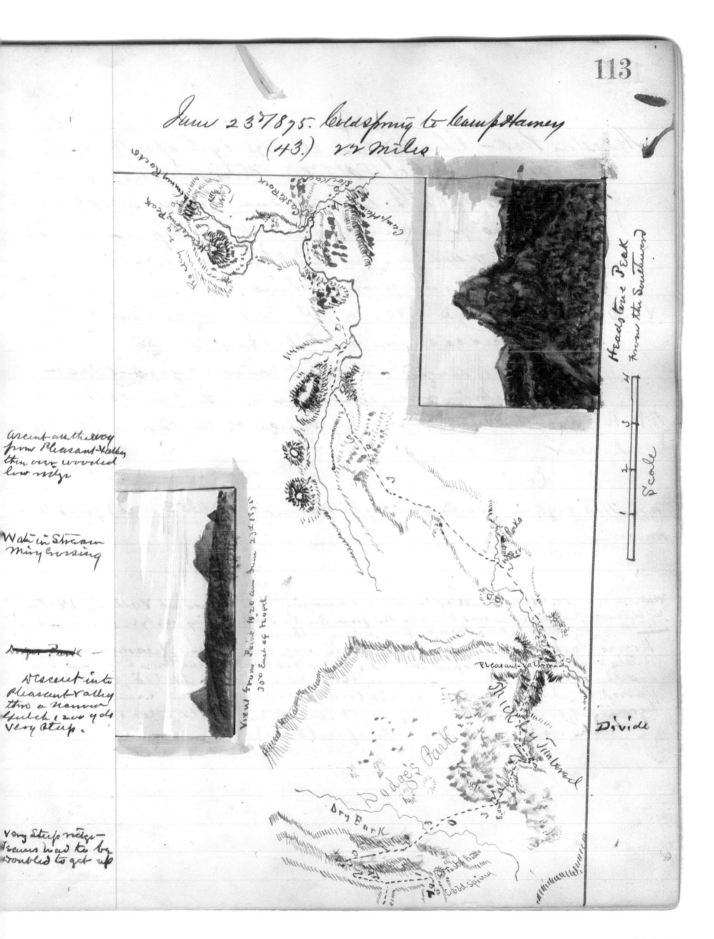

June 23rd 1875. Coldspring to Camp Harney
(43.) 22 miles

Ascent all the way
from Pleasant Valley
then over wooded
low ridge

Water in Stream
Many Crossing

Descent into
Pleasant Valley
thro a narrow
Gulch 200 yds
Very Steep.

Very Steep ridge—
teams had to be
doubled to get up

Headstone Peak
from the Southward

Scale

Divide

Dodge's Park

Dry Fork

View from Point 1920 am June 23d 1875
30° East of North

FIG. 4.10.

Castle Rock from Camp Harney

Looking N.N.W.   June 28th 1878

View from Summit of Headstone Peak
Peak in distance supplies the Rawhide
17° W of South.   June 26th 1875

to Rummey Rocks
from 3 miles West of Camp
Harney on French Creek
from 2 84 873.6

FIG. 4.II.

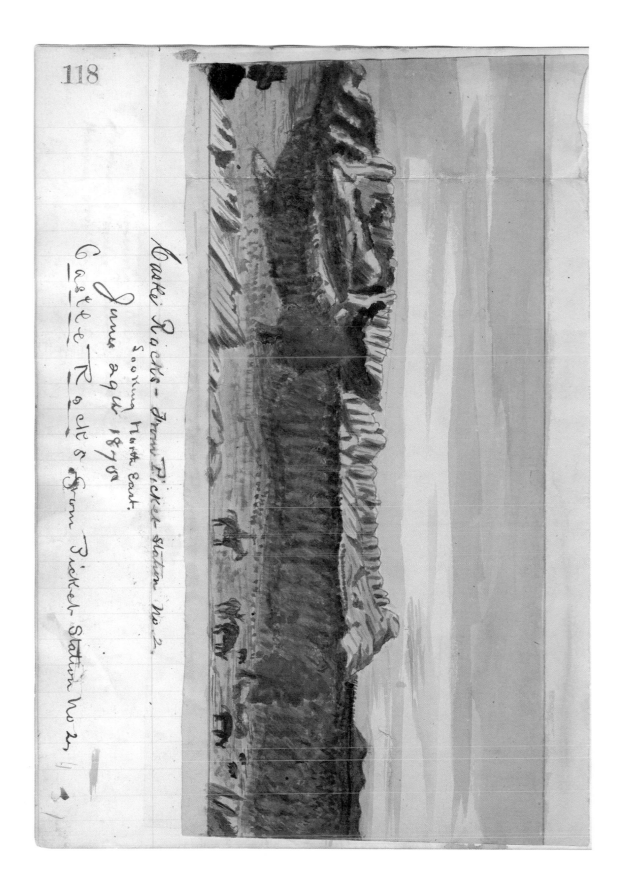

FIG. 4.12. For several seasons, Castle Rock was the great army campgrounds of the Black Hills. The Custer expedition camped in its vicinity in 1874, the Jenney expedition in 1875, and the Big Horn and Yellowstone Expedition in 1876. Located two miles east of Custer, Castle Rock is today known as Calamity Peak.

troops on the march were to select an officer to make field notes, sketches, and a journal necessary to later prepare a map of the route traversed. The officer selected was to be relieved of his routine duties to map and record. Officers on this duty were variously referred to as "Acting Engineer Officer," "Topographical Surveying Officer," "Topographical Officer," or by the common nickname, "Topog."[34]

During the five weeks the expedition was at Camp Harney, the topographers accomplished much work. Survey parties returned to camp every five or six days to check in and obtain supplies and change escorts. Although no native tribesmen were actually sighted thus far, Foster, while on a survey to the south, spotted Indian signs and reported back to Colonel Dodge that the prairie had been fired (burned off) around the Cheyenne River.[35] Upon return, his map drawn of the country scouted was pronounced by Dodge as "more than acceptable," and that "He (Foster) does remarkably well for a beginner." Several days later Dodge wrote Captain Hawley praising Foster's work. Hawley was the senior officer of the Third Cavalry on the expedition, and Colonel Dodge wanted to keep his new "topog" on the job.[36]

Finally, Dodge decided it was time to advance the base camp. Satisfied with the work accomplished out of Camp Harney, he boasted the vicinity of the camp had been "explored and mapped with almost the accuracy of an eastern township."[37] On July 19, he left with headquarters and two cavalry companies and headed north to locate the next camp. Two days later, "Camp Crook" was established thirty-five miles north on Rapid Creek, at a point where Jenney had found gold several weeks earlier.

By this time hundreds of miners were in the Hills working the streams. Several weeks beforehand, newspaper correspondents with the expedition had announced gold was in the Hills. Although prohibited from entry, adventuresome miners crept in, and were increasingly noticed by Colonel Dodge's survey parties. Scores had been seen on French Creek, leading Dodge to write in the expedition journal, "They seem to have suddenly sprung from the earth."[38]

In order to share supplies and escorts, Foster was paired up with McGillycuddy and sent out to explore and map specific areas. On July 23 they left Camp Harney with pack animals, to examine the area north of Castle Rock to the new camp on Rapid Creek. Astronomer Tuttle, Professor Newton, and photographer Guerin accompanied the party. After several days they were near Harney Peak, and prepared to climb it. After a perilous traverse up, they made camp a scant sixty feet below the summit.[39]

That night, a severe thunderstorm "shook the rocks like an earthquake." With heavy rain and lightning, several of the party quickly retreated two

"Thirty-six colors in that 'ere pan, stranger."

COLD SPRING CANON —ENTRANCE TO CUSTER CITY.

FIG. 4.13. While in Omaha after the Jenney Expedition, Foster prepared several illustrations, here and following, which appeared in the *Omaha Daily Bee*, May 13, 1876.

FIG. 4.14. *Omaha Daily Bee*, May 13, 1876

HARNEY'S PEAK, LOOKING S. E. FROM RAPID CREEK. 17 MILES AWAY.

FIG. 4.15. *Omaha Daily Bee*, May 13, 1876

hundred feet lower to a less exposed position (fig. 4.16). The next morning, most of the party returned to camp at the base of the mountain, but McGillycuddy, Newton, and Lieutenant Foster were determined to reach the top. That morning they set out to scale the highest peak in the Black Hills, as described by expedition surgeon J. L. Lane:

> The extreme summit consists of a tower-rock 60 feet in height, with almost smooth, perpendicular sides, that are most dangerous to climb; but the party proved equal to the occasion by going below and cutting a pine tree with branches for steps, which was used as a ladder to climb part of the distance, and a lariat-rope was then thrown over a projecting point of rock, and the Doctor made the first ascent up this perilous steep. Prof. Newton followed. Lieut. Foster came next, and, when half-way up, his feet slipped, and he launched out into space over the abyss below, hanging by his hands to the rope, and was hauled to the top in that way by the two men above.

They were the first white men to reach the true summit of Harney Peak. To commemorate their feat, Guerin took a photograph of the climbers atop the summit (fig. 4.17). In addition, Tuttle painted in red the signs of the Zodiac and a large red cross on a smooth face of the tower rock. The members of the climbing party then wrote their names on paper and enclosed it in a pint-flask left near the summit. They descended the mount, and moved on to Camp Crook.[40]

On July 28, Foster and McGillycuddy made it into Camp Crook. With

FIG. 4.16. View number 24 entitled "Surveying party at Breakfast on Harneys (*sic*) Peak." Foster is likely one of the group to the right. J. Leonard Jennewein Collection, McGovern Library/ DWU Archives, Dakota Wesleyan University, Mitchell, South Dakota

FIG. 4.17. View number 27, "Surveying Party on the summit of Harney's Peak." Foster, McGillycuddy, and astronomer Tuttle can be seen on the summit. J. Leonard Jennewein Collection, McGovern Library/ DWU Archives, Dakota Wesleyan University, Mitchell, South Dakota

the storm and all, they had "a hard time" on their adventure and lost three mules (subsequently recovered) in the process. After a day's rest they were sent out to map Spring Creek, returning to camp five days later.[41]

In the last part of July, General Crook arrived in the Black Hills. His intent was to meet with the illegal miners and inform them they all had to leave the Hills. Colonel Dodge was called on to assist in this touchy matter, and also to organize hunting excursions for the general and other guests. Before a large crowd in Custer on July 29, Crook issued a proclamation ordering all unauthorized citizens to leave by August 15. But he also encouraged those miners to file claims and return when permitted by the government. Later, to show that the army meant business, a military camp was established nearby with an infantry company and two troops of cavalry, to patrol and enforce the proclamation.[42] Lieutenants Morton and Foster were to pass on word of the eviction to any prospectors they met while exploring. Morton began to inform miners on his survey of the headwaters of Rapid Creek. Foster did the same as he moved up and down Spring Creek with McGillycuddy.[43]

Several days later Foster and Dr. McGillycuddy were back to camp. They reported their pack train had been lost and all hands had had nothing to eat for the past twenty-four hours. Tuttle did not come back with them, and Newton could not be found. Dodge sent out a detail to hunt up and bring in the mules and missing men. The lost were safely found after spending a day without food and "a night's lodging on a mountain side without even a blanket."[44]

An understandably perturbed Dodge felt that Jenney and his scientists were not concerned about proper management of the government pack trains or of their men. Jenney was determined that all of their time should be spent on exploration, not on any aspects of routine camp or field accountability and discipline. Generally, as a rule the soldiers and civilian members of the scientific corps got along fine—but every once in a while, Dodge found it necessary to have a sit-down with Professor Jenney. On this occasion Jenney agreed with the colonel's reasoning and advice to take more responsibility for his equipment and men. Dodge then issued orders placing Lieutenants Foster and Morton in full charge of the pack trains and escorts on their surveys. With the reorganization of the surveying parties complete, they were sent out again.[45]

After three weeks at Camp Crook, Dodge felt ready for the expedition to move on into the northwest section of the Black Hills. While at this camp, Foster mapped Spring Creek and its branches, Rapid Creek below Camp Crook, Box Elder Creek and its branches, and the head of Elk Creek.

FIG. 4.18 This loose page from Foster's journal contains typical field notes that he recorded in his field book to construct a map of a particular region. The field book held the compass readings and sketches of the topography encountered along his route throughout the day. At camp he would transcribe the observations onto a large sheet of paper and begin creating a working map. Both sides of the page are shown in actual size. It is rare to find original field notes as those were usually discarded after the map was drawn.—*Gene Thomsen, Nebraska Deputy State Surveyor.*

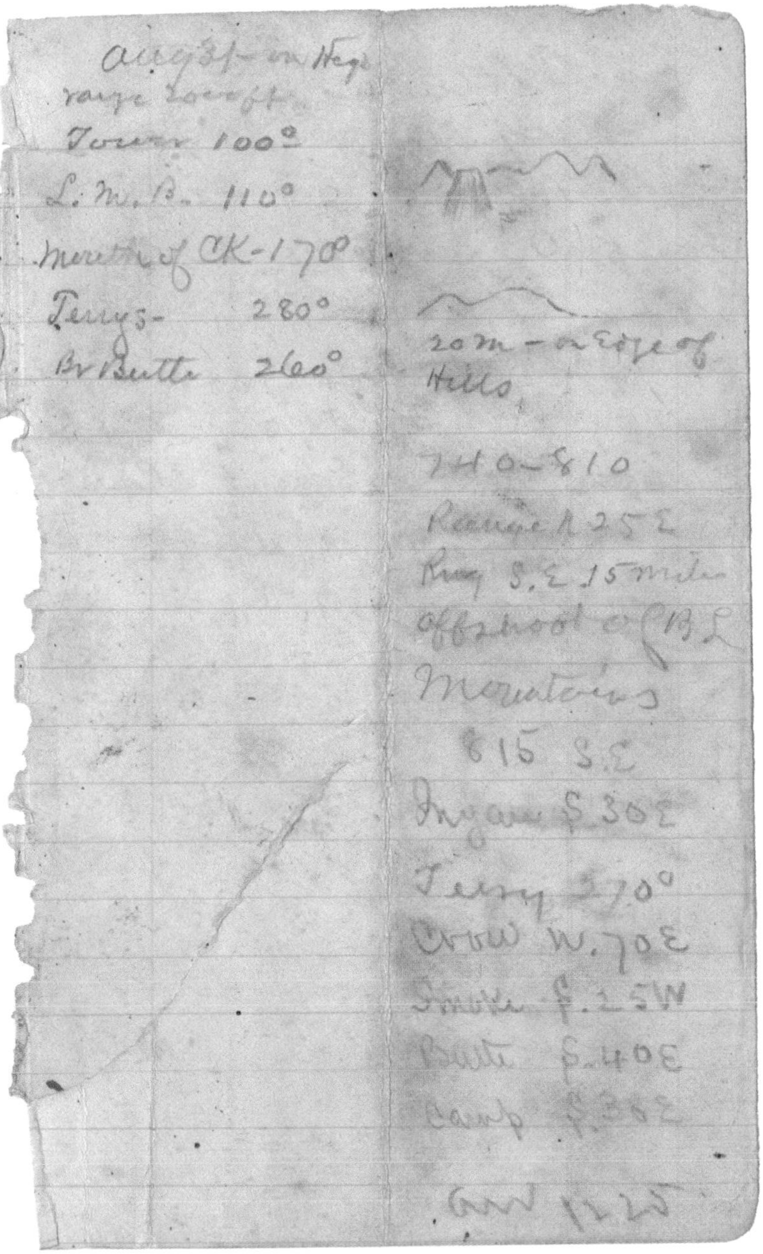

4.18A Shown on the front of the page are the selections of prominent peaks and buttes Foster used for reference points: Tower (Devils Tower), L.M.B. (Little Missouri Buttes), Terry's (Terry Peak), and Br. Butte (Bear Butte). These points were used for observations and compass readings which would be the foundation of his map. By use of triangulation, Foster could determine his location by observing those features, and plot additional field notes for the densification of the map. These notes appear to have been taken at a location about eight miles north-northwest of Sundance, Wyoming, more than likely from atop Warren Peak. [*G. T.*]

Latitudes —
Aug 10 . 1875

Lennox	44 ⊙ 3. 51	
Camp O	44. 0 3 22	
Noon	44, 2, 32,,	Aug 11th
Camp "P"	44, 3, 12,,	
157	44, 58, 35,,	Spg Ck
158		Rapid Ck
159	44, 8, 16,,	
Camp 8	44, 7, 6,,	

4.18B The back side of the page shows the locations and latitudes of observations made on August 10–11, when Foster mapped Spring Creek. At that time the main expedition was still at Camp Crook on Rapid Creek, thirty-five miles north of Camp Harney.

After several days' march to the northwest, the expedition halted for four days near Terry's Peak, to rest while the surveyors climbed the peak to take and verify readings from it. When this was completed, Dodge moved down to Floral Valley, and then west by north to where he established a new base camp, named Camp Bradley, on August 25.[46]

The new camp was on Inyan Kara Creek, just north of the peak with the same name. Dodge's plan was to explore the northwestern hills up to Bear Lodge (Devil's Tower), then move along the Belle Fourche, or North Fork of the Cheyenne River, and south along the eastern periphery of the Hills. On August 26 he ordered Foster to make a survey of Inyan Kara and Bear Lodge Creeks. He was assigned an escort of two noncommissioned officers and ten enlisted men, rationed for seven days with seventy rounds of ammunition each.[47] California Joe accompanied Foster as a guide on this trip. For the next week, they trudged through the country around the Tower, and then moved down the Bear Lodge Range.

Meanwhile, Dodge left camp to meet a supply train coming north from Fort Laramie, and to send his empty wagons back for more. To commemorate the rendezvous and transfer of supplies, he named the new camp "Camp Transfer." On September 1, Capt. William H. Andrews of Company I, Third Cavalry, joined the command, and the next day Lieutenant Foster's party returned. When he was introduced to Andrews, it was the first time in nearly two years of service that Foster had met, and would serve under, his actual company commander.

At Camp Transfer, Dodge wrote a report to General Crook on recent operations. Regarding the activities of his survey parties, he wrote:

> I have kept 2 parties of surveyors under Lts Morton & Foster in the field all the time, & have materials by which we can make as perfect a map, as can be made without surveyors compass & chain. I am very sure that no part of the wilderness is as well known as the Black Hills now are.[48]

He then laid out his plans for the rest of the expedition, planning to re-concentrate the exploring and survey parties near Bear Butte on September 20. He also requested that on the completion of the expedition, Lieutenants Foster and Morton report to Department Headquarters in Omaha, there to assist Dodge in drawing up the final maps. He felt with Lieutenant Bourke also at headquarters, it would prove helpful if all the officers who compiled the information would be present for the work.

When the Jenney Expedition was in its last weeks of exploration and survey, expedition manpower and material began to decrease. On

FIG. 4.19. Expedition photographer Guerin's photos were later marketed as a stereoscopic series entitled, "Professor Jenny's (*sic*) Expedition to the Black Hills 1875." This unnumbered view shows a mapping party at work in the hills. J. Leonard Jennewein Collection, McGovern Library/DWU Archives, Dakota Wesleyan University, Mitchell, South Dakota

VIEW OF THE BLACK HILLS.—VIEWED FROM THE BELLE FOURCHE.

FIG. 4.20. Foster's profile drawing of the northern hills picturing Bear Butte, and Custer's, Terry's, Warren's, and Crow Peaks. *Omaha Daily Bee*, May 13, 1876

September 4, Lieutenant Morton had made application to return to Sidney Barracks, his regular duty station. Dodge reluctantly approved his request.[49] This left the expedition one topographical officer short for the duration of its time in the field. The next morning a train prepared to return to Fort Laramie, transporting Morton, the two Ninth Infantry companies, the artillery, and all wagons not necessary for future use of the command. By the next time the expedition needed supplies, it would be in position to receive them from Camp Sheridan, in Nebraska, rather than via Fort Laramie.

As the troops moved forward, Foster mapped the Red Water and Crow Creek drainages. After ten days' travel through the mountainous country of the Wyoming Black Hills, the expedition moved in quest of the Belle Fourche River. Upon reaching a questionable water course, expedition members placed bets on its proper identification. Foster was sure the drainage was the Belle Fourche, but was proven wrong. To commemorate his miscalculation, a fellow officer composed a satirical limerick:

> There was a young topog named Foster,
> Who found La Belle Fourche and then lost her
> Getting mad, bet his pile
> Which Sam took with a smile
> And scooped this young topog named Foster.[50]

By mid-September the expedition was moving down the Belle Fourche. On the eighteenth, they reached its junction with Bear Peak Creek, the point where Dodge planned for the survey parties to rejoin the main body. For several days the command halted at Camp Raynolds, named for the officer whose expedition marched past the area in 1859. Jenney, however,

Custans from Bald Peak

failed to make it by the rendezvous date. This was the first time on the trip that a survey party missed an assigned gathering point. With his command (and Dodge himself) suffering from bad water, Dodge concluded to leave supplies for Jenney and move on.

Two days later, Camp Warren, the last of Dodge's base camps, was established two miles from where Rapid Creek emerged from the Hills. This campsite was occupied September 23–30, while the scientists explored the drainages of the eastern slopes of the Black Hills. Foster's field work included plotting the locations of Custer's Peak, Elk Butte, Kamelque Buttes, and other elevations along the eastern frontage.

By this time the expedition had run its course in the Black Hills, and exited out onto the Plains. As the column moved into more open country, Foster continued his topographical work. He mapped the route from Camp Warren through the Bad Lands, to the White River, which they reached on October 5, then up that river to Camp Sheridan, Nebraska, arriving there on the seventh. Although the rest of the way from Camp Sheridan was previously recorded, he continued to map their route of march from Sheridan to Camp Robinson (arrived October 9), and from there to Fort Laramie.[51]

The Jenney Expedition went into camp at Fort Laramie on October 13, nearly five months after it departed. While the headquarters wagon passed over 795 miles, the army had opened up 1,500 miles of wagon road, and the survey parties had made some six thousand miles of horse trails, all carefully mapped. Of the near four hundred mules taken on the expedition, only five were lost or died — not a single head of cattle from the beef herd was lost.[52]

* * *

After resting for several days, Dodge issued general orders that officially disbanded the Jenney Expedition. The infantry and cavalry units which comprised the escort were reassigned to stations in the Department of the Platte. On October 15, Companies A, H, and I of the Third Cavalry left for Fort D. A. Russell, where Company A took station. While Company H moved on to Fort McPherson, Foster's troop joined the garrison at Sidney Barracks on October 25.[53] He would have had barely enough time to settle in before orders arrived that sent him and Lieutenant Morton off to department headquarters. General Crook had approved Dodge's earlier request to have both officers assist in compiling the final maps of the new Black Hills explorations. On November 1, Foster joined Morton on the east-bound train for Omaha and detached service at headquarters.[54]

FIG. 4.21. In this view of Custer Peak, Foster included himself wearing a blue army blouse, and using a surveyor's transit.

Duty at department headquarters often provided a welcomed break from the monotony, isolation, and hardship frequently faced by the officers of the frontier army. And, particularly for those coming off hard field service, being surrounded by the benefits and excitement of city life was truly a return to civilization. By the mid-1870s Omaha was a large, thriving metropolis with a population of nearly twenty thousand, with many of the amenities found in eastern cities. While on this duty, Foster and Morton were quartered in downtown hotels or boarding houses, rather than in drab military housing.

Omaha was the most important military town in the department. Just north of town was Omaha Barracks, a post large enough to accommodate an entire regiment in garrison. Whenever necessary, troops from there were quickly sent out by rail to provide protection and scouting duty along the Union Pacific in Nebraska. Another key installation was located at the north end of the Union Pacific shops. This was the main quartermaster and commissary depot, a sprawling complex of offices, shops, warehouses, and stables, which supplied the thousands of soldiers in the Department of the Platte.

Headquarters proper was located in the Withnell Building, a four-storey brick office building located at Fifteenth and Harney Streets. Built for government use by the Withnell brothers, it was first occupied by the Department of the Platte on November 3, 1868. It contained offices for the department commanding general and staff, and for the adjutant general, chief medical officer, judge advocate, chief engineer officer, and other departmental bureau chiefs, all occupied by staff officers and numerous enlisted and civilian clerks.[55]

Both Foster and Morton drew recognition for their services during the expedition. While still in the field, Dr. McGillycuddy wrote a report to the Commissioner of Indian Affairs which in part acknowledged their valuable assistance in reconnaissance and trail survey. Regarding their work, Colonel Dodge wrote in his report of operations: "On the Topographical Officers of the expedition the heaviest burden of labor fell. With scanty pack-mule outfits, a shelter tent and blanket, hard tack and bacon, they penetrated to every portion of the Hills, exploring everywhere, examining everything, locating with fidelity and care every stream and mountain range." Publicly, their mapping work was complimented by an expedition correspondent for the *Chicago Tribune;* Professor Jenney also noted their topographical work in the press. Later published reports thanked the accompanying army officers for their co-operation, "as well as a recognization [sic] of topographic assistance by Lts. Morton and Foster."[56]

FIG. 4.22. Located at the southwest corner of Fifteenth and Harney streets, the Withnell Building housed the Department of the Platte headquarters from 1868 to 1878. NSHS RG2341-2, p. 36.

After nearly seven weeks of cartographic work, Morton was excused and returned to his proper station.[57] During the course of the expedition, Foster mapped much more territory than either Bourke or Morton. As a result, he spent the next two months at headquarters on compiling notes and sketches, and map work with Colonel Dodge.

1   For more on the Warren Expedition, see James D. McLaird and Lesta V. Turchen, "Exploring the Black Hills, 1855–1875: Reports of the Government Expeditions: The Dacota Explorations of Lieutenant Gouverneur Kemble Warren, 1855–1856–1857" *South Dakota History* 3 (Fall 1973): 360–389.

2   McLaird & Turchen, "Exploring the Black Hills: Reports of the Government Expeditions: The Explorations of Captain William Franklin Raynolds, 1859–1860," *South Dakota History* 4 (Winter 1973): 19–62. The most recent study of the 1874 Custer Expedition is Ernest Grafe and Paul Horsted, *Exploring with Custer: The 1874 Black Hills Expedition* (Custer, SD: Golden Valley Press, 2002).

3   Henry Newton and Walter P. Jenney, *Report on the Geology and Resources of the Black Hills of Dakota* (Washington, DC: Government Printing Office, 1880), 18.

4   Newton & Jenney, *Report on the Geology*, 19.

5 For a fine biography of Dodge, see Wayne R. Kime, *Colonel Richard Irving Dodge: The Life and Times of a Career Army Officer* (Norman, OK: University of Oklahoma Press, 2006).

6 Charles M. Robinson, ed., *The Diaries of John Gregory Bourke, Vol. I, November 20, 1872–July 28, 1876* (Denton, TX: The University of North Texas Press, 2003), 160.

7 Lesta V. Turchen and James D. McLaird, *The Black Hills Expedition of 1875* (Mitchell, SD: Dakota Wesleyan University Press, 1975), 31.

8 Post returns, Fort McPherson, April 1875.

9 Ibid., May 1875; Regimental Returns, Third Cavalry, May 1875.

10 Wayne R. Kime, ed., *The Black Hills Journals of Colonel Richard Irving Dodge* (Norman, OK: University of Oklahoma Press, 1996), 56.

11 General Orders (GO) No. 2, May 24, 1875, Headquarters, Black Hills Expedition (BHE); Robinson, *Bourke Diary, Vol. I*, 173–74.

12 GO 2, May 24, 1875, BHE.

13 Robinson, *Bourke Diary Vol. I*, 174; Turchen & McLaird, *Black Hills Expedition*, 34–35.

14 Kime, *Black Hills Journals*, 48.

15 Robinson, *Bourke Diaries, Vol. I*, 170.

16 Ibid., 171.

17 Kime, *Black Hills Journals*, 50.

18 Ibid., 51; Robinson, *Bourke Diaries, Vol. I*, 172.

19 Robinson, *Bourke Diaries, Vol. I*, 172.

20 Ibid.

21 Kime, *Black Hills Journals*, 53.

22 Ibid., 54; Turchen & McLaird, *Black Hills Expedition*, 35.

23 Kime, *Black Hills Journals*, 58.

24 Robinson, *Bourke Diaries, Vol. I*, 176–77.

25 Turchen & McLaird, *Black Hills Expedition*, 36.

26 Robinson, *Bourke Diaries, Vol. I*, 179.

27 Newton & Jenney, *Report on the Geology*, 34–35; John G. Bourke, *On the Border with Crook* (New York, NY: Scribner's Sons, 1891), 242–43.

28 Turchen & McLaird, *Black Hills Expedition*, 38.

29 Ibid., 44.

30 Kime, *Black Hills Journals*, 97; SO 8, June 27, 1875, BHE.

31 Unfortunately for Foster, the name did not stick. Today there is no landform or peak named Foster's Butte in the Hills.

32 Moses Milner (California Joe) once held the reputation of "Custer's Favorite Scout." He was hired on as a packer on May 21, but three days later was discharged for drunkenness. Joe nevertheless accompanied the expedition. Dodge soon realized that he had an uncanny ability to find a good route and rehired him as guide. Joe served in that capacity until the end of the expedition.

33 SO 11, July 4, 1875, BHE; Turchen & McLaird, *Black Hills Expedition*, 46.

34 The Secretary of War, *Regulations of the Army of the United States and General Orders in Force on the 17th of February, 1881* (Washington, DC: Government Printing Office, 1881), 97.

35 Kime, *Col. Richard Irving Dodge*, 206–07.

36 Kime, *Black Hills Journals*, 129, 135.

37 Turchen & McLaird, *Black Hills Expedition*, 46.

38 Ibid., 47.

39 The story of this escapade appeared in the *Chicago Tribune*, Aug. 17, 1875.

40 The material quoted in the preceding paragraph and the details here are from the August 17 article.

41 Kime, *Black Hills Journals*, 152.

42 Kime, *Col. Richard Irving Dodge*, 213–17.

43 *The New York Herald*, Aug. 20, 1875.

44 Kime, *Black Hills Journals*, 160; Turchen & McLaird, *Black Hills Expedition*, 51.

45 Kime, *Col. Richard Irving Dodge*, 215; SO 24, Aug. 8, 1875, BHE.

46 "Authorities" listed on the "The Black Hills of the Cheyenne, Map of Explorations & Surveys made under the direction of Lt. Col. R. I. Dodge, 23 U. S. Infantry, 1875."

47 SO 28, Aug. 26, 1876, BHE.

48 Dodge to Gen. Crook, Sept. 4, 1874, in Kime, *Black Hills Journals*, 206.

49 With his wife near childbirth, Morton had applied for leave in August. After the child was born, Dodge could not disapprove the leave. Kime, *Black Hills Journals*, 188, 197–98.

50 Ibid., 248; Kime, *Col. Richard Irving Dodge*, 221.

51 Information on Foster's mapping activities is from the "Authorities" section published on the Black Hills map.

52 Turchen & McLaird, *Black Hills Expedition*, 92, 79.

53 GO 6, Oct. 15, 1875, BHE; Post Returns, Sidney Barracks, October 1875.

54 *Army and Navy Journal*, Nov. 6, 1875.

55 *Omaha Weekly Republican*, Nov. 4, 1868.

56 Turchen & McLaird, *Black Hills Expedition*, 22, 92; *Chicago Tribune*, Aug. 21, 1875; Capt. George M. Wheeler, *Report Upon United States Geographical Surveys West of the One Hundredth Meridian, Vol. I—Geographical Report* (Washington, DC: Government Printing Office, 1889), 719.

57 Morton returned to Fort D. A. Russell from detached service at Omaha on Dec. 24, 1875. Post Returns, Fort Russell, December 1875.

SKETCH BY
LIEUT. J.E.FOSTER U.S.A.

ROAD TO BLACK HILLS

CHICAGO ENGRAVING

CHAPTER 5

The Great Sioux War, 1876–1877

With the completion of his Black Hills cartographic assignment, Lieutenant Foster received orders dated February 18 to return to his proper duty station "without delay." After nearly four months of detached service at department headquarters, he was on his way back to rejoin his unit at Sidney Barracks, in western Nebraska. Two days later he reported to the post commander, and also received his quarters assignment from post quartermaster and fellow company subaltern, Lt. Albert King.

Sidney Barracks was one of the eighteen army posts then in active service in the Department of the Platte. Established in late 1867, it was one of four posts that were specifically built in western Nebraska and Wyoming for protection of the new Union Pacific Railroad. Positioned between the main Indian crossing points of the railroad, its troops could be quickly dispatched by rail to trouble spots. In the 1870s, troops from the post were sent out on scouts and pursuits of depredating native bands roaming south from the northern Nebraska agencies. Sidney Barracks proved a useful troop station: a permanent garrison was maintained there well into the 1890s.[1]

The post contained excellent facilities to comfortably house three companies of troops. With its location immediately east of the town of Sidney, and within easy view of the railroad, Sidney Barracks was a well-maintained post with a number of new buildings. Irrigation ditches provided a green parade ground, as one officer later recalled that the post was "a wonderful thing out there, being a green spot in the yellow plains country."[2] When Foster arrived at post, the garrison still consisted of three companies of the Third Cavalry Regiment, which numbered nearly two hundred officers and enlisted men, plus a number of dependents.

FIG. 5.1. Foster's view of Sidney, Nebraska. Sidney Barracks is on the left background; the road to the Black Hills is on the right. *Omaha Daily Bee,* May 13, 1987. NSHS RG 2548-10

In 1876, Sidney was the most important railroad town between North Platte and Cheyenne, Wyoming. Sporting a population of about five hundred inhabitants, Sidney was a freight division for the Union Pacific, with a roundhouse and shop facilities located there. It was also the county seat and an established, *lively* frontier town. Of Sidney, the post surgeon's wife wrote home in January 1876: "I don't believe there is so utterly bad a place in the whole United States. Nothing but whiskey & vice & wickedness. I wouldn't live in Sidney for the wealth of the whole state." Lucky for her, her home on post was not in Sidney, but three blocks away![3]

Significantly, its location on the Union Pacific made Sidney the closest rail point for the shipment of government supplies to the large Indian agencies and their adjoining military posts in northwestern Nebraska. At the time Foster was there, Sidney was on the verge of becoming a major gateway to the Black Hills. When the Hills were opened to the miners, the route established to deliver agency and military goods was extended further north into the Hills to become the legendary Sidney-Deadwood Trail of the gold rush period.[4]

Upon Foster's arrival, commanding officer Capt. Frederic Van Vliet appointed him post adjutant. Foster had proven administrative skills, and previously served as adjutant while at Fort McPherson. Additionally, with all three of his company's commissioned officers present, he was not directly needed for company duty. Thus, he was free to fill this important, yet time-consuming job, which was necessary at every army post.

On the post level, the adjutant position was usually held by a junior lieutenant, appointed by the post commander to assist in all details of post operations. The adjutant served as the channel of communications to the commanding officer, had all orders or instructions written up and delivered, and was in charge of all books, files, and rosters. He inspected the daily guard and other armed parties before departure on duty, and received the company reports at the daily evening parade. At Sidney Barracks, Foster's cartographic skills were put to further use. Van Vliet requested him to draw up a large wall map of the country north and south of the post. Such a map would aid in the deployment of scouts and patrols and also record new geographical information for future reference. To help prepare the map, Foster wrote to the department engineer office and asked to borrow any reports and maps of scouts made out of Sidney. His request quickly received General Crook's approval, and the materials were forwarded on.[5]

The only change from Foster's regular routine at Sidney came in March, when an order arrived detailing him for general courts-martial duty at Cheyenne Depot, Wyoming. Sitting on a military court was a frequent cause of detached service for army officers. There were two basic courts that soldiers could be tried before. On the local level, garrison courts were presided over by one officer, and heard lesser cases such as insubordination, drunkenness, or absence from roll calls. On the other hand, general courts were convened for more serious offences which involved long-term sentences, and could only be authorized by the department commander. General courts were presided over by five or more disinterested commissioned officers, brought in from other posts to hear the case. One of the officers would be appointed to serve as the judge advocate. Although general courts-martials were cumbersome affairs with time-consuming procedures to follow, the soldiers charged received fair trial and were sentenced accordingly.[6]

The court Foster served on consisted of three Third Cavalry officers from Sidney Barracks, and four Twenty-third Infantry officers: one from North Platte Station, one from Fort Russell, and two from Cheyenne Depot. The post of Cheyenne Depot was located halfway between Fort Russell and the town of Cheyenne, and was the point where military supplies coming from the east on the Union Pacific were unloaded and shipped north by wagon train. Although the court spent the rest of the month and into April hearing cases, Lieutenant Foster was relieved from this duty on April 1 and returned to Sidney.[7]

While Foster was on detached service at Omaha, he apparently began work on a series of sketches of the Black Hills, more than likely intended for publication in the *Omaha Daily Bee* newspaper (figs. 4.13–14, 4.16, 4.20). Because this project was not a part of his official assignment, he apparently made the sketches on his own during off-duty times. His Black Hills views included scenes from the climbing of Harney Peak, view of Devils Tower, a profile view of the northern Hills from the Belle Fourche River, and other interesting terrain along the expedition's route. Although some of his drawings were made off Guerin's photographs, others were strictly freehanded.[8]

Foster continued the project, and probably made several drawings of Black Hills-related subjects while at Sidney Barracks. That spring he created a detailed bird's-eye view of Sidney from the high bluff just above town (fig. 5.1). Importantly for Sidney boosters, his sketch showed the railroad facilities, business district, the military post, and the beginnings of a trail labeled "Road to the Black Hills." He also prepared a view of Red Cloud Agency, and the recently completed Sidney Bridge over the North Platte River, which was built by Omaha businessman Henry T. Clarke (fig. 5.2).

His submitted sketches were converted to engravings, and printed in a two-page illustrated promotional spread titled "The New Short Cut to the Black Hills," published as a supplement to the May 13, 1876, issue of

SCETCH BY LEIUT J.E.FOSTER.U.S.A.

CHICAGO ENGRAVING CO.

THE SIDNEY BRIDGE, Across the North Platte River on the Custer City Route. Erected by H. T. Clarke.

the *Bee*. Additionally, his drawings of Sidney and the Red Cloud Agency were subsequently reprinted in the *Sidney Telegraph* on October 28, where they appeared in several later issues. As a result, Foster's drawings provided many westerners with their first visual impressions of the mysterious Black Hills. Publication of his drawings added a new dimension to the record of Foster's experiences in the American West.

The War Begins

War with the Sioux over possession of the Black Hills was brewing on the horizon. In the fall of 1875, government attempts to purchase the Hills from the Teton Lakotas failed miserably. Plans were next set in motion to win the Hills militarily in a final war of conquest for control of the Northern Plains.

For years, large numbers of Lakotas had always remained away from their agencies on the Great Sioux Reservation. Those nonagency, traditional bands resisted changes brought by the government and free-roamed the Yellowstone and Powder River countries. They preferred to cling to their traditional lifestyles of the hunt and, when necessary, war. This resistance often brought them into conflict with the encroaching whites, particularly with those now wanting to enter the Black Hills. Generally called northern Indians, those bands were influenced by Sitting Bull, Crazy Horse, and other traditionalists; others at the agencies left to join the Northern camps.

In November, a decree was sent out by the Indian Bureau that all tribesmen were to return to their proper agencies by January 30, or be considered hostile and face the consequences. Although some did come in, getting the word out to all the nonagency camps in the dead of winter proved an impossible task. On February 8, Philip Sheridan, commanding general of the Division of the Missouri, forwarded instructions to Brig. Gen. Alfred Terry at the Department of Dakota, and General Crook at the Department of the Platte, to begin military operations against the Northern warriors. The overall military strategy called for three strong troop columns to enter the Yellowstone/Powder River country from the west, east, and south, to locate and force nonagency Indians back to the reservation. As it had been for the Black Hills Expedition, Department of the Platte troops were close to areas of operations, and Crook was free to move and command in Terry's department.[9]

It was Crook who made the first move of the war. In late winter he amassed a strong force of ten cavalry and two infantry companies at Fort Fetterman, Wyoming Territory, to strike into the Powder River country. On March 1 the Big Horn Expedition, commanded by Colonel Reynolds, Third Cavalry, and accompanied by Crook, departed Fetterman and headed north. Seventeen days later they attacked a village believed to be that of Crazy Horse along the Little Powder River. The soldiers quickly captured the village and the Indian horse herd of seven hundred head. Seemingly with victory in hand, Reynolds ordered his forces to withdraw from the field before the village was destroyed. And also later that night, the warriors recaptured the horse herd—the soldiers were in essence left with nothing for their efforts but casualties. In disgust, Crook ordered the expedition back to reorganize and try again.[10]

On that same day Crook struck the village on Powder River, a second troop column headed for Sioux country. That day, five Seventh Infantry companies at Fort Shaw in northwest Montana Territory, headed south to Fort Ellis, where they joined an additional infantry company and four troops of the Second Cavalry. Under command of Col. John Gibbon, Seventh Infantry, the so-called "Montana Column" marched eastward into the Yellowstone River country to search for any bands of northern Indians and engage them if the opportunity arose.[11]

Later that spring, three companies of the Sixth and Seventeenth Infantry regiments, and the entire Seventh Cavalry regiment (commanded by Lt. Col. George A. Custer) marched out of Fort Abraham Lincoln at Bismarck, in Dakota Territory. The "Dakota Column" made its way west to link up with Gibbon's Montana Column. Both troop columns were under General Terry's overall command.[12]

Crook's next foray, the Big Horn and Yellowstone Expedition, brought together fifteen cavalry and five infantry companies, which totaled forty-seven officers and 1,002 enlisted men, all from posts in the department.

Crook once again used Fort Fetterman, the closest military post to the Powder River, as the expedition point of departure and of supply. The troops were supplied by 120 wagons and one thousand pack mules, manned by nearly three hundred civilian teamsters and packers. Of the cavalry troops on the expedition, four companies of the Second Cavalry and five of the Third were veterans of the earlier Powder River campaign. Most of the companies ordered to the field were from posts along the Union Pacific. This included the three companies of the Third Cavalry stationed at Sidney Barracks. Foster was in line for the longest and arguably hardest Indian Wars campaign on the Northern Plains.[13]

The ultimate goal of the Big Horn and Yellowstone Expedition was to find the non-agency Sioux—more specifically, Crazy Horse and his allies. Once located, Crook's force was to engage them in battle, or to drive them eastward toward the strong column moving west from Dakota. All of this fit into the broad strategy employed by the army during the Plains Indian wars; a strategy which included converging troop columns, relentless pursuits, and complete destruction of captured resources. The end result of such harsh tactics was the forced return of resisting northern bands to their agencies.[14]

According to a letter of instruction dated May 8 from department headquarters, two companies of the Twenty-third Infantry from Omaha Barracks arrived at Sidney on the 11th. They were the replacement units for Companies C, G, and I of the Third transferred for field service. Foster was relieved as post adjutant on May 12 to prepare for the field. At 9:00 a.m., on May 13, the cavalrymen boarded a train and proceeded via the Union Pacific for Medicine Bow, Wyoming Territory. Once on board, they joined two other companies of the Third from Fort McPherson, also on the way to join the expedition. Later that day the cavalrymen arrived at Medicine Bow, and went into camp for several days to await the arrival of other troop units, department staff officers, and other officers assigned to the expedition.[15]

On May 21, under the command of Maj. Andrew W. Evans, the troops marched north eighty-five miles—with a portion of the route through high elevations—to Fort Fetterman. Three days later, they camped within sight of the post, and the next day (25th) joined the expedition camp directly across from the post on the north side of the Platte. There, the busy preparations for field service were vividly described by Lt. John Bourke:

> Bustle and activity prevailing in camp: officers, orderlies and detachments of men passing constantly to and from the Garrison... Wagon loads of grain, ammunition, subsistence and other stores crossed the

Platte to the camp on the other side which spread out in a picturesque panorama along the level meadow, surrounded by a bend of the stream. The long rows of shelter tents, herds of animals grazing or running about, trains of wagons and mules passing from point to point, made up a scene of great animation and spirit.[16]

After several days in camp, the expedition moved out at noon on May 29. The cavalry column alone stretched out for more than a mile. Lt. Col. William B. Royall, Third Cavalry, was in command of the expedition cavalry forces, with Major Evans in charge of the Third Cavalry battalion, and Capt. Henry E. Noyes commanding the Second Cavalry battalion. The first several days were uneventful, as men and animals adjusted to campaign routine.[17]

After struggling through a pelting snowstorm on the first of June, the column reached the site of old Fort Reno of the Bozeman Trail days on the second. There the command had expected to meet a body of Crow Indian scouts coming down from Crow Agency in Montana. No scouts were there, and not wanting to wait, the troops pushed on. As they neared the site of Fort Phil Kearny several days later, signs of Indians moving north were spotted. After that, the officers paid more attention to the posting of pickets, and the wagons were corralled at night. On June 7 Foster's company was on pioneer duty. That day was particularly hard work, as they prepared the road with an amount of excavating, embanking, corduroying, and grading that was "rather unusual and most laborious."[18]

Crook had intended to go on to Goose Creek, but his guides were absent and a wrong turn was made. The column had headed north along Prairie Dog Creek, away from the forks of Goose Creek. Crook decided to continue down the creek to Tongue River; camp was made that night on the confluence of Prairie Dog and the Tongue. Realizing that his men and animals were exhausted from the hard march and steep grade, he decided to remain in camp there for a couple days to rest and wait for the Crow scouts. But by this time the soldiers had been spotted by a small party of Cheyennes. Two days later, James Foster came under fire for the first time since the Civil War.

At six o'clock in the evening of June 9, several hundred Sioux and Cheyenne warriors gathered on a high bluff across the river and began firing into the camp. The cavalry companies were grooming their horses on the picket line, so the infantry companies, with their longer range rifles, returned the warriors' fire. Although the camp endured the hostile fusillade for half an hour, no serious damage was done. Bourke noted,

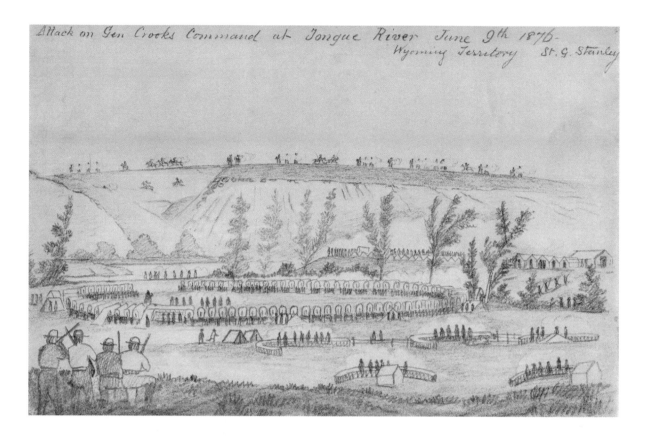

"Bullets passed through canvass [sic], tent-poles, stove-pipes and wagons and struck the ground amidst our troops, but no further casualties were received."[19] Nevertheless, three horses and one mule were wounded. During the attack, a party of warriors attempted to cross the river above the camp to capture horses. They were quickly driven back by the alert pickets.

To prevent more serious damage to the command, Crook ordered Capt. Anson Mills to take a battalion of Third Cavalry and clear the bluff. Companies A, E, I, and M crossed the river, dismounted and moved up the steep slope. Company I, led by Captain Andrews and Lieutenant Foster, cleared the left, while the other three companies swept the middle and right. The warriors retreated when they saw the size of the attacking force. Twenty minutes after the appearance of the cavalry on the bluff, the fight was over. One warrior was seen shot and carried off the field and another possibly wounded. On the other side, two soldiers were slightly wounded. Accordingly, many officers were glad the attack had been made, for if it did nothing else, "it proved we were not going to have our marching for nothing."[20]

The next morning Foster was placed in temporary command of E Company, and sent to relieve Captain Vroom's company, which had spent

FIG. 5.3. The Tongue River Heights fight, as sketched by Charles St. George Stanley, *Frank Leslie's* field illustrator who accompanied the Big Horn and Yellowstone Expedition. Courtesy of Mark E. Miller

the night atop the bluff. With a shortage of grass in the vicinity, Crook decided to move camp nearer to the mountains. The next morning (11th) the command moved out. Foster's company remained on the bluff with pickets out until everyone was out of camp, and then joined the rear guard on the opposite side of the river. That night the expedition camped on a pleasant spot near the Goose Creek confluence, seventeen miles south of the Tongue River campsite.[21]

At the new camp the command anxiously waited for their belated Crow allies. With official duties and drills only taking up a couple of hours each day, officers played whist, read (Bourke later recalled newspapers were "read to pieces"[22]), talked, and told stories. Both officers and enlisted men fished and went hunting, particularly those from Capt. Mills's company, who brought in several bears they bagged in the Big Horn Mountains. Foster spent much of his time making sketches of points of interest along their march and the scenery around Goose Creek. According to Bourke, he hoped to send them to *Harper's Weekly* for publication. However, most of the illustrations that came out of the campaign were drawn by Charles St. George Stanley, the field artist for *Frank Leslie's Illustrated Newspaper*.[23]

Somewhat surprised at the aggressiveness of the Sioux and Cheyenne at the Tongue River fight, Crook improved his camp security. As a precaution against surprise daylight attack, Crook placed whole companies at protective locations, to defeat small attacking parties and hold larger ones in check. However, with no northern warriors in the neighborhood, those preparations proved unnecessary.

Just before dusk on June 14, the Crows, numbering 176 warriors, finally arrived in camp. Additionally, two hours after this, 80 friendly Shoshoni braves rode in, giving Crook over 250 auxiliaries to find and fight the northern warriors. The next day the Crows informed Crook that a large Sioux village was located on Rosebud Creek, about forty-five miles north of the Goose Creek camp. That night at retreat he laid out his battle plans for his battalion and staff officers. Crook's objective was simply to strike the Indians on the Rosebud. In the morning the command would cut loose from its wagons and pack train, with each man carrying four day's rations of coffee, hard bread, and bacon. Also each man would carry one hundred rounds of ammunition and was allowed to carry one blanket. To increase the attack force, 175 infantrymen were mounted on pack mules to accompany the cavalry. One hundred men were left to guard the camp, with the wagons corralled for defense. At 5:00 a.m. on June 16, the march to the Rosebud began.[24]

Crook's force numbered more than 1,300 soldiers, Indians, civilian packers, and a few miners who had been permitted to travel with the column. As it marched out of camp, the column was led by five companies of mule-mounted infantry, divided into two small battalions. They were followed by Colonel Royall's cavalry force, which was divided into four battalions, each commanded by senior captains. Foster's company was in Capt. Mills's battalion. The Crow and Shoshoni auxiliaries were at the front and flank of the column, with the civilian packers and miners riding at the rear.

The column marched down the Tongue River till early afternoon, and then crossed the divide to the extreme headwaters of Rosebud Creek, a "feeble rivulet of snow water" at that point.[25] Camp was made on the Rosebud at dusk after a march of thirty-five miles. The camp was formed in a hollow square for defense, with horses and mules held in the square for protection. Unknown to Crook at the time, the village he sought was not below on Rosebud Creek, but some thirty miles to the northwest on Reno Creek, a small tributary of the Little Big Horn. By this time the northern warriors were aware of the coming soldiers, and by that night hundreds of Lakota and Cheyenne fighters rode out to meet them; the Lakota led by the great warrior-chieftain Crazy Horse, and the Cheyenne by Two Moon and Old Two Moon.

The Battle of the Rosebud

Early the next morning, the command arose at 3:00 a.m., and by 5:00 a.m. was on the march, continuing its hunt for the village. As they followed along the Rosebud, so-named for the thick growth of wild roses along its banks, the headwaters turned into the main stream. At 8:00 a.m. the column arrived between two bends of the stream, five miles below their camp of the 16th. Here the valley opened up with a bottomland almost half a mile wide. While on the north side of the creek, a series of low ridges that gradually arose toward the northwest, on the south side were bluffs five hundred feet above the valley floor. The terrain was open, rolling hills, with rock outcroppings and scattered timber found at the higher points. Just to the east, the second bend of the Rosebud made an abrupt turn to a narrow canyon to the north.

At this point, Crook halted the troops in their marching order to give the men a break and allow the horses to graze. Crook with the mounted infantry and the Second Cavalry units remained on the north side of the creek; the Third Cavalry, with Mills's battalion in the lead, remained on the south. As soldiers relaxed and some prepared coffee,

Crook played whist with Lieutenant Bourke and several infantry officers. Crow scouts suddenly came charging down from the hills, pursued by Lakota and Cheyenne warriors. Just like that, the fight was on.[26]

The Battle of the Rosebud lasted for the next six hours, in what was described as a "battle of ebb and flow" where "Charge met with counter charge."[27] Quickly sizing up the situation, Crook realized he needed to control the high ground to the north and west, plus the south bluffs, to prevent his command from falling into a crossfire. The troops on the north side of the Rosebud formed a dismounted skirmish line over a mile long, and advanced on the Sioux there. While two companies of the Third took the south bluffs, Mills's battalion fought off the attack on the east end, then cleared the highest ridge running to the northwest. Colonel Royall led five companies of the Third to the west end of the field to engage the Indian attack on the rear of the camp. Foster's company rode with Royall.

Colonel Royall sent Andrews's company to drive off mounted warriors from the heights west of the camp. Captain Andrews ordered Foster and I Company's second platoon to drive the Sioux from a ridge on the left of his position. With eighteen men, Foster charged the left, seized the ridge, dismounted his men and fired a volley at warriors in his front and then charged and seized that point. Foster's men forced other Indian warriors back from the high ground they occupied beyond. But, by this time his platoon was far to the west, and with mounted Sioux and Cheyenne swarming about, was in serious danger of being cut off. When he saw this threat, Andrews quickly ordered his subaltern to return to his company on the ridge where Royall was forming a new line. Foster led his men back through a withering fire to rejoin Company I. Throughout the entire escapade, his platoon only suffered casualties of two men and one horse wounded. For the next several hours Royall's battalion held their position on the left flank against hostile charges and heavy rifle fire. Foster and the other Third Cavalry officers remained mounted to direct the fire of their men through what became the hardest fighting of the entire battle.[28]

By 10:00 a.m., Crook had occupied the highlands north of his morning camp and held the bluffs south of the Rosebud. Meanwhile, the main problem on the battlefield remained the same: the soldiers could drive the Indians off, but could not fix and destroy them.[29] He needed to find a new strategy to win the day. All along Crook believed the Indians' main camp further down the Rosebud was the key to the issue. Determined to capture the village, he had Captains Mills and Noyes prepare their battalions to push downstream, to find and destroy the nonexistent village he thought there.

However, at the west end, the Sioux and Cheyenne began to make concentrated attacks on Colonel Royall's Third Cavalry battalion, which included Foster's troop. For over an hour, Royall continued to fend off aggressive attacks from the high ground of his second position. Crook, wanting to change the course of battle, ordered Royall to withdraw eastward to his (Crook's) position, and sent Mills to execute his drive in search of the village. Over the midday, Royall pulled back as Crook had ordered, but subsequently fell under attack on three sides. Realizing the present danger, Crook sent word for Mills to give up on the village and come around to strike the Indians attacking Royall. From 12:30 to 1:30 p.m., the last hour of the battle, Mills struck the Sioux and Cheyenne flank and scattered hundreds of warriors that were massing for another attack. Immediately after Mills's charge, the Indian forces abandoned the field and left. The Battle of the Rosebud was over.

Because he held the field, General Crook claimed victory. Of course to the warriors who met and engaged him that day, it meant little difference if Crook held the field or not. To them, the important point was that the soldiers were stopped long before they were a threat to the village on Reno Creek. The northern Indians were not defeated. Army losses at the Rosebud totaled 10 killed and 21 wounded. Nearly 80 percent of this total number came from Royall's four companies of the Third Cavalry.[30]

FIG. 5.4. The Battle of the Rosebud—the charge on Col. Royall's third position. *Frank Leslie's Illustrated Newspaper,* August 1, 1876.

Foster's company alone lost 2 men killed and 7 wounded. According to one account, Company I "had a more arduous duty and suffered more severely than any other portion of the command."[31] During the engagement, one Indian scout (a Shoshoni) was killed, and four Crow scouts and two Shoshoni were wounded. As for the Sioux and Cheyenne, who carried off their dead and wounded whenever possible, 13 dead were found in "close proximity" to the soldier lines. In a later interview, Crazy Horse reported the northern Indian casualties at 39 killed and 63 wounded.[32]

After a last attempt at a foray down the Rosebud Creek, the command returned to the field hospital set up by the medical officers at the site of the morning rest halt. Here the entire command bivouacked for the night. That evening the dead were buried with fires built over the graves to conceal them. The next morning Crook decided to return to the Goose Creek camp for several reasons. His wounded could receive better care and be sent on to Fort Fetterman for recovery. Secondly, his troops had entered the field carrying only four days' rations each. And lastly, the ammunition supply of the command needed replenishment. According to one source, 25,000 rounds of rifle and carbine ammunition had been expended at the Rosebud; additionally, the Indian scouts and allies fired some 10,000 rounds.[33] Crook abandoned his advance and returned to Goose Creek. His withdrawal removed a military force that "fatefully altered the dynamics of the war," and largely disrupted any chance of success for the tactic of converging columns.[34] One week later the invigorated warriors destroyed the Custer command at the Little Big Horn.

On June 20, all the officers who held field commands in the fighting, including General Crook, dutifully wrote their reports on the Rosebud battle. Foster received recognition for his part in the combat. Colonel Royall commended Lieutenant Foster (and Lieutenant Morton, who was then acting regimental adjutant) and his other officers for their conduct in his report. Additionally, on the night after the battle, he personally complimented Foster for his gallant conduct under fire. Captain Andrews's report described how Foster, under heavy fire, drove the Indians from three ridges, and also under heavy fire, withdrew his platoon in good order and avoided being cut off and possibly annihilated. In closing Andrews declared, "I desire to mention the distinguished gallantry of 2nd Lieut J. E. H. Foster who acted throughout the whole affair in the most efficient manner, displaying courage and bravery of a very high-order."[35]

While the officers wrote their official battle reports, the accompanying newspaper correspondents hurriedly filed dispatches for eastern readers. Several weeks later, readers in "the states" could thrill how Lieutenant

Foster, "With an abiding faith in his men and horses" advanced and carried another ridge, and read with assurance that Captain Andrews's men, "with all their officers, displayed a most honorable degree of fortitude and bravery."[36] While the country reeled from news of Custer's defeat on the Little Big Horn, the Third Cavalry, and Foster, received their share of glory.

Five different correspondents representing thirteen different newspapers traveled with the Big Horn and Yellowstone Expedition. Two of the correspondents, Reuben B. Davenport (*New York Herald*) and Thomas C. MacMillan (*Chicago Inter-Ocean*), had accompanied the Jenney Expedition.[37] Additionally, two officers wrote for newspapers. One was Capt. Andrew S. Burt, Ninth Infantry, whose dispatches were published in the *Chicago Tribune* and *Cincinnati Commercial*. The other officer/correspondent wrote a colorful, descriptive account of the Rosebud battle that was published in the July 13, 1876, issue of *The New York Graphic*. Wishing to remain anonymous, he simply signed his name "Z."

The anonymous correspondent can be none other than James Foster. There are some very strong clues for this conclusion. To begin with, part of the article's heading stated, "By an Officer of His (Crook's) Command." The article is centered on the role played by Company I on that day, and handed out laurels to its men. Additionally, because of the amount of detail given, the author had to have been standing on the line fighting with the troop. It is evident that the writer had a familiarity with the enlisted component of I Company. In the list of casualties, all the men from "I" had their first names and middle initials (when applicable) listed—not so with the men from the other companies. Foster accomplished several things in writing the article. He praised the enlisted men of the company, the common soldiers who fought with "splendid courage" and were "imbued with the very highest grade of soldiery discipline." Foster also played homage to the two longtime company veterans who died in combat like true soldiers, one "standing . . . firing coolly with his carbine" to the end. He speaks with pride about his regiment and the esprit de corps they displayed that day which "sustained the ancient reputation of the "Old Mounted Rifles." He was a young officer, proud of his men and also proud of his role in battle.[38] With a dateline of "Camp on Goose Creek, June 20," what follows is Foster's third-person account of the Rosebud.

* * *

From Crook's camp on Goose Creek to the point on the Rosebud where he first struck the river it is upwards of forty miles, and the command made the march in about fourteen hours, and one-half of the route was over a country that for ruggedness and utter sterility almost equals the worst part of the Bad Lands. Upon going into camp on the night of the 16th the command was formed in a hollow square, with the animals in the centre. The morning broke without incident worthy of special mention, and at six o'clock the column—the Third Cavalry on the left bank and the Second Cavalry and infantry on the right—began its march down the stream. The Crows and Snakes[39] deployed in the advance and on the flanks. After marching about three miles in this order the command was halted, unsaddled, and ordered to graze their horses, it being understood that the Crows and Snakes had found signs indicating that we were in the vicinity of the large village that we were in search of.

At this time the common opinion was that we were to remain where we were all day *en bivouac* and at night make a swift march on the enemy, attacking at daybreak in the morning. But Sitting Bull, whom we afterwards found was then waiting for us to enter the narrows of the Rosebud a few miles further down, he having occupied the crests of the precipices on either side, finding that we had halted and evidently intended to remain where we were for the present, gathered his warriors and, sending a large body around to occupy the bluffs south of us, made a strong push with the main force right for our camp, evidently hoping to be upon us before we could saddle up and to sweep the field in one grand rush.

A dropping, desultory fire on our right first announced that the Sioux were in the vicinity, and this rapidly swelling to a heavy skirmish fire, together with the return of the Snakes and Crows who came rushing pell-mell into camp closely pursued, showed that we had before us one day earlier than we had anticipated a fight with the main fighting force of the Sioux nation. In the mean time we had all saddled up. The Second Cavalry dismounted, and the infantry—all deployed as skirmishers—pushed for and recaptured the heights north of camp, and the infantry swinging to the left gallantly carried the high hill marked "A" in the sketch of the field. [Capt. Frederick] Van Vliet, with his own and [1st Lt. Emmet] Crawford's troops of the Third, charged for the bluffs south of the camp, reaching them just in time to repulse a strong body of the enemy who had been sent to occupy them, and held the position until ordered positively to withdraw by General Crook, who desired to concentrate the whole command on the hill and ridge marked "A," in order to make a dash at the village, which was said to be seven miles further down the creek.

Colonel Royall, with Mills's battalion, consisting of Mills's, [Capt. Alexander] Sutorius's, Andrews's, and [Capt. Joseph] Lawson's troops of the Third, pushed into the valley between the ridges marked respectively

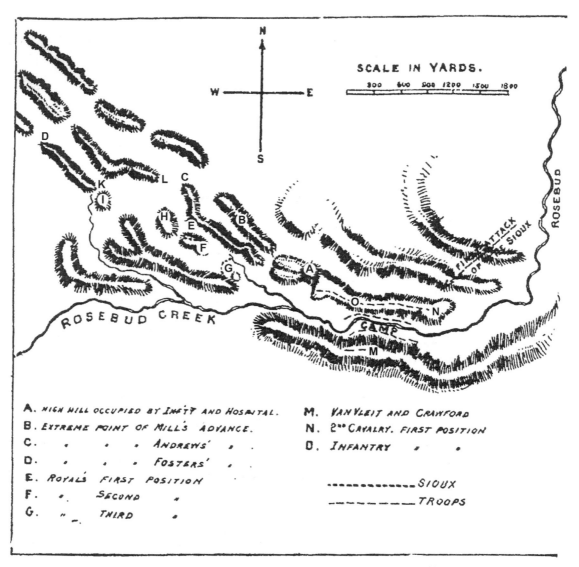

SCALE IN YARDS.

300 600 900 1200 1500 1800

ROSEBUD

FIRST ATTACK OF THE SIOUX

ROSEBUD CREEK

CAMP

A. HIGH HILL OCCUPIED BY INF.T.Y AND HOSPITAL.
B. EXTREME POINT OF MILL'S ADVANCE.
C.   "   "   " ANDREWS' "   "
D.   "   "   " FOSTERS' "   "
E. ROYAL'S FIRST POSITION
F.   "   SECOND   "
G.   "   THIRD   "

M. VAN VLEIT AND CRAWFORD
N. 2ND CAVALRY. FIRST POSITION
O. INFANTRY   "   "

---·---·---·---·--- SIOUX
--- --- --- --- --- TROOPS

BATTLE GROUND OF ROSEBUD HILLS, JUNE 17.

FIG. 5.5. Map of the Battle of the Rosebud, more than likely based on a sketch map by Foster, published in the *New York Graphic*, July 13, 1876. (The letters marking locations have been enhanced for legibility.)

"B" and "C," and going left front into a line at a gallop, ordered Andrews, with I Troop, to carry the ridge on the left, and Mills, with the remainder of his battalion, to take the one on the right, both of them being held by a strong body of the enemy. The plateau was gained, and reforming, the charge was sounded and the crest cleared with a dash and spirit worthy of all praise, the officers riding gallantly in advance of the platoons, although the retreating enemy were all the time delivering a sharp fire on the advancing line. Mills pushed on to the point marked "B" when he was ordered to halt and hold the ground won. This he did until ordered by General Crook to join him on the hill occupied by the infantry. Andrews, after detaching his subaltern Lt. Foster, with the second platoon, to charge a body of the enemy further to the left, dashed on under a strong fire with the remainder of I Troop and carried the point marked "C," holding it until preemptory orders came to fall back and rest his left at the point marked "E." The point taken so gallantly by Andrews is a natural redoubt, commanding everything within range, and the enemy afterwards occupied it and annoyed Royall's first line terribly by an enfilading fire.[40]

In the meanwhile Foster, in accordance with his orders, led his platoon, charging as foragers[41] over the valley to the left, and gaining the crest of the ridge marked "H," drove a body of the enemy that held it pell-mell from their position. Continuing his charge, the next ridge was carried in the same style, when wheeling to the right in order to conform to the general direction of the main line, he swept along the plateau, the enemy, though superior in numbers, running before him, firing from their ponies as they gave way. The rocky knoll marked "I" was next charged for and taken, and a sharp fire coming from a timber-clad point of a ridge marked "K," the plucky little party—numbering less than twenty men—was placed under cover behind the knoll marked "I," from whence issued some of the best shots fired on the enemy occupying the point "K." With an abiding faith in his men and horses Foster again advanced, charging and carrying the point "K" and following the retreating enemy along the crest of the ridge, both pursuers and pursued fired rapidly as the movement was executed. Occupying the end of this ridge (D) it was determined to halt and await the advance of the line, but finding that a body of the enemy were moving along the ridge to his right (L) with the evident intention of intercepting the party the retreat was ordered. The moment this retreat began the Indians followed rapidly, delivering a heavy fire as they advanced, but they were kept at a respectful distance by the fire of the retreating platoon, who fell back deliberately and in perfect order to a point just south and east of "K," which position it was determined to hold. At this moment an orderly from Colonel Royall, and Private [Herbert W.] Weaver, of I Troop, from Captain Andrews, came up, after running the gauntlet of a sharp fire from the enemy, with preemptory orders to fall back at once and as rapidly as possible, as the Indians were trying to cut off the platoon. Starting at a trot down the hill, at the base of which ran the dry bed of a stream about eight feet wide and as many deep, with steep banks on either side, the platoon had gotten half way to the bottom when the advance of the pursuing Indians reached the crest just abandoned and poured a scattering volley into the party. The order was given to take the charging gait and make it for our own lines. A board valley had to be crossed to reach the left of Royall's first position, and in doing so two men, Privates [James] O'Brien and [Charles W.] Stewart, and one horse were wounded. The platoon now joined their troop on the left about the point marked "E."

In the meanwhile [Capt. Guy V.] Henry's battalion, consisting of his own, [Capt. Charles] Meinhold's, [Capt. Peter D.] Vroom's, and [2nd Lt. Bainbridge] Reynold's troops of the Third, had occupied this line, but Meinhold being ordered back to report to General Crook, I Troop extended their line, and the ridge was held as before. The left now suffered from a front fire from the ridge "B" and a fire by the Indians that occupied "L" and "C." At one time a number of men in this part of the line started to go back. Being strongly appealed to by the officer in charge, one of them turning about said: "All right, Lieutenant, if you say stay, we'll stay." They went back and remained without a murmur until the positive order came to abandon the position and fall back.

This retrograde movement[42] was made on foot, and the enemy, occupying the position just abandoned, fired steadily and heavily on our retreating line. Occupying the second line, the enemy not only pressing us in front but getting on our flanks, Royall refused the left of his line[43] and held on stoutly against from 500 to 700 Indians, until again the order came to fall back from the commanding general. The men and officers, not knowing the object of the withdrawal and knowing well that Royall's immediate command were not whipped, naturally supposed that some disaster had happened on the right. Again the retreat began. This time the enemy, emboldened by our withdrawal a second time and evidently reinforced, pressed on even harder than before, coming in on the left flank. The line was promptly halted, faced about, and the braver of the savages who had pressed on in advance of the others compelled to retire. The retreat was then continued to the last position, which was destined to be the scene of the fiercest encounter that has ever taken place between Indians and United States troops.

The officers with the four companies under the immediate command of Colonel Royall—Henry, Andrews, Vroom, Reynolds, and Foster—remained mounted, and, although a conspicuous mark for the enemy's rifles, were on the line with their men, who were fighting on foot, during the whole engagement. First Sergeant John Henry, of I Troop, Third, also remained mounted in the line doing effective service and displaying courage of the highest order. He has been recommended to the consideration of the department commander. The affair now became serious, and the men cautioned to husband their ammunition and to fire only when they had a fair assurance of hitting their man. A few minutes had only elapsed when, with their wild yell, firing as they came, a vast mass of savages dashed at the line. The men received them steadily and, pouring in volley after volley, drove them back in confusion to their cover in the rocks and ravines beyond the slope. One warrior was left dead on the field within fifty yards of the line, the others that were hit either holding on to their ponies or being carried back by their companions. By this time the four companies, that had averaged about forty men each at the opening of the fight, were so depleted by casualties and details necessary to carry the wounded to the hospital, as well as losing the services of every fourth man who had been detailed in the morning to hold the lead horses, did not number in all more than sixty or seventy men, whilst in their front, if the estimate of experienced officers who could see the whole field from higher ground further back is to be considered, there were upwards of 700 Sioux warriors.

The Indians, who all the while had kept up a steady rolling fire from the front, now extended their line down a ravine on our right flank, rendering it necessary to refuse that portion of our line, which was done promptly. Colonel Guy V. Henry,[44] of the Third Cavalry, was wounded by this enfilading fire, being shot through the head immediately below the eyes, the ball striking the apex of the right cheek bone and coming out at the apex of the left cheek bone. The gallant fellow never lost his seat in the saddle, but rode slowly back to the field hospital, and would have returned after having the wound dressed but that the surgeon in charge positively refused to permit it. Poor Henry knew not how badly he was hurt, and was ready even after his wound to go back and share the then probable fate of Royall and the battalion of the gallant Third horse. The slanderous assertions that were made in regard to the regiment for the alleged acts of one of its companies at the affair of Powder River, which assertions had been published in journals like the New York *Tribune*, induced the line officers with Royall to expose themselves unnecessarily—facing death with a laugh and a passing joke, and with utter recklessness that may be charming to those who admire high courage and unquestionable pluck, but that induced General Crook to say that he did not desire that *such* officers throw their lives away. He knew the stuff they were made of and felt satisfied that they would "stay put" wherever they might be ordered. And so it can be said of the balance of the Third and the gallant old Second Dragoons.[45] If either had been on "Royall's line" that day they would have behaved as bravely as the men who, with their brave commands, so nobly held their position against ten to one.

The firing was now terrific, the repeating rifles used by the Indians enabling them to make it one continuous volley. Officers who were through the war and were there say that they never in their experience saw anything hotter. Again the Sioux advanced. With their "Yip! Yip! hi-yah! hi-yah!"[46] urging their ponies to their utmost speed, they came in myriads from the ravine on our right. Facing by the right flank and breaking to the right and left in open order the men gallantly poured in volley after volley, and again the pride of the Sioux nation were dragged in the dust and drenched with their best blood. Returning to their cover, they again endeavored to shake the everlasting courage of the gallant little band by their scorching fire. Men, brave men and true, were falling every moment. The wounded were carried back to the hospital by details called from the line, which, growing thinner and thinner, seemed to be dwindling so constantly that annihilation was apparently but a question of time.

"Better to die right here than back in the ravine," said one officer to another. "It's only a question of cartridges," said a soldier to his comrade who stood by him in the line.[47]

Royall sent [2nd] Lt. [Henry R.] Lemly, of his staff (who already had a horse shot), at a gallop back to General Crook asking for help. Already the order had come to retire, but seeing no way to withdraw he asked for assistance to cover the retreat of his men to their horses. Morton, acting adjutant of the Third Cavalry, after carrying orders all day through the hottest of the fight, as calmly as though on a pleasure ride, now took charge of the headquarters escort and with them did good service.

At last the supreme moment arrived. The Sioux, massing in all their strength, charged with a yell on the right flank and on the front. For an instant it looked as through Royall and his little band were doomed. The Indians never flinched under our fire, but pressed on, and the worn-out, harassed little battalion gave way. The officers with one accord dashed forward. Sergeant Henry's clear, ringing voice was heard high above the tumult shouting, "Face them, men! [D]____ them, face them!" whilst some officers calling out, "Great God, men; don't go back on the old Third!"

raised a cheer, and the line faced about, fired into the enemy at such short range as to almost burn the noses of their ponies, and drove them back almost 200 yards over the slope on their front, the officers riding with and ahead of the charging line.[48]

A lull followed—a season of rest thankfully welcomed by the officers and men. Again it was broken by the enemy, who opened fire as before from the rocks and ravines on our front and right. The order was given to make for the horses and mount in the ravine below, and then fall back rapidly to the hill on which the field hospital had been established and that was now occupied by the infantry and C, G, and B troops, Third Cavalry. This movement was executed at once, [Capt. Andrew S.] Burt and [Capt. Thomas B.] Burrowes, of the Ninth Infantry, coming down from the hill and each firing a volley into the mass of savages that had again advanced when they saw our line withdraw. This aid, though late in coming, checked the main body who were rushing over the crest, but a party of Sioux that had started down the ravine had killed and wounded a number of our men while mounting.

In the meanwhile, before Royall's first position had been abandoned, Mills, with M, E, and a part of A troop, of the Third—twenty men and the first sergeant of A troop having been detached to act with the friendly Indians—and the battalion of the Second Cavalry, consisting of [Capt. Henry E.] Noyes, [Capt. Elijah R.] Wells, [Capt. Thomas B.] Dewees, [1st Lt. William B.] Rawolle's, and [1st Lt. Samuel M.] Swigert's troops, was sent down the Rosebud to march on and charge the village which was supposed to be located seven or eight miles below. They had gone five or six miles when they were overtaken by Captain [Azor H.] Nickerson, with orders from General Crook to change direction to the left, come out of the creek valley, and by a detour regain the main body, which was done.[49]

Having assembled the whole command on the hill and ridge to the eastward, marked "A," General Crook started with the cavalry down the stream, but arriving at the head of the canyon or narrows of the Rosebud the Crows and Shoshones lost their courage and refused to go further, saying that the Sioux were as many as the blades of grass on the prairies and would destroy them if they entered the canyon. The column then returned to the hill on which the field hospital, guarded by the infantry, still was, and from thence marched to the old camp, each company burying its dead that evening.

The loss of the enemy can only be estimated. The Crows and Shoshones took fourteen scalps, but as the enemy, owing to our continued withdrawal after Royall's gallant advance in the morning, had every opportunity to

Lieut. Schwatka.
Capt
G.W. Pach Photographer

get their dead and wounded off the field, their loss in killed alone must number not less than fifty, and perhaps will reach 100.

The ground in front and on the flanks of Royall's last stand was found to show unmistakable signs of the rough handling that the enemy had undergone. Clotted pools of blood back behind the rocks showed where their killed and wounded had been carried before final removal from the field. Sitting Bull evidently intended to have another Phil Kearny massacre; but the breech-loading rifles and the pluck of the officers and men, who fought with such magnificent courage under Royall's able command, gave him a setback.[50]

Colonel Royall has highly commended the gallant conduct of the officers who were with his immediate command, and personally complemented Lieutenants Reynolds and Foster on the evening after the engagement. There can be no doubt that any portion of the command similarly situated would have behaved as well, but as troops D, I, L, and F happened to have the opportunity and fought throughout with such splendid courage they certainly deserve and will doubtless receive the honors for the affair of Rosebud Hills. The Third Cavalry have in this affair sustained the ancient reputation of the "Old Mounted Rifles."[51] Soldiers who, when in full retreat before an enemy superior in force, with advantage of position and in arms, will face the foe and fire as steadily and deliberately as though on the drill ground when an officer rides out and commands, "Skirmishers, halt!" must be imbued with the very highest grade of soldiery discipline. Men who will turn again and charge the advancing enemy when to all appearances all is lost and everything in confusion at a simple appeal to their regimental pride cannot be lacking in *esprit de corps*. Both these things this noble little battalion did.

That evening the sad duty of committing the bodies of the dead to the earth was performed. Fires were built over their last resting places in order that the savages might not find where they had been buried. The night passed without incident and in the morning the column began its march up the Rosebud, it having been determined to return to the wagons in order that our wounded might be taken care of and that additional supplies might be procured. A feeling of sadness seemed to spread over the companies whose ranks had been depleted of some gallant spirits. Especially were Allen, of I Troop, and Sergeant Marshall, of F, mourned by officers and men. Old soldiers—both of over twenty years' service in the regiment—they were well known and respected by all. They died like true soldiers, facing the enemy gallantly, and their memories will long be green among the commissioned and enlisted of the Third Horse.

FIG. 5.6. Lt. Frederick Schwatka, Foster's fellow officer from the Fort McPherson days, served through the campaign as the junior officer in Captain Mills' company M. Courtesy of Paul L. Hedren

The following is a full list of the killed and seriously wounded:

THIRD CAVALRY, D TROOP — Wounded –Colonel Guy V. Henry, seriously, head.

I TROOP — Killed — Privates William W. Allen and Eugene Flynn. Wounded — Sergeant Andrew Groesch, seriously, head, arm, chest, leg; Corporal Tobias Carty, leg; Privates Francis Smith, breast and leg; Charles W. Stewart, hand and arm; James O'Brien, arm; John Loscibroski, arm; James Riley, chest.

L TROOP — Killed — Sergeant Antoine Neukirchen; Privates [George] Potts, [Richard] Bennett, [Allen J.] Mitchell and [Brooks] Conner. Wounded — Trumpeter [William H.] Edwards, side; Private [John] Kramer, shoulder; Sergeant [Samuel] Cook, thigh.

F TROOP — Killed — Sergeant David Marshall, Private Gilbert Rowe. Wounded — Privates [Phineas] Town, side; Robeson [Otto Brodersen] and [William] Featherly.

Individual acts of heroism were of frequent occurrence during the progress of the action, among which was the feat performed by Old Crow, chief of the Crows, who with his people did good service during the day. First Sergeant [John W.] Van Moll, of A Troop, Third Cavalry, being detached with twenty men to act with the friendly Indians, was left at one time far in advance of our own people, dismounted and exhausted. A party of the enemy seeing his desperate position made a dash at the sergeant, when Old Crow, with great heroism rushed down and, taking the sergeant up behind him, galloped back to our lines amidst the cheers of the troops, the triumphant shouts of our allies, and the disappointed yells of the enemy.

Farrier [Richard] O'Grady, of F Troop, Third Cavalry, accompanied by a small party of that gallant command, displayed great courage in dashing back and bringing off the corpse of Sergeant Marshall in a shower of bullets from the then rapidly advancing enemy, thus saving from mutilation the remains of a gallant old soldier whose service in the regiment had extended over a period of twenty-five years.

William W. Allen, of I Troop, Third, died as such a soldier might be expected to. His horse was shot twice and he was dismounted, and being hard pressed by the enemy he turned upon them, determined to sell his life as dearly as possible. Nobly the brave fellow fought, standing all the while and firing coolly with his carbine, until the Sioux, coming in on either side, shot him down. Allen then tried to draw his pistol, but one of the Sioux, clubbing his carbine, struck the poor fellow over the head, thus ending the unequal contest.[52] Sergeant Groesch, who lay desperately wounded nearby, witnessed this scene, and was saved from a similar fate by the timely arrival of the Crows and Shoshones, accompanied by a number of men of his own company, who took him back to the hospital.

Private Herbert W. Weaver, of I Troop, displayed high courage in carrying the order for Lieutenant Foster to withdraw, as in doing so he had to pass over open ground commanded by the rifles of the enemy, thus running the gauntlet of their fire at the imminent risk of his life.

Trumpeter [Elmer A.] Snow, of M Troop, having both hands disabled by a bullet through the wrists, rode his horse for the hospital. The animal becoming frightened at the balls striking around him broke into a run, and the trumpeter being afraid he would carry him too far and into the enemy's lines threw himself off as he passed near the hospital on the hill.

Private [Michael] McMahon, of I Troop, also deserves special mention. He was in the charge made by the Second Platoon on the extreme left in the morning, and when the third and last charge was made, rode alongside the chief of platoon, and was first on the ridge just abandoned by the enemy. McMahon was reprimanded for riding ahead of an officer [Lt. Foster] whilst he was leading a charge and complimented for his courage at the same time. Z.

* * *

The Stern Chase

While the command made camp on Goose Creek, Crook realized he faced larger numbers of better armed northern warriors than on the Powder River fight earlier that spring. After the Indians had engaged his soldiers with surprising aggressiveness at Powder River, Tongue River Heights, and the Rosebud, Crook now showed caution. Additionally, the Crow and Shoshoni allies had returned to their agencies and Crook was without scouts. Fearing he was greatly out-numbered by the Sioux and Cheyenne, he called for reinforcements of five additional infantry companies, and also requested the Fifth Cavalry companies recently brought up from Kansas and now working to secure the Black Hills road.

On the 21st, the wagon train for supplies left for Fort Fetterman guarded by three infantry companies. The wounded were transported back in wagons with freshly cut grass padding the beds. Crook figured the column would have to wait a minimum of fifteen days for the infantry reinforcements and supplies to arrive. So, the expedition basically came to a halt and waited. With little to do in camp, officers explored the mountains and hunted big game, elk, mountain sheep, and bear. Enlisted men also had opportunities to hunt—but the big sport was fishing, and everybody fished. The waterways flowing out of the Big Horns were loaded with trout; soldiers caught them by the score. On the twenty-eighth Bourke wrote in his diary, "It is estimated that fully 500 trout have been brought into camp to-day. Colonel Mills and squad caught one hundred and forty six." The next day he reported buffalo and elk killed for meat, but added very many trout caught, fifty-five by Lt. John Bubb alone. For the next six weeks, trout became a component of the expedition daily ration.[53]

Eighteen seventy-six was a presidential election year, and new officers who arrived to join the expedition were plied for news of the summer's Republican National Convention. Rutherford B. Hayes, who received the presidential nomination, was a personal friend of General Crook. James Foster also had political connections. Bourke reported that William A. Wheeler, the Republican candidate for vice president, was a "cousin to Lieut. Foster of our command."[54]

Although Crook's camp became known as "Camp Cloud Peak," named for the towering mountain in the Big Horns, it was not situated in one single location. With a continual need to provide fresh grass for grazing, the command had to move every four to six days. Additionally, the officers felt the breaking up and establishing of camp was good practice for the men: the "details of camp life are learned by constant practice." The first of several moves came after four days at the initial camp site, when the cavalry moved three miles up Tongue River to a new place which provided grass for its horses. All in all, the camp was moved some half-dozen times before the expedition moved on.[55]

After seventeen days of inactivity, Crook decided to send out a scouting detachment to search toward the northwest for signs of Indians. On the sixth, Lt. Frederick W. Sibley with twenty men, scout Frank Grouard, and correspondent John Finerty, rode out on what became known as the "Sibley Scout." After they left, Crook returned to business as usual, and departed the next morning with a party of officers on a four-day hunt to the summit of the mountains. The following day, word was received in camp to send on pack mules to carry in fourteen elk taken by the hunters.

Three days later, Sibley and his men were brought into camp. The day after their departure, they ran into and fought with a large party of Lakota and Cheyenne warriors. In order to make their escape, the soldiers abandoned their horses and retreated on foot through the mountains. The men were hungry and exhausted, but survived.[56]

Meanwhile, Colonel Royall and other officers feared that the warriors who engaged Sibley might have found and followed the pack mule trail to Crook's mountain camp. He dispatched the first battalion of the Third under Captain Mills to find the general and escort the hunters back to the base camp. Mills's battalion included Company I, on this outing commanded by 2nd Lieutenant Foster. With Captain Andrews on sick leave and Lieutenant King on detached service, Foster was left in command. The cavalry battalion located Crook's hunters and everyone was back in camp by five o'clock. Earlier that day (June 10), couriers from Fort Fetterman appeared with word of Custer's monumental defeat on the Little Big Horn. By this time northern warriors were in the close vicinity; on the nights of July 9 and 10 the camp had been fired on, further putting nerves on edge.[57]

After endless waiting, events finally began to develop. The following day (eleventh) several hundred Shoshonis under Washakie arrived and joined the column. On the twelfth three couriers from Terry's column arrived bearing additional news on the Custer fight, and an offer from General Terry to cooperate with Crook in future operations. On the thirteenth the supply train from Fort Fetterman rolled in accompanied by five companies of infantry, four from the Fourteenth Infantry at Fort Douglas near Salt Lake City, Utah. One of the second lieutenants who arrived with the Douglas reinforcements was Frederic S. Calhoun, the brother of 1st Lt. James Calhoun, who commanded Company L, Seventh Cavalry. He was also the brother-in-law of Lt. Col. George Custer. Both James Calhoun and Custer died at the Little Big Horn. Also among the new arrivals was Dr. McGillycuddy, Foster's fellow topographer from the Jenney Expedition, who had been hired as an additional acting assistant surgeon (civilian contract surgeon) for the campaign.

Crook sent Terry a dispatch likewise extending his cooperation, but wanted to delay field operations until the arrival of the Fifth Cavalry. The expedition continued to drill, fish, and wait at the Cloud Peak camp. General Sheridan at division headquarters had begun to grow impatient with Crook's inactivity. On July 25 he wrote Crook, "As soon as [Col. Wesley] Merritt joins you, I think it will be well to push out without further delay." Then to another dispatch three days later he added, "Terry and you should unite your forces."[58]

With Andrews still sick and King gone on detached service, Foster again commanded the company from July 18 to 27. That summer he wrote home about his Sioux War adventures, and his friends in Pittsburgh read in the papers of his actions in the Rosebud battle. After the Custer disaster, Alexander Foster lobbied for his son's advancement. In late July he wrote several political friends asking them to urge the secretary of war to transfer

James to the Seventh Cavalry, and his promotion to a first lieutenancy in a regiment in which "unhappily so many vacancies now exist."[59]

Promotion in the Indian War army came from date of commission and time in grade. Company grade (second lieutenant, first lieutenant, captain) promotions were made within the regiment; field grade (major, lieutenant colonel, colonel) promotion was made within the service branch. The *Army Register*, published annually, listed every officer by current rank and date of promotion. When an officer was promoted, retired, resigned, or died, his name was stricken and the others below moved up one place. As a consequence, promotion was slow and not made until one's time came. Because James served in another regiment, he had no chance of being transferred into the Seventh Cavalry to receive a higher rank.[60]

On August 3 the Fifth Cavalry arrived under the command of Colonel Merritt, expanding Crook's strength from twenty-five to thirty-five companies, totaling 1,800 soldiers, 250 Indian allies, and 200 packers and volunteers. Along with meeting officers of a new regiment, Foster probably had opportunity to meet the Fifth's famed scout, William F. "Buffalo Bill" Cody.

Crook realized that the northern Indians had the jump on him, and were probably long gone. The campaign now became a "stern chase," a focused, determined pursuit. According to one veteran of Indian warfare, a stern chase was "a long chase—unless you have the lead at start."[61] In order for any chance to catch up, his men needed to travel light, which deprived men of the few comforts found in field service. Each soldier, officer or enlisted man, only carried the essential items: overcoat, blanket, poncho or rubber blanket, one hundred rounds of ammunition, four days' rations, and the clothes on his back. No tents were taken. While the wagon train stayed behind, 240 pack mules carried extra ammunition and rations (hardtack, bacon, coffee, sugar, and salt) to last fifteen days. The reorganized Big Horn and Yellowstone expedition marched out of Camp Cloud Peak on August 5 and traveled north to unite with General Terry's column.[62]

For several days the column followed the meandering Tongue River, on one day crossing it thirteen times. On the seventh, the troops crossed the divide to the Rosebud and passed the battlefield. The next day they rode through thick smoke caused by Indians firing the grass. Two days later on August 10, they met the advance guard of Terry's Dakota column. The united columns, now under General Terry's command, made camp on the Rosebud.[63]

The next morning the massive column, numbering over four thousand men, moved down the Rosebud in a somewhat cumbersome manner, to

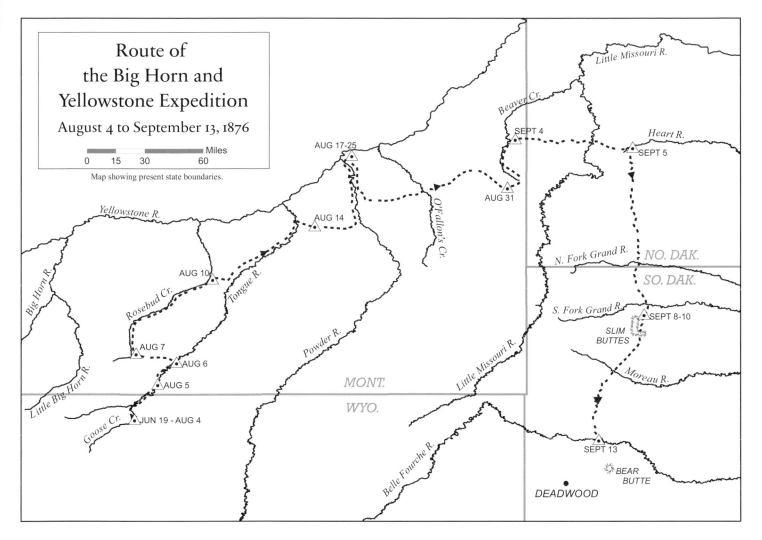

FIG. 5.7.

pursue an elusive and seemingly long-vanished foe. It rained the whole night of the first day's march, a foretaste of what was to come. Being in light marching order without tents, the men spent a miserable night. When dawn broke, one Third Cavalry officer recalled: ". . . and the 'clerk of the weather,' as if to add insult to injury, gave us a bitter cold morning in which to enjoy our wet clothing."[64]

By August 15 the column reached the Powder River, and arrived at the Yellowstone two days later. Crook's command remained there from the seventeenth to twenty-fourth. Part of the delay was caused by having to wait to replenish his rations for another fifteen days in the field. By this time several of Crook's officers were critical of the cautious Terry: under his (Terry's) leadership the command "would never catch, kill or scare 40 Indians."[65] It also became evident that the joint expedition was too large and hopelessly unwieldy for any kind of offensive operation.

Thoroughly soaked and chilled from yet another night storm, the troops left the Yellowstone on the twenty-fourth and moved back up the Powder in search of Indian trails. Two days later, Terry and Crook split their forces up by mutual agreement. While Terry and his army moved north of the Yellowstone in search of northern bands there, Crook intended to follow a trail that headed east toward the Little Missouri River. When Crook's column marched out of the Powder River valley, it began the infamous "starvation march," one of the hardest marches on men and animals in American military history. For the next three weeks, Crook's men plodded for miles through almost continual heavy rains and gumbo mud in pursuit of northern warriors. Each day they suffered from inadequate rations and clothing, lack of firewood, and no protective tentage. Likewise, horses and pack mules languished from hard riding and continual exposure. For Foster and the rest of the command, the ordeal had just begun.[66]

After the commands split up, Crook's column crossed over to O'Fallon's Creek, a stream distinguished according to correspondent Finerty for having "the most adhesive mud on the American continent."[67] After three-some months in the field, signs of approaching illness appeared in several officers and enlisted men, and cases of rheumatism, diarrhea, and neuralgia increased on morning sick reports. That evening the command was drenched by a heavy rain and hail. Finerty remarked that the men gave up on sleep and were glad to keep moderately warm. The troops remained in camp the next day to dry clothing and blankets.[68]

The last day of August found the column caught in a freezing Norther. The troops fled into a sheltering valley near the head of Beaver Creek to wait out the storm. It was evident to Crook's scouts that they were following a large trail, but as they followed it down the creek, the trail split up, indicating the Indians moved off in different directions. However, while following a trail toward Sentinel Buttes, the column's advance had a running fight with a small group of warriors, thought to be a rear-guard of the main group, and killed one or two of their horses. The next day the scouts picked up a fresh trail; that night camp pickets fired on approaching Indian scouts.

On September 4, the column marched through rain all day before striking the Little Missouri. The soldiers harvested half-ripe plums and bull berries growing along the river, which were boiled and eaten, both for nutrition and as a valuable anti-scorbutic. The command spent another night, cold and shivering, as the rain poured in torrents. Although some officers began to question the wisdom of Crook's decision to move further off from sources of supply, one stoically noted, "We are following those Indians to the bitter end."[69]

The next day (fifth) the weary troops marched thirty miles and made camp on Heart River. Once again the advance scouts ran up on a small war party of Sioux and exchanged shots before the warriors escaped. Morale of the command continued to deteriorate. By this time the soldiers had not had a change of clothing in a month, but the nagging fear was that Crook's neglect of supply would only bring disaster. At this point, only two and one-half days' rations remained. Fort Abraham Lincoln was four or five days away and the supply depot at Glendive Creek was not much further. But Crook decided to turn south and follow a "hot" trail heading toward the Black Hills. This decision caused apprehension on the part of officers who were concerned about crossing the large expanse of unexplored land between them and the Hills. The commissary issued only half-rations that night.[70]

The stern march was especially hard on the expedition's livestock; horses and mules suffered from fatigue and were played out. Additionally, grain-fed animals weakened without their daily grain ration. Each day, gaunt, exhausted horses dropped down and refused to rise and were abandoned. Abandoned animals were ordered to be shot. By the fifth of September, about one-third of the cavalrymen were afoot, including officers who did not take along an extra mount. The day before Bourke had noted, "the conviction is forcing itself upon our minds that we cannot avoid the alturnative [sic] of starvation or killing and eating our mules and horses."[71]

On the sixth the column turned south. In a continuous drizzle, the troops struggled through gumbo, which brought straggling and break-downs. Moving ahead, the scouts were fired on again by warriors. By the end of the day, the weary, soaked soldiers had marched thirty-five miles to the north fork of the Grand River. Finerty remembered that "The whole country was as wet as a sponge, but without elasticity."[72] That night camp was made in a pelting rain with no fuel except for what grass could be made to burn.

The next day (seventh) the situation grew desperate. The command covered twenty-four miles to the South Fork of the Grand, within sight of the Slim Buttes. The rain had lasted all day, but they did have fuel at this camp. The men received a quarter of the regular ration each that evening; this was the beginning of horsemeat rations. There was nothing to do "...but to eat one another or our animals."[73] Orders came from Crook that abandoned animals were to be shot for food at the daily rate of three per battalion. The officers selected animals to be shot and butchered for issue to the weary, hungry soldiers. Lieutenant Bourke, trying to make the best of everything, commented on the new camp staple: "In taste and appearance, no difference of great extent could be discovered between it and beef or old antelope. Hunger gave it a goodly flavor and our men ate it greedily."[74]

Crook decided to send a detachment commanded by Captain Mills to rush to the settlements in the northern Black Hills and obtain provisions for his famished command. Mills selected fifteen men with the strongest horses from each of the ten companies of the Third Cavalry, as escort to Lieutenant Bubb, Crook's chief of commissary, to buy supplies. That night the detachment hurried south. The next day they discovered a fresh trail heading the same direction. At this point there were probably more hostile northern warriors near the expedition than at any time since the Rosebud battle. While Mills continued on, the main column struggled to reach a camp site with at least some available firewood. That night the men warmed themselves around a fire and cooked horsemeat. The day was also General Crook's birthday.[75]

About 3:00 p.m. Frank Grouard, riding in advance of Mills's relief party, spotted the horse herd and lodges of a village on the east edge of Slim Buttes. He quickly passed this information on to Mills. The village was a mixed camp of Minneconjous, Oglalas, Brules, and Cheyennes that numbered thirty-seven lodges, probably 260 people, who were on their way back to the Spotted Tail agency in northwestern Nebraska. They were camped on a tributary of the Moreau River, in a broad depression surrounded on three sides by the buttes. After a conference with his officers, Captain Mills decided to attack the village in the morning. He then moved off his command to a concealed position for the night. The Indians were completely unaware of the soldiers' advance, or their closeness. Although Mills was unaware of the size of the village, he still planned to attack.[76]

At dawn on September 9, a group of mounted soldiers led by Lieutenant Schwatka charged through the camp, while dismounted troops under Lieutenants Von Luettwitz and Crawford moved in from the northwest and north and opened fire on the lodges. Just before the attack, the Indian horse herd startled and ran through the camp. Following the horses, Schwatka charged through during the confusion as warriors and their families fled to the higher ground to the south and west. The village was captured, including a large supply of dried meat and other foodstuffs, and items captured at the Little Big Horn battle, which included several army horses, military clothing, and a Seventh Cavalry guidon.[77]

Firing from the bluffs and other hidden areas, warriors targeted soldiers in the camp, resulting in casualties. Mills quickly sent a message to General Crook explaining he "had a village & was trying to hold it and needed assistance." The expedition had left their camp at dawn, and met Mills's messengers with news of the fight seventeen miles ahead. Crook directed Colonel Merritt to move with all the cavalrymen who still had serviceable mounts. Led by Crook, some 250 men and 17 officers, including Company I and Lieutenant Foster, rode off at 8:00 a.m. The infantry and dismounted cavalrymen pressed on as fast as possible. The relief force arrived at 11:30. The infantry battalion, anxious to take part in the expected fight, arrived at the village just behind the cavalry. Their arrival was timely—by mid-afternoon, Crazy Horse led hundreds of warriors to continue the fight.[78]

Just as the troops were beginning their bivouac, hostile rifle fire came from the bluffs to the west and spread to the southwest. Between 600 and 800 warriors occupied the bluffs and highlands, opening fire on the soldiers below. After securing his horses and mules, Crook quickly organized a counterattack to clear the bluffs. While part of the infantry battalion took the higher ground north of the village, the other section swept toward the south. Meanwhile, the cavalry forces moved forward dismounted toward the Indian positions to the southwest. The Third Cavalry troops advanced from their camp (the camp furthest northwest on the line), to the west. As darkness fell, the fight was over. However, just before the end of the fighting, the warriors charged the Third Cavalry portion of the skirmish line, but were quickly repulsed. That night, the soldiers enjoyed the warmth of fires and buffalo robes, and dined on dried meat and other foodstuffs captured in the village.

The next morning the soldiers buried their dead and destroyed the village. Slim Buttes was an example of the army's total war philosophy where everything left in the village was either broken up or burned so nothing could be used again. After the fight had ended, most of the stricken inhabitants were taken in by the Crazy Horse camps, while others joined Sitting Bull. The soldiers captured twenty-three Indians, mostly women and children who had joined five warriors fighting from a nearby ravine. While half the captives decided to remain with Crook's column until they reached an agency, two men and nine women voluntarily chose to leave. One captive warrior remained with the command and later enlisted as an army scout.[79]

During the Slim Buttes fight, two soldiers and one scout were killed, and one officer and fourteen enlisted men were wounded, one of whom died during the night.[80] On the other side, there were probably fewer than twenty Indians killed or wounded; most of those casualties occurred in the afternoon fighting. Of the men who rode with his battalion, Captain Mills recommended twelve men from the Third Cavalry (including two from company I) for the Medal of Honor. However, only two medals were actually awarded for the Slim Buttes fight.[81] The Big Horn and Yellowstone Expedition moved out of the village at 9:00 a.m. The rear guard had one last skirmish with the northern warriors; in this encounter two soldiers were wounded and five Indians were believed killed.

Although provisions had been captured at the village, the poor condition of his men, plus having many sick and wounded to care for, compelled Crook to hurry along to the Black Hills mining towns. The rain continued throughout the day's march before camp was made twenty miles south. Deadwood and Crook City were still nearly a hundred miles distant.

On the eleventh, Mills, Bubb, and fifty men, mounted on Indian ponies with all the strong mules, were dispatched to Deadwood to secure food. Crook was well aware that the command was still moving among the Sioux, and arranged stronger advance and rear guards, with a line of skirmishers on each flank for protection. By this time there was a string of nine travois and three two-mule litters transporting the expedition's wounded. To help ease the invalid soldiers along, Foster's troop was detailed as both escort and guard company, and was to control the animals and prevent injury. Even though the weather was overcast the guides were able to make out two of Foster's old landmarks, Bear Butte on the east and Inyan Kara to the west.[82]

The march from Owl Creek (Moreau River) to Willow Creek was remembered as one of the worst of the whole campaign. The troops were on the march from daylight until after dark. They were driven on by the fact that the Belle Fourche River lay ahead, and across it, the Black Hills settlements. That day the column had to destroy seventy horses; a large pit was dug to bury their saddles and horse equipments.[83] Bourke recorded the unending march to the Belle Fourche:

> . . . the mud was so tenacious that every time foot or hoof touched it there would be a great mass of "gumbo" adhering to render progress distressingly tire-some and slow. Our clothing was in rags of the flimsiest kind, shoes in patches, and the rations captured at the village exhausted.
>
> On we trudged, mile succeeding mile, and still no sign of the fringe of cottonwood, willow, and elder which we had been taught to believe represented the line of the stream of which we were in search. The rain poured down, clothes dripping with moisture, horses reeled and staggered, and were one by one left to follow or remain as they pleased . . .
>
> It was half-past ten o'clock that never-to-be-forgotten night, when the last foot soldier had completed his forty miles . . .[84]

FIG. 5.8. After the campaign ended, photographer Stanley J. Morrow took group photos of the expedition officers. This view pictures the Third Cavalry officers. Denver Public Library, Western History Collection, X-31756

1. First Lieutenant Joseph Lawson;
2. Second Lieutenant James F. Simpson;
3. Second Lieutenant Charles Morton;
4. Captain Frederick Van Vliet;
5. First Lieutenant Emmet Crawford;
6. Major Julius W. Mason;
7. Lieutenant Colonel William B. Royall;
8. Second Lieutenant George F. Chase;
9. Major Andrew W. Evans;
10. Captain William H. Andrews;
11. First Lieutenant Augustus C. Paul;
12. Captain Anson Mills;
13. Second Lieutenant Frederick Schwatka;
14. Second Lieutenant Henry R. Lemly;
15. Captain Charles Meinhold;
16. First Lieutenant Alexander D. B. Smead;
17. **Foster**;
18. First Lieutenant Albert D. King;
19. Dr. V. T. McGillycuddy;
20. Second Lieutenant Bainbridge Reynolds.

Throughout that day, men and horses fell out of the ranks as the rain poured down, "quenching every particle of spirit and enthusiasm." Regardless, it was necessary to reach the Belle Fourche or any tributary with firewood. Some soldiers, frantic with suffering, "cursed the God who made them." After a thirty-five mile march, the column stopped short of the Belle Fourche. Stragglers struggled in to camp all night and into the morning, but relief was on the way. Lieutenant Bubb had reached the Hills, and in Crook City and Deadwood, had purchased fifty beeves on the hoof and thirteen wagon loads of provisions.[85]

Receiving word of Bubb's successful mission on the morning of the thirteenth, the inspired column marched five miles to the Belle Fourche. That afternoon the troops heard the lowing of the cattle "which then seemed sweetest music to our ears."[86] The beeves were quickly shot and butchered. Excluding what foodstuffs had been captured at Slim Buttes, Crook's men had lived on horse or mule meat for more than a week. The wagons arrived shortly afterward. Bubb had bought up all the bacon, flour, and coffee to be had, plus, the local merchants had "loaded up with every eatable then in their establishments. Company commanders secured everything the men could need."[87]

About this time the sun broke through the clouds for a good hour, "the first fair look we had of his face for ten dreary days." For the men of the Big Horn & Yellowstone Expedition, the nightmare ordeal of the "Starvation March" had ended.[88]

1 Thomas R. Buecker, "Fort Sidney: Its Role on the Upper Plains" *C.A.M.P. Periodical* II (March 1981): 22–36.

2 Philip H. Sheridan, *Outline Descriptions of the Posts in the Military Division of the Missouri* (Ft. Collins, CO: Old Army Press, 1969), 75–77; *Sidney Telegraph*, Oct. 12, 1917.

3 Thomas R. Buecker, "Letters of Caroline Frey Winne from Sidney Barracks and Fort McPherson, 1874–1878," *Nebraska History* 62 (Spring 1981): 19–46.

4 For more on freighting out of Sidney and the Sidney-Deadwood Trail, see William E. Lass, *From the Missouri to the Great Salt Lake: An Account of Overland Freighting* (Lincoln, NE: Nebraska State Historical Society, 1972), Chapter VIII, "The Sidney-Black Hills Trade."

5 Paul L. Hedren, *Great Sioux War Orders of Battle: How the United States Army Waged War on the Northern Plains, 1876–1877* (Norman, OK: The Arthur H. Clark Company, 2011), 214; Letter, Foster to Capt. W. S. Stanton, Feb. 29, 1876.

6 Rickey, *Forty Miles a Day*, 142–43; S. E. Whitman, *The Troopers: An Informal History of the Plains Cavalry 1865–1890* (New York, NY: Hastings House Publishers, 1962), 91.

7 *Army and Navy Journal*, March 18, 1876; April 8, 1876.

8 Foster's drawings published in the *Bee* are clearly marked with his name.

9 For an excellent overview of the beginnings of the Great Sioux War, see John S. Gray, *Centennial Campaign: The Sioux War of 1876* (Ft. Collins, CO: Old Army Press, 1976).

10 For a full assessment of the expedition and its later ramifications, see J. W. Vaughn, *The Reynolds Campaign on Powder River* (Norman, OK: University of Oklahoma Press, 1961).

11 Hedren, *Orders of Battle*, 81–84.

12 Ibid., 48–50, 96–100.

13 Ibid., 50–52, 100–104.

14 Jerome Greene, personal conversation, March 13, 2013; Hedren, *Orders of Battle*, 38.

15 Post Returns, Sidney Barracks, May 1876; Regimental Returns, Third Cavalry, May 1876.

16 Robinson, *Bourke Diaries, Vol. I*, 289–90.

17 *Chicago Tribune*, July 5, 1876; Robinson, *Bourke Diaries, Vol. I*, 291.

18 Ibid., 302.

19 Jerome A. Greene, *Battles and Skirmishes of the Great Sioux War, 1876–1877: The Military View* (Norman, OK: University of Oklahoma Press, 1993), 20–25; Robinson, *Bourke Diaries, Vol. I*, 305.

20 *Chicago Daily Inter-Ocean*, June 27, 1876; John G. Bourke, *On the Border With Crook* (New York, NY: Scribner's Sons, 1891), 296–97.

21 *Chicago Tribune*, July 5, 1876.

22 Bourke, *On the Border*, 299.

23 Robinson, *Bourke Diaries, Vol. I*, 308; Bourke, *On the Border*, 299; *Frank Leslie's Illustrated Newspaper*, Oct. 14, 1876.

24 Neil C. Mangum, *Battle of the Rosebud: Prelude to the Little Bighorn* (El Segundo, CA: Upton & Sons, 1987), 42–45, 47.

25 Robinson, *Bourke Diaries, Vol. I*, 325.

26 Mangum, *Battle of the Rosebud*, 53–54.

27 Ibid., 55.

28 J. W. Vaughn, *With Crook at the Rosebud* (Harrisburg, PA: Stackpole Co., 1956), 54–55; *Chicago Tribune*, July 5, 1876; *New York Daily Graphic*, July 13, 1876.

29 Charles D. Collins, *Atlas of the Sioux Wars, Second Edition* (Ft. Leavenworth, KS: Combat Studies Institute Press, 2006), Map 22.

30 Collins, *Atlas of the Sioux War*, Map 23.

31 *New York Herald*, July 6, 1876.

32 Capt. Henry R. Lemly, "The Fight on the Rosebud," John M. Carroll, ed., *The Papers of the Order of Indian Wars* (Ft. Collins, CO: Old Army Press, 1975), 18; Collins, *Atlas of the Sioux War*, Map 23.

33 John Finerty, *War-Path and Bivouac: The Big Horn and Yellowstone Expedition* (Lincoln: University of Nebraska Press, 1966), 141; Lemly, "The Fight on Rosebud," 18.

34 Hedren, *Orders of Battle*, 53.

35 Vaughn, *With Crook at the Rosebud*, 229–30, 234; *New York Daily Graphic*, July 13, 1876.

36 *New York Daily Graphic*, July 13, 1876; *New York Herald*, July 6, 1876.

37 The best study of Sioux War correspondents remains Oliver Knight, *Following the Indian Wars: The Story of Newspaper Correspondents Among the Indian Campaigners* (Norman, OK: University of Oklahoma Press, 1960).

38 *New York Daily Graphic*, July 13, 1876. Before being re-designated as the Third Cavalry in 1861, the regiment was originally the Regiment of Mounted Riflemen. Heitman, *Historical Register*, 68. Also see Marc Abrams, *Sioux War Dispatches: Reports from the Field, 1876–1877* (Yardley, PA: Westholme Publishing, 2012), 92–101.

39 At the time the Shoshoni were commonly known as "Snakes."

40 In battle, enfilading fire was to shoot down the line or fire diagonally across it, instead of facing the line frontally and firing.

41 A foragers' charge is made in pairs of men armed with the pistol. The interval between men in a charging platoon was nine feet between pairs.

42 A retrograde movement is to retreat or fall back.

43 "To refuse any part of the line in battle, as the centre or a wing, to keep that part retired, while the remainder is advanced to fight." Thomas Wilhelm, *A Military Dictionary and Gazetteer* (Philadelphia, PA: L. R. Hamersly & Co., 1881), 481.

44 Although Henry was only a captain in the regular army, Foster uses a brevet rank awarded for his service in the Civil War. The .44 caliber bullet actually entered below his left eye and exited below the right. Mangum, *Battle of the Rosebud*, 79. Henry survived the horrific wound and served in the army until his death as military governor of Puerto Rico in 1899.

45 The Second Regiment of Dragoons was organized in 1836. It was re-designated the Second Cavalry on August 3, 1861. Heitman, *Historical Register*, 66.

46 This war-cry also appeared in the July 5 *Chicago Tribune* article written by correspondent Robert E. Strahorn, who had evidently interviewed Foster.

47 Again, these quotes are all very similar to those used by Strahorn.

48 While the first quote is exact, the second is very similar, also indicating Foster had been interviewed.

49 Like many of his officers, Crook still maintained there was a large northern village farther down the Rosebud.

50 Sitting Bull might have been present at the battle, but just as an observer and not in a leadership role. Mangum, *Battle of the Rosebud*, 50.

51 Organized in 1846, the Regiment of Mounted Riflemen was re-designated the Third Regiment of Cavalry on August 3, 1861. The words "Brave Rifles" are today on the Third Cavalry's distinctive unit insignia, from an accolade given the regiment by Gen. Winfield Scott for its actions at the Chapultepec in the Mexican War.

52 William W. Allen was the same soldier who had served as first sergeant of I Company at Fort McPherson in 1874.

53 Robinson, *Bourke Diaries, Vol. I*, 345.

54 Ibid., 342. Wheeler was probably a cousin to one of Foster's parents, not directly to him.

55 Mark E. Miller, *Military Sites in Wyoming 1700–1920: Historical Context* (Laramie, WY: Wyoming Department of State Parks and Cultural Resources, 2012), 121–22; Bourke, *On the Border*, 328.

56 Gray, *Centennial Campaign*, 199–200.

57 Bourke, *On the Border*, 334; *Chicago Tribune*, Aug. 1, 1876.

58 Robinson, *Bourke Diaries, Vol. I*, 387; Gray, *Centennial Campaign*, 207.

59 A. W. Foster to Senator S. J. R. Williams, July 24, 1876, ACP 1873.

60 For example, see *Official Army Register for January, 1876* (Washington, DC: Adjutant General's Office, Jan. 1, 1876). Foster is listed on page 55.

61 Capt. Charles King, *Campaigning with Crook* (Norman, OK: University of Oklahoma Press, 1964; second printing December 1967), 77.

62 Bourke, *On the Border*, 348; Greene, *Slim Buttes*, 23. For the reorganization of the Big Horn and Yellowstone Expedition, see Hedren, *Orders of Battle*, 111–17.

63 Bourke, *On the Border*, 349; Hedren, *Orders of Battle*, 112. Crook consented to his command: Terry was the senior officer and the troops were in his department.

64 Jerome A. Greene, *Slim Buttes, 1876: An Episode of the Great Sioux War* (Norman, OK: University of Oklahoma Press, 1982), 28–29.

65 Ibid., 30.

66 The best recounting of the "Starvation March" is in Greene, *Slim Buttes*, 33–58.

67 Finerty, *War-Path and Bivouac*, 266.

68 Ibid., 266–67.

69 Bourke, *On the Border*, 365; King, *Campaigning with Crook*, 93.

70 Gray, *Centennial Campaign*, 243–44; Bourke, *On the Border*, 365–66; Greene, *Slim Buttes*, 37.

71 Greene, *Slim Buttes*, 41; Charles M. Robinson, ed., *The Diaries of John Gregory Bourke, Vol. II, July 29, 1876–April 7, 1878* (Denton, TX: The University of North Texas Press, 2005), 96.

72 Finerty, *War-Path and Bivouac*, 277.

73 Ibid., 278.

74 Robinson, *Bourke Diaries, Vol. II*, 106.

75 Bourke, *On the Border*, 368; Greene, *Slim Buttes*, 46, 49; Robinson, *Bourke Diaries, Vol. II*, 102.

76 Greene, *Slim Buttes*, 49, 54.

77 Robinson, *Bourke Diaries, Vol. II*, 108; Bourke, *On the Border*, 371.

78 Greene, *Slim Buttes*, 64; Finerty, *War-Path and Bivouac*, 280.

79 Greene, *Slim Buttes*, 80, 92. For examples of the army's application of the total war strategy, see R. Eli Paul, *Blue Water Creek and the First Sioux War, 1854–1856* (Norman, OK: University of Oklahoma Press, 2004); Jerome A. Greene and Douglas D. Scott, *Finding Sand Creek: History, Archeology, and the 1864 Massacre Site* (Norman, OK: University of Oklahoma Press, 2004); Jerome A. Greene, *Morning Star Dawn: The Powder River Expedition and the Northern Cheyenne, 1876* (Norman, OK: University of Oklahoma Press, 2003).

80 Greene, *Slim Buttes*, 127–29.

81 On October 16, 1877, medals were awarded to Sgt. John A. Kirkwood and Pvt. Robert Smith, both of Co. M, Third Cav., for their bravery in dislodging warriors entrenched in a ravine adjoining the village. Some of Mills's soldiers received certificates of merit for distinguished service at Slim Buttes. Greene, *Slim Buttes*, 176n46.

82 Gray, *Centennial Campaign*, 251; Robinson, *Bourke Diaries, Vol. II*, 117; Bourke, *On the Border*, 376.

83 Finerty, *War-Path and Bivouac*, 306.

84 Bourke, *On the Border*, 378.

85 Robinson, *Bourke Diaries, Vol. II*, 118.

86 Finerty, *War-Path and Bivouac*, 306.

87 King, *Campaigning with Crook*, 133.

88 Robinson, *Bourke Diaries, Vol. II*, 120.

Wyoming Duty

For two full days the men of the expedition ate, dried out, and rested along the Belle Fourche River. By this time Crook had received word to proceed to Fort Laramie to confer with General Sheridan on future field operations. Before he departed on the sixteenth, Crook turned over command of the expedition to Colonel Merritt. Two days later (eighteenth) the expedition moved to Centennial Park, just above Crook City. The next morning they began the march through the center of the Hills for Custer City, where it had been planned to ship the expedition's rations, supplies, forage, and company wagons (which held their tents, camp equipage, and clothing that had been left at Camp Cloud Peak). As the column moved south, Foster moved through familiar territory, retracing some of the same country he mapped the year previous.

As soon as the troops entered the Hills, the attention of the cavalrymen turned to the recuperation of their surviving horses.[1] Well-grassed campsites were selected along the Whitewood and Rapid Creeks, with easier marches and better weather to travel through. On September 23, the column arrived at Custer City and went into camp east of town on French Creek. Their bivouac area was the same one used by Custer's 1874 Black Hills expedition, and by the 1875 Jenney expedition for Camp Harney.

The expedition remained there through the first half of October, regaining the strength of men and horses. Camp was only moved when necessary to obtain fresh grass. After the three hardest months of field service (August-October), the Third Cavalry alone reported 106 animals lost, having either died or been destroyed, with 180 horses classified as unserviceable. Basically, camp life was dull work, but with no drills and plenty to eat, the men enjoyed it immensely. Their extended stay in the Black Hills was well-recorded by frontier photographer Stanley J. Morrow, who came to the Hills to photograph the gold rush. As the troops rested, Morrow's candid and posed photography documented camp life of the troops and some of the hardships they faced. In his group photos of officers, many, including Lieutenant Foster, still show the haggard and worn appearance of long months of hard campaigning (figs. 5.8, 6.1).[2]

Crook always had it in mind to disarm and dismount the agency camps, but decided to delay any such operation until he had a larger force on hand. By September the four company garrison at Camp Robinson was augmented with the arrival of fourteen companies, including six companies from Col. Ranald S. Mackenzie's Fourth Cavalry. In mid-October, Merritt received word to move his command south to Camp Robinson and Red Cloud Agency. General Crook planned to surround the camps of Red Cloud and Red Leaf, which had moved off some twenty-five miles southeast of their agency. With Merritt's force of thirty-five companies arriving from the north, any escape in that direction by those bands (or any agency Indians) could be blocked. The date set for the surround was October 24th.[3]

However, Crook realized the bands could bolt at any time, and decided to begin operations before Merritt's command had arrived. On the early morning of the twenty-third, Mackenzie's cavalry with the assistance of Frank North's Pawnee Scouts surrounded the camps of Red Cloud and Red Leaf, disarmed them, and marched the sullen warriors back to the agency. The next day Crook telegraphed Sheridan with word of his success, "I feel that this is the first gleam of day-light we have had in this business."[4] After a spring and summer of disappointment and defeat, the tide of the Sioux War was beginning to turn.

Later in the day of the twenty-third, Merritt's command, including Foster's troop, arrived and went into camp. The next day the long-serving Big Horn & Yellowstone Expedition was officially disbanded. Many of Crook's soldiers had been in the field for nearly six months. That day Crook issued General Orders No. 8, which dissolved the command, noting the physical and mental strain suffered by its officers and enlisted men:

> In the campaign now closed he [Gen. Crook] has been obliged to call upon you for much hard service and many sacrifices of personal comfort. At times you have been out of reach of your base of supplies; in most inclement weather you have marched without food and slept without shelter; in your engagements you have evinced a high order of

discipline and courage; in your marches, wonderful powers of endurance; and in your deprivations and hard-ships, patience and fortitude.[5]

After this congratulatory message, Crook immediately began plans for a winter campaign. Orders were issued that sent Merritt's thirty-five cavalry and infantry companies in to winter quarters. Those troops were not called for field service, but were held in reserve and assigned to posts near the agencies or seat of war—for the time being, they (the Big Horn & Yellowstone veterans) had served their time.

On October 25, Company I of the Third Cavalry left Camp Robinson and marched via Fort Laramie to its new assigned station, Fort Fetterman. Foster's troop was accompanied by Company F, Fourth Infantry, also bound for Fetterman, and Company A, Second Cavalry, returning to its post. With Captain Andrews absent moving company property from Sidney Barracks and King still on duty with Company B, Foster was the only company officer present and commanded his troop on the trip. Seven days later, the troops arrived and took station. Company A of the Second was immediately transferred to Fort Sanders near Laramie City. Their departure on November 9 left Foster's troop and two Fourth Infantry companies to form the new garrison. The next week, twenty-nine recruits arrived at Fetterman to help fill the ranks of Foster's Troop, depleted over the months by battle casualties, sickness, and desertion.[6]

During the five-month course of the campaign, Foster's company marched a grand total of 1,887 miles. With the arrival of its companies in Wyoming Territory, one last campaign accolade came, this time from the Cheyenne paper, which wrote: "The Third Cavalry especially distinguished itself in the recent campaign. Capts. Henry, Vroom, and Mills, and Lieuts. Chase, Schwatka, Crawford, Foster, Reynolds, Simpson, and Morton, made splendid reputations for good conduct and gallantry."[7]

Fort Fetterman was established on July 19, 1867, on a broad plateau above the south bank of the North Platte River. The site was near the mouth of La Prele Creek, at the point where the Bozeman Trail turned north and crossed the Platte into the Powder River Country. With its elevated position, the post commanded an extensive view of the surrounding country, but also exposed its garrisons to storms and gales from every quarter. Six months after the fort was established, the post commander requested moving his post below the plateau to the creek bottom for better shelter from the wind; his request was denied. As a consequence, Fort Fetterman was a desolate duty station where "high winds and low temperatures" prevailed during the winter, and July and August were "very warm."[8]

Outside of being known as the most uninhabitable location for a military post in the Department of the Platte, Fort Fetterman was also one of the most isolated. The supply depot at Cheyenne was one hundred and sixty miles southeast; Fort Laramie, its closest army post, was eighty miles south and east. Medicine Bow, the nearest railroad station, was eighty-five miles south. Furthermore, those roads were frequently obstructed by heavy snows during the winter months.[9]

In later years Correspondent Finerty left this description of Fort Fetterman: "It was a hateful post—in summer, hell, and in winter, Spitzbergen. The whole army dreaded being quartered there . . . Its abandonment was a wise proceeding on the part of the government."[10] For the next two years this was James Foster's duty station and home.

Fort Fetterman was laid out the same as any typical plains army post. On the west and southwest sides of the parade ground were four company barracks that could house three hundred soldiers. Officers' quarters were on the north, northeast, and south sides of the parade. Quarters at Fetterman for officers and enlisted men were structures with "no pretentions to architectural elegance" built either of log, frame, or adobe construction.[11] While commissary and quartermaster storehouses were built north of the main post, the hospital and stables for cavalry and quartermaster animals were to the east. Quarters for married soldiers and civilian employees and post shops were spread along the northern edge of the plateau. At this time all water for garrison use had to be hauled up by wagon from the river.

FIG. 6.2. Winter scene at Fort Fetterman, November, 1876. In this illustration, General Crook's personal designating flag flies above the commanding officer's quarters. *Harper's Weekly*, December 16, 1876. Courtesy of High Plains Press

As was the normal procedure, officer housing was assigned by rank and availability. During the period Foster was stationed at the post, Fort Fetterman's garrisons were reduced, at times to half of its designated capacity. Upon arrival, he was assigned to the east half of quarters two, the last set on the north side of the parade. Built in 1871, this log building was a story and a half duplex, with a veranda across the front, an enclosed yard, and, like the other units, painted with a yellow wash. Foster's quarters were more than adequate for a single junior subaltern.

The year 1876 proved to be the pivotal moment in Fort Fetterman history. During the Great Sioux War the post was the jumping off point for the seat of war in the Powder and Yellowstone river countries. Both Crook's early and summer expeditions against the northern tribesmen set out from Fetterman. For the troops in the field, the post was their logistical link to supply depots along the railroad. Throughout the summer and fall, supplies were received, inspected, stored, and then freighted on to the troops. Commanding officer Capt. Edwin A. Coates estimated that over 1,300,000 pounds of supplies and equipment had been received at Fetterman in July and August alone.[12] In addition, hundreds of soldiers and Indian allies were assembled at the post before departure for the front.

In November 1876 Fort Fetterman for a third time became a point of departure for an expeditionary force, this time for Crook's Powder River Expedition. Devised as a winter campaign to strike at Crazy Horse, the force was comprised of eleven companies of cavalry, eleven of infantry, and four of artillery (deployed as infantry). In all, it numbered 1,750 officers, enlisted men, civilians, and Pawnee, Sioux, and Cheyenne auxiliaries. Commanded by Col. Ranald Mackenzie and Lt. Col. Richard Dodge (from the 1875 Black Hills Expedition), and under overall command of General Crook, the expedition marched out on November 14. Ten days later the soldiers stuck a decisive blow, not against Crazy Horse, but against Dull Knife's Northern Cheyenne. Along with the persistent campaigning of Col. Nelson Miles in Montana, Crook's capture of the village on the Red Fork of the Powder River proved a turning point in the Great Sioux War.[13] The end was near for the traditional free-roaming lifestyle of the Lakota Sioux and their Cheyenne allies.

Among the items captured by Crook's men at the Dull Knife fight were a number of Seventh Cavalry souvenirs from the Little Big Horn battle. Also found was a hat, marked on the inside of the sweatband as belonging to Pvt. William Allen, the old soldier from Foster's troop who had been killed at the Rosebud in June.[14]

Although Foster was not a direct participant, he played an important role in keeping the expedition's supply line open and moving. Any military operation, particularly a winter campaign, requires careful logistical calculations for the timely arrival of provisions, forage, and other necessary supplies. The Powder River Expedition proved no exception. As with the Big Horn & Yellowstone Expedition, all supplies into the Powder country for the winter campaign had to come up from the railroad, and then through Fort Fetterman. Although the trail from Medicine Bow station on the Union Pacific to Fetterman was the shortest known supply route, travel between December and June was prone to be irregular on account of snow.

To provide a closer supply base for operations in the Powder River country, Crook had ordered the establishment of a post near the site of old Fort Reno on the Bozeman Trail. But by November the new post was still under construction and unable to support Crook's third campaign. As a result, escort duty for supply trains was a major duty for Fort Fetterman garrisons. Eventually supplies could be stockpiled at the new post, christened Cantonment Reno, for transport further north.[15]

Since the earliest days of Fort Fetterman, the army had used the trail from Medicine Bow Station to move its supplies up from the Union Pacific railroad. Although the route involved less travel distance, its major obstacle for wagon transport was the rugged Laramie Range, particularly during the winter season. After leaving the railroad, for the first forty miles the road basically followed the Medicine Bow River across the broad Laramie Plain. Then the trail ascended the Laramie Mountains for half a dozen miles before the eight thousand foot divide was reached. After crossing the pass, the road wound down the Boxelder Creek canyon for nearly fifteen miles before it reached La Prele Creek. From the crossing of the old Overland Trail, it was a short ten-mile ride to Fetterman. The total distance of the trail from Medicine Bow to the fort was eighty-five-and-a-half miles.[16]

Foster's first detached service at Fort Fetterman came late in November. Several contract supply trains moving north from Medicine Bow were snowbound in the high elevations. On November 26 Lieutenant Foster, with a detachment of one non-commissioned officer and nine enlisted men, were ordered south to find the stalled wagons and assist and urge them on to Fetterman. In this case, Foster was to provide all assistance possible and to "use his own judgment as to the best means of urging forward the train." He was to take command of a similar detachment previously sent out and give particular attention to trains carrying grain. The mission was successfully completed and Foster's detail was able to return to post after only three days' absence.[17]

After their victory over the Cheyenne, General Crook's command moved northeastward up Foster's Belle Fourche River in search of the elusive Crazy Horse and the camps of his followers. Regardless of the cold weather, supply trains regularly moved north from Fetterman. Crook had estimated the expedition would require 26,000 pounds of forage per day. To meet this need, 200,000 pounds of grain were freighted to Cantonment Reno and 300,000 pounds were stored at Fetterman. In December two trains were dispatched to Cantonment Reno while four trains traveled to the Belle Fourche. Between November 28 and the twenty-fifth of December, 634,000 pounds had been shipped through Fort Fetterman for the expedition's use.[18]

For several weeks the expedition marched and camped along the Belle Fourche. With forage running low, the men grew impatient with the campaign. Finally on December 21, after being notified that his transportation costs were more than double what had been estimated, and with the weather growing unpredictable, animals failing, and no enemy in sight, Crook decided to turn back to Fort Fetterman. The campaign was over.

Meanwhile, Lieutenant Foster and twenty enlisted men had been detailed on December 16 as escort for a grain train bound for Crook's supply camp designated on Wind Creek, south of the Pumpkin Buttes. The Powder River country was still a dangerous area, and Foster's men were supplied with one hundred rounds of ammunition each.[19]

With daily temperatures ranging from highs in the teens to lows below zero, the train moved out. After nine days of travel, Foster and his men spent Christmas Day on Wind Creek awaiting the expedition. On the twenty-sixth Crook's column, by this time completely out of grain, arrived at the supply base. With food for their animals, Lieutenant Bourke noted with satisfaction, "... we turn in to bed, happy to know that our mules and horses, their stomachs well filled with corn, will not sound in the stillness of the midnight air their appeal to a powerless Q[uarter]. M[aster]. to aid them."[20] As a bonus, the train also brought newspapers and a welcomed mail for the expedition.

Back at Fort Fetterman, transportation was in such short supply that every available wheeled vehicle was pressed into service. To make up for a shortage of draft horses and mules, post commander Maj. Caleb H. Carlton, Third Cavalry, ordered the portion of Company I which remained at post, to be dismounted and their horses substituted in for draft duty.[21]

Foster's detachment returned to post on December 29. The trip was hard; the minimum temperature that day reached minus twenty-nine degrees. He was immediately reported as sick in quarters. To help occupy his time while on sick leave, he drew up a plan and made sketches of a proposed cavalry stable for the consideration of the post quartermaster. A week later he was healthy enough to return to duty.

Upon his return to duty, Foster was ordered to assume command of one of the infantry companies at post. Company grade officers from one service branch were occasionally called upon to temporarily command organizations of another branch. This was particularly the case when there was a shortage of officers in garrison. Ten days later Foster resumed company duty with his proper organization.

A week later he received orders for more detached duty in the field. On February 20 Foster and eighteen enlisted men were detached as escort for a train of twelve wagons bound for Cantonment Reno. When a supply train with eleven wagons was dispatched to Reno in January, twenty-two horses and two of its wagons had to be abandoned. On the march to Reno and return, Foster and his detail were also to search the vicinity and recover any government stock or property for return to Reno or to be brought back to Fetternan.[22]

After they had arrived at the cantonment, the lieutenant and the mounted portion of his detail were ordered to report to the post commander, Maj. Edwin Pollock. Several days before Foster's detachment left Fort Fetterman, Maj. Carlton had heard there was a camp of civilians near Reno with abandoned or stolen government animals in their possession. He ordered Foster, under Pollock's advisement, to inspect the stock in the camp for illegal horses or mules. By this time, Cantonment Reno had grown large enough to house four companies of infantry; with stables, storehouses, and other support buildings, the post had more than forty log structures in all. For the months ahead, Fort Fetterman soldiers rode on escort details there, transporting supplies for soldiers in the field in the Powder River country.[23]

Although the empty supply wagons arrived back at Fetterman on March 2, Foster and six enlisted men from his company remained at Reno to provide an escort for Maj. Thomas T. Thornburgh, the department paymaster. Foster's detail arrived back on March 4 and the Fetterman garrison was paid the same day.[24]

After the winter war, Sioux and Cheyenne warriors began to return to the agencies to surrender. By the spring of 1877 Fort Fetterman was no longer directly involved in the northern Plains Indian wars, but was part of a second line of forts around the Great Sioux Reservation. Although far from the scene of any combat, a shortage of manpower at the post was soon apparent. With its troops continually detached on logistical support duties, there were fewer men available at post for the normal garrison tasks, much less for any construction work, drill, or to maintain a reserve. As a result, when they were not on detached duty, Foster's troop was occupied with regular garrison duties. In January men from the infantry companies and Company I began ice harvest. An important winter job, cutting ice for summer use began when the ice on the North Platte River averaged twelve to fourteen inches thick. Whenever possible details harvested ice and stored it in post ice houses. Another important duty for Fetterman garrisons was cutting and hauling logs in from the wood reserve. During the first part of February Company I spent time moving wood in from the log camp, thirty miles distant on a tributary of the La Bonte.[25]

Detached service continued to occupy much of Foster's time. During the last part of March he accompanied a small escort for several Third Cavalry officers to Fort Laramie for general court martial duty. On the trip to and from Laramie, Foster was ordered to "use every effort in his power" to locate and arrest deserters from the post. Eight days later the detail returned bringing prisoners belonging to Company I. Another major occupation for the fort in 1877 was pursuit of horse thieves who raided post herds. Officers believed there were several camps of suspected culprits in the hills south of the post in the Laramie Range. In April, Foster and soldiers from Company I were ordered to join a Fourth Infantry detail commanded by Capt. Gerhard L. Luhn to pursue horse thieves. The soldiers unsuccessfully trailed the outlaws to the head of La Bonte Creek before returning to post three days later.[26]

Foster's work as a topographer proved more successful than his brief stint as a building architect. In late February he had submitted the stable plan he drew up while on sick leave to post quartermaster John Bubb. His proposed plan was a somewhat unorthodox design for stable construction. Primarily built of adobe, Foster's stable could be described as two single rectangular shed-roofed structures, which faced each other to form a central open-air alleyway. It contained twenty-five double stalls with four rooms for saddles, grain, general supplies, and sleeping quarters. Bubb eventually rejected the plan, claiming it would prove cheaper to use pole construction rather than adobe. Later that fall, a more conventional stable was built of wood with a roof enclosing the central alleyway.[27]

Later that spring Foster had an opportunity to put his topographical and road building skills to work. Although the supply road to Medicine Bow was a direct route to the railroad, as mentioned it was generally blocked by heavy snow drifts in winter months. In May instructions were received from Department Headquarters to locate a new route which would be

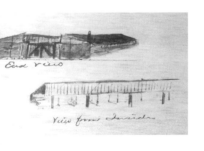

FIG. 6.3. Foster's design for a stable. National Archives, H-134, Fort Bridger and Fort Fetterman Consolidated Correspondence File

less susceptible to winter drifting. Lieutenant Foster and Captain Coates were ordered to survey a route east of the present trail, which would head north from Rock Creek station, twenty-two miles east of Medicine Bow. A route in that area was thought more passable for winter travel.[28]

On May 16, Foster, who had been in command of Company I, was relieved by Lieutenant King, and left the same day with Captain Coates and a detachment of seven cavalrymen and five infantrymen from their respective units, to examine and report on the "practicability" of a new road. The post engineer officer was to issue to Foster any instruments or materials needed for making a map of the route. The detachment returned after nearly three weeks in the field. In addition to being a shorter shipping distance by rail, the new route from Rock Creek was two miles shorter overland, and passed through a lower summit on the mountain divide. Coates enthusiastically reported the Rock Creek route would provide a better road and also had better wood, water, and grass, three necessities army officers looked for when establishing overland routes.[29]

Several weeks later Foster was able to see the new route in practical use. On June 13, he was detailed in command of an escort for a wagon train to Rock Creek station to pick up government supplies. Besides providing protection for the wagons, Foster could also observe actual use of the road, and determine where improvements for travel would be needed. On June 28 the train and escort returned to Fort Fetterman.

To assist with the road project, 1st Lt. Joseph Keeffe, Fourth Infantry, and twenty enlisted men from Fort Fred Steele were sent by rail to Rock Creek Station. From there they worked their way over the divide, using blasting powder when necessary to remove obstructions. At the same time Lieutenant Foster was sent south from Fetterman to meet up with Keeffe's detachment. Foster gave him information on places where improvement work had to be done. As a junior lieutenant, he was to *suggest* to his senior the necessity if working the road through the canyon beyond the summit first. This way loaded trains could have easier passage and the road improved toward the fort. After completion of this assignment, Foster returned to post on the twenty-first.[30]

A week later Foster was sent out again to advise the Fort Steele work detail. By this time Keeffe's men had reached the upper crossing of La Prele Creek, in the canyon beyond the divide. Here again, Foster advised his counterpart on how to straighten the road to avoid a temporary detour. By the end of the month Keeffe was able to report the road through the canyon was complete. But even with the new route, moving supplies over the Laramie Range during winter months continued to be a challenge.

Several weeks after this, Foster was again sent out as an escort for the chief department quartermaster, Maj. Marshall I. Ludington, who had arrived at Fort Fetterman wanting to see the new route to the railroad. Lieutenant Foster and a detail of one noncommissioned officer and twenty-one privates of Company F, Fourth Infantry, were sent to escort the major to Rock Creek station. Although the new route was also liable to winter blockage, it replaced the Medicine Bow road as the main supply route from the Union Pacific Railroad.[31]

During the summer of 1877 Foster was ready to take some time off and applied for a leave of absence. Army officers were entitled to thirty days' leave per year at full pay. This leave time could be accumulated for a period not to exceed four years. In his nearly four years of service time, James had only used sick leave, not leave of absence time. Orders from division headquarters dated August 9 granted him two months of leave with permission to request an extension of an extra three months.[32]

Before he could go on leave, Foster had other obligations at Fort Fetterman. In addition to regular company duties, on August 9 he was designated acting post adjutant and also post treasurer, commissary officer (Acting Commissary of Subsistence), and signal officer. He also had the escort for the department chief quartermaster's visit. Finally, on August 27 Foster was relieved from duty at Fetterman and two days later departed for the east on leave. While passing through Cheyenne, he applied to the Adjutant General in Washington for the three months' extension. His request was granted and Foster was free to be absent on leave until the end of January. According to regulation, he reported his contact address while on leave as "Care [of] A. W. Foster, Craig Str. (Bellefield) Pittsburgh, Pa."[33]

* * *

It was probably a good thing that Foster was able to take leave and live at home for a while. The year 1877 found Congress in crisis over the army's fiscal situation. With trouble with the Apache in the Southwest, the Nez Perce outbreak, and the railroad strike, 1877 was an especially busy year for the U. S. Army. In spite of that, Republicans and Democrats were in a political squabble over army size and its deployment in the southern states during Reconstruction. When the Congressional session ended on March 4, no military appropriation bill had been passed. Consequently, when the fiscal year ended on June 30, neither enlisted men nor officers were able to draw their pay.

For the next five months Congress, in essence, directed the army to hold their own financially. Although the men received no pay, the War

FORT FETTERMAN
FROM C.G. COUTANT'S HISTORY OF WYOMING.

Department was still able to provide contracts for subsistence, clothing, fuel, and forage for its enlisted ranks. But the loss of pay was especially hard on the officer corps, who had always paid for those personal necessities out of their own pockets, even before the recent financial difficulties. Finally, on November 12 a bill was passed to maintain the army at its normal size (it had been threatened with reduction), and with the appropriation bill signed by President Hayes eight days later, the soldiers received their pay.[34]

Foster's leave lasted for four months. In December he chose to return to duty and relinquished the remainder of his leave. In the latter part of the month, he had been assigned to serve on a general court martial to meet at Fort Russell. Foster sat on the court from December 29 until he was relieved at the end of January and ordered to rejoin his company at Fetterman. The next month he was again detailed for court martial duty, now to Fort Laramie. This session was much shorter, and he was able to return to post after only ten days of detached duty.

On February 9, Lieutenant Foster was appointed post adjutant, replacing Lt. Leonard A. Lovering, Fourth Infantry, who was returned to company duty. With his experience of adjutant in the Greys and in the regulars,

FIG. 6.4. Bird's-eye view of Fort Fetterman, looking north toward the Powder River country. Labels have been added showing, 1) Foster's quarters, 2) Adjutant's Office. Wyoming State Archives, Department of State Parks and Cultural Resources

Foster was a natural for the job. Gen. Charles King, who spent his share of time as an adjutant when serving with the Fifth Cavalry, best summarized the qualifications for the post:

> We all know what the adjutant should be,—a soldier in everything, in carriage, form, voice, and manner, the soul of parade and guard mounting, the reliable authority on tactics and regulations, the patient student of general orders, the rigid scrutinizer of returns and rolls, the scholarly man of the subalterns, the faithful adherent and executive in spirit and in letter of the commanding officer.[35]

The post headquarters building, which housed the adjutant's office where Foster worked, was the third such structure built at Fort Fetterman. It was situated at the southeast corner of the parade ground, conveniently just behind the post commanding officers quarters. Built in 1874, it was a frame structure, lined with adobes, which measured seventy feet by twenty-nine feet, five inches in size, and had ceilings fourteen feet high. On the inside were offices for the adjutant, post quartermaster, the commissary of subsistence, and quarters for the ordnance sergeant, telegraph operator, and quartermaster's clerk. When completed, the new building was described as "commodious and comfortable."[36]

One of Foster's first tasks was to correct a record number that was typical of nineteenth century military bureaucracy. A simple clerical error by his predecessor gave the same number to two post orders, which were copied and submitted to Department Headquarters. After the error was noticed at headquarters, the copies were sent back to post where they were corrected, and then returned to headquarters. To his credit, Foster proved to be one of the most capable officers to serve as post adjutant.[37]

At times the post adjutant had to be a martinet who strictly adhered to established procedures, rules, and regulations. On one occasion he officially scolded his senior company lieutenant for missing the regular Sunday morning inspection. In reply, Lieutenant King explained Company I was not paraded on account of inclement weather and that the first sergeant had the guard detail formed and forgot about inspection. Several months earlier, Foster had been similarly berated by the post adjutant for missing a roll call.[38]

Although Foster was responsible for the daily function of the military post and for creating and submitting correct daily records, he was frequently required to serve on administrative boards. When necessary, the post adjutant had the authority to call several different officer boards for oversight of accountability of post operations and finances. During the period Foster was stationed at Fort Fetterman, he served on or presided over fifty separate boards of survey, boards of officers, and councils of administration.

Boards of Survey were convened to fix responsibility for public (meaning government) property lost, damaged, stolen, or destroyed. Due to its strategic location on the Powder River supply line, many boards held at Fetterman dealt with losses of stores or supplies in transit. A board in January 1877 was called to determine responsibility for the loss of potatoes, and one hundred cans of green peas and twenty-five of tomatoes. Other boards fixed blame for shortages of grain shipped, deficiencies of bacon, and losses of mules at Rock Creek Station. Boards of Survey were also called to record items taken by deserters or lost by troops in the field. On one occasion Foster called a board to determine responsibility for the loss of a Springfield carbine, "the property of the United States," for which he was responsible.[39]

Whereas Boards of Survey were formed to determine responsibility for loss, Boards of Officers were held to inspect local contract goods, fuel, hay, lumber, after their delivery at post, and also to evaluate condition of public animals. Just after he arrived at Fetterman, Foster served on a board to inspect a herd of beef cattle offered by a civilian for purchase. Other board work included inspection of quartermaster animals and ordnance supplies. Officer boards also reported on destruction of buildings by fire, such as the burning of the post shingle mill in September 1878.[40]

In the summer of 1878, Foster presided over a Board of Officers investigating the circumstances of the death of Pvt. Lewis P. Bauer, Company C, Fourth Infantry. At that time the post sawmill was operated by a civilian employee named R. L. DeLay. On June 7, one of his soldier assistants warned him that the steam-powered saw was in need of repair, to which Delay replied, "Oh, if it kills anyone, it will only be a soldier." That afternoon while sawing wood for his company's monthly supply, the blade broke and struck Bauer "squarely in the eyes, killing him instantly." The men of Company C immediately placed full blame on Delay. After threats against his life, including placing a noose around his neck, Delay soon left the country. As a result the department engineer was ordered to inspect all steam machinery at post.[41]

A Council of Administration was a board of two or three officers periodically assembled to conduct certain post business. While he served as post adjutant, Foster presided over ten such councils. Councils were concerned with financial matters, and usually held to audit the accounts of the post treasurer. They also met to determine the amount of post funds properly due to company units when they were transferred to new duty stations. Councils were also called to administer the effects of deceased soldiers. On June 25, Foster and another officer met to rule on the effects of the late Private Bauer, killed at the sawmill. Although boards generally consisted of three officers, at times it was not easy to turn up that number. Adjutant Foster issued a general order on April 29, 1878, that stated, "A Council of Administration consisting of Lieut. Foster, no other officer being available for the duty, will meet at this post at 1:00 o'clock tomorrow." At that time Foster was the only Third Cavalry officer on duty and commanded his company plus the duties as adjutant and post signal officer. He in fact carried this work load from May 21 to November 29 of that year.[42]

During this period Foster was interested in professional development and advancement. In 1879 he became a member of the Military Service Institution of the United States. Organized in 1878, this was a voluntary organization of officers of the army for mutual improvements, and the promotion of the military interests of the United States. There was interest in such an organization—in addition to naval officers, a quarter of the army's officer corps immediately joined. The institution also initiated a quarterly journal, *The United Service*, in 1879.[43]

Lieutenant Foster was like other progressive officers of the post-Civil War army, who came up with new ideas to improve both training and performance in combat. While at Fort Fetterman he devised a system of signaling troops under battle conditions. For eons of time, line troops received their orders either vocally or by bugle or trumpet call. From his experiences in the Civil War and at the Rosebud in 1876, he realized that battle noise in skirmish formations was greatly increased due to modern rapid-fire weaponry. Under such conditions vocal orders were frequently not heard. Additionally many soldiers did not recognize all the different bugle calls.

To counter the problem, Foster suggested the shrill sound of a whistle could be used. His system was based on long and short whistle blasts, similar to Morse code. To ease training, a small manual listing the calls could be prepared for the soldier's convenience and study, rather than the old method of memorizing musical tunes. Other officers were interested in this innovative approach and it quickly passed through levels of administrative approval. But, William T. Sherman, the commanding general of the U. S. Army, was a long-standing traditionalist and nixed the plan. His blunt rejection stated that because current tactics prescribed commands by word and bugle, "the method by whistles is not approved."[44]

A section of the 1878 Army appropriation bill provided that an officer's time served as an enlisted man during the Civil War, could be added to his service time as a commissioned officer for longevity pay. In June 1878, Foster requested the adjutant general to provide the dates of his enlistments and discharges from the First Pennsylvania Artillery Battalion, and the 155th and 191st Pennsylvania Infantry regiments. This service gave him just over six months of extra time, which advanced his ten year service anniversary from October 1883 to April of that year. The extra time in grade could prove handy for future assignment or promotion.[45]

By this time Foster had full intentions of making a career in the U. S. Army. He had proved a dedicated and talented officer; a true leader of men and capable subaltern, whose place in his chosen profession already was established. With everything seemingly going his way, Foster's only Achilles' heel was a nagging health problem. The respiratory illness contracted during his first winter service at Fort McPherson continued to haunt him, and was only exacerbated by hard duty during the 1876–77 campaigns and subsequent field service. As a result, his health was on the decline.

Foster was able to spend most of 1878 on duty in garrison with little time away on detached service. During the year he spent several days at Fort Robinson on court martial duty, and sat at least half a dozen times on garrison courts at Fetterman, serving as judge advocate. However, in October he was detached in command of a detail of two noncommissioned officers and nine privates from his regiment and the Fourth Infantry, as an escort for Lt. Col. William B. Royall, the department inspector general, to Fort Laramie.

For a sufferer of bronchial problems, Fort Fetterman was about the worst place to be stationed. Its exposed position on the plateau above the North Platte River, plus the extremes of Wyoming weather, only worsened Foster's health. For instance, when he was sent out on field service in December 1876, the temperature at Fetterman ranged from a high of twenty degrees to a low of minus twenty-six degrees. The prevailing sickness at the post was afflictions of the air passages, mostly catarrhs. Army physicians felt the great amount of ozone and dryness of the atmosphere, plus an abundance of dust, accounted for those afflictions. In Lieutenant Foster's case, by the spring of 1879 it was obvious a change was necessary.[46]

In the spring of 1879 he was encouraged by post surgeon John V. R. Hoff, to go on an extended sick leave. Hoff diagnosed that Foster was suffering from a chronic follicular pharyngitis complicated by chronic nasal catarrh. In other words, inflammation of the throat and infection of the mucus membrane with increased production of mucus, affecting the nose; the affliction was of four years' standing. He also declared if there was any chance for Foster's recovery, it was necessary for him to spend time in a Southern insular climate, a milder environment than that of the northern Plains. On April 16 Foster applied to the Department of the Platte for a one month's leave on a surgeon's certificate. His application also requested permission to apply for an extension of five months, and for permission to go beyond the limits of the department. Dr. Hoff prepared a surgeon's certificate with his recommendations which was filed with Foster's request.[47]

Foster's request for sick leave was passed through the department adjutant general and medical officer for approval, and then moved on to division headquarters in Chicago, where commanding general Philip Sheridan's endorsement sent it on to Washington. Here it was given formal approval on May 22 by Gen. Edwin D. Townsend, the adjutant general of the army.

As Foster awaited authorization to depart on leave, he spent his last days on duty at Fort Fetterman. On April 19 he was relieved as post adjutant and signal officer. His replacement was fellow Third Cavalry officer Lt. Charles Chase. The next day the post commander, Maj. Julius W. Mason, granted him a seven days' leave of absence from duty, which he spent sick in quarters. When he returned to duty, Foster was put on garrison court martial duty. As expected, Foster's request for one month's leave was granted, but before leaving post, he had one last duty assignment at Fort Fetterman to perform. On May 9, ". . . in order to avail himself of a leave," he received orders to inspect the telegraph line to Fort Laramie, and there to report on its condition. Three days later, he arrived at Laramie, filed his report, and on the thirteenth left post for Cheyenne and the railroad east. While in Chicago, he applied for the five months' extension, which was fully approved by army headquarters. Even had he not departed on leave, Foster's days at Fetterman would have been numbered. Three weeks later, Company I was relieved of duty there and left post to take station at Fort Robinson, Nebraska.[48]

Foster spent the summer and fall recuperating at the family home and in nearby New Castle in Lawrence County. His health did improve, but with winter coming on, any improvement might be put in jeopardy. While he was on sick leave, Foster was attended by H. P. Peebles, a New Castle physician. Dr. Peebles advised that all progress made would be lost if he returned to active duty, and encouraged Foster to continue on sick leave. If this course was followed, the doctor assured him that in the spring of 1880, ". . . he would be capable of resuming and continuing active duty."

Knowing a change in climate would be beneficial, Peebles also recommended Foster pass the coming winter season in Bermuda.[49]

On October 25 Foster applied to the Adjutant General in Washington for a seven month's extension with permission "to go beyond sea." Because there was no medical officer in Pittsburgh to provide a surgeon's certificate to accompany his application, a statement from Peebles was submitted. Foster informed the Adjutant General he intended to spend the winter in Nassau, on New Province, the most populated island in the Bahamas. As his application passed through army headquarters, a sympathetic endorsement, probably penned by General Townsend, simply noted, "It is well known that Lieut. Foster is a sick man." Additionally, Assistant Surgeon Hoff at Fort Fetterman reiterated, "I am convinced that a return now to field duty in this climate would place his case beyond all hope of permanent recovery." He also stressed that Foster's extension be granted.[50]

After ten days Foster had not received word on his leave extension. With his authorized leave time running short, he requested the Adjutant General's Office to inform him of the final action on his application by telegraph, at his own expense. Two days later a telegram arrived that notified Foster that his leave extension was approved. True to his request, the War Department sent the telegram collect. By December Foster was comfortably situated in the balmy climate of Nassau in the Bahamas. With his residence now out of the Department of the Platte and the United States, he had made arrangements through the First National Bank of Omaha to have his pay accounts forwarded. Far removed from winter campaigns and garrison and field service on the northern Plains, Foster hopefully waited for his health to improve so that he could return to active service.[51]

At the end of the year, 2nd Lt. James Foster was in line to receive his first lieutenancy. His advancement was due to the promotion of 1st Lt. John P. Walker of Company B, to the rank of captain. Walker was promoted within the regiment to replace William H. Andrews, Foster's company commander, who retired on November 30. Foster's promotion was nominated by President Hayes on December 9 and referred to the Committee on Military Affairs the same day. On January 12 the committee reported favorably on his promotion, which was verified by the Senate two days later. By the first of February Foster received his ornate commission certificate, and the formal oath of office statement. He duly signed the oath and had it attested at the American Consul in Nassau before returning it to the War Department. Foster's promotion brought him a raise to sixteen hundred dollars per annum. It also brought assignment to a new company organization and duty station.[52]

While James was in the Bahamas, his father, Alexander W. Jr., died on January 24, 1880. The cause of his death was listed as an embolism, an obstruction of a blood vessel, generally due to a blood clot. George S. Foster, the second son, had served as his attending physician. The senior Foster was buried in the family plot in Allegheny Cemetery, the main cemetery in Pittsburgh, next to his eldest son Pearson, who died in 1867.[53]

The appearance of *The United Service* journal in 1879 gave Foster an opportunity to express his views on the size and role of the post-Civil War army, a question faced by every officer who saw the strength of the army reduced. While either at Fort Fetterman or on his 1879 leave, he wrote an article for the journal which appeared in the April 1880 issue. In Orwellian style, Foster painted a grim, futuristic view of the weak condition of the regular army and of the national guard and militia units. Titled "The Battle of Kiskiminetas," his story was a fictitious recollection of a war with England and of the joint British and Canadian invasion of the United States in 1881, as told by an American veteran of the conflict in 1901.[54]

A number of details in Foster's story are drawn from his own personal experiences. He has the veteran telling his story as a member of a Pittsburgh guard unit, called into action when the British moved south through western Pennsylvania. The members of his brigade had to furnish their own gray uniforms, the same as Foster did in the Duchesne Greys. The volunteer units were poorly armed and poorly supplied with field equipment. Knap's Battery even made an appearance in the battle. The gist of his story is that the American military failed miserably. The emergency units composed of raw levies were totally worthless; ill-trained, they broke and ran. The small regular army was badly outnumbered and out gunned, and mostly scattered across the western states.

After the defeat on the Kiskiminetas River, the British advanced to Pittsburgh. There the Americans dug defensive works through the suburbs, as Foster had seen during the Civil War. Pittsburgh, as well as most northeastern cities, was captured. In the last fight the veteran is knocked unconscious, and had no memory of the end of the disastrous campaign. The old guardsman summed up the sorry state of America's unprepared military: "... but I cannot but think how much more economical it would have been to have kept up a regular army sufficient to have made a rallying-point for the volunteers, with a volunteer force well enough organized, equipped, and trained to have been available as soldiers when needed ..."[55]

Lieutenant Foster was due to return from his sick leave in June to join his new troop, Company B, commanded by Capt. John B. Johnson, which was stationed at Fort Sanders, Wyoming Territory. The post on the

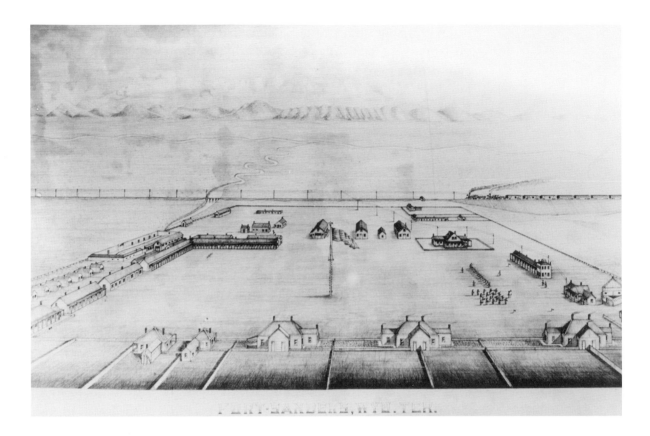

FORT SANDERS, WY. TER.

FIG. 6.5. Fort Sanders, Wyoming Territory. Barracks for six companies on left; officers' row in foreground. Wyoming State Archives, Department of State Parks and Cultural Resources

Laramie Plain was established in June 1866 to protect the overland travel routes, and became one of the key posts for the protection of Union Pacific construction crews. After the completion of the Union Pacific, Sanders continued as an important troop station on the railroad. Although in its last years of occupation, Fort Sanders was still one of the largest posts in the department. In 1880 three companies of the Third Cavalry and three of the Fourth Infantry were stationed there.[56]

Foster returned from his leave on June 13 and immediately reported sick in quarters. Evidently his condition was still weakened and the trip was harder than expected. The next day the Tenth U. S. Census enumerated the population of Fort Sanders and recorded James as bed-ridden with bronchitis, and he apparently remained sick in quarters for the rest of the month. He returned to duty in July, but spent the last week of the month on sick leave in quarters.[57]

In August Foster was ordered to sit on a general court martial at Fort Fred Steele, 124 miles west on the railroad from Fort Sanders. The court, which consisted of four Third Cavalry and four Fourth Infantry officers, was in session for three days before it was dismissed. It was Foster's last opportunity to serve with his old friend Lt. Albert King, from Company

I, and also Capt. Edwin Coates from Fort Fetterman. On his return trip to Sanders, General Crook and several members of the department staff were aboard the train returning to Omaha from Ogden, Utah. Foster had his last chance to see the general and his aide, Lt. John Bourke, from the 1875 Black Hills Expedition days. As it turned out, this was the last time Foster was sent out on detached service where he was able to perform duty.[58]

During his term at Fort Sanders, Foster came to the realization that his days of active service in the army might be numbered. Clearly his health was deteriorating. For some time his medical problem was classified as chronic bronchitis coupled with catarrh. It was hoped that the time he spent on leave would contribute to his full recovery; unfortunately this was not the case. Lt. James P. Kimball, the Fort Sanders post surgeon, diagnosed his illness as pulmonary phthisis: tuberculosis. Kimball identified the affected area as the lower portion of the left lung, which had increased during the time James had been under his care.

In August Foster took an unusual step. Instead of applying for sick leave, he requested transfer to the Post of San Antonio, Texas, in hopes that the change to a mild climate might be of benefit and enable him to continue duty. He asked for a travel route from Omaha down the Missouri River to St. Louis, then down the Mississippi to New Orleans, and from there through the Gulf of Mexico to Galveston, Texas. He suggested that traveling by a water route would avoid long railroad journeys with "the unfavorable fatigue connected therewith." While Dr. Kimball provided a certificate in support of Foster's request, Captain Johnson, his troop commander gave his full endorsement adding, "it is so rare for officers to choose the duty status in preference to sick leave" that he hoped the request would be granted.[59]

While his unusual request made its way through the Departments of the Platte and Texas and Division of the Missouri headquarters, Foster left Fort Sanders for temporary assignment at Fort D. A. Russell. Upon recommendation of the department medical director he was to report to the commanding officer at Russell for "such temporary duty as the post surgeon of that post may find him capable of performing." Foster desperately wanted to be useful to the army and arrived at Cheyenne on September 11 for his new assignment. Fort Russell was his last posting on the Northern Plains.[60]

Foster was among friends at Russell. The post was regimental headquarters for the Third Cavalry, with the field staff, band, and four troops stationed there, which included officers he had served with during the

Great Sioux War and on the "Starvation March." One was Lt. Augustus Paul, visited by Foster and the others at North Platte Station while on his first scout back in the winter of 1873. While this temporary assignment could not include any regular troop duties, which by now he was incapable of doing, it more than likely consisted of staff or office type work.

Meanwhile, his request for duty in Texas was approved by department Adjutant General Williams and Acting Medical Director William H. Forwood, and forwarded through the division headquarters to Adjutant General Townsend in Washington. In September Gen. E. O. C. Ord, the commanding general of the Department of Texas, was asked if he would have any duty for Lieutenant Foster at San Antonio. On the twenty-third, General Ord replied that there was nothing for Foster there, but he could make use of him at the Post of San Diego, 145 miles south of San Antonio. Established in April 1878 to protect area settlers and ranchers from Indian and Mexican raiders, the Post of San Diego was a small station, garrisoned by a single Eighth Cavalry troop. At that time only the company captain was there; both of his subordinates were on leave or detached service. Ord welcomed the opportunity of having an available cavalry lieutenant to send to assist him. The general noted the good climate around San Diego and recommended sending Foster there "for such duty as his physical condition will permit." On October 7 Foster left Fort Russell to report to the Department of Texas for duty.[61]

As he traveled enroute, orders were issued on October 20 for him upon arrival at Galveston to go to San Diego and report to the commanding officer there. However, in early November, the order was revoked. Perhaps after rethinking the situation, it was determined an officer fully capable of assisting with all troop duties was needed, and in his condition, Foster did not fill the bill. As soon as he arrived at the port of Galveston, Foster was notified instead to report to San Antonio. According to his new orders, he was to proceed to the post there for whatever duty assignment he was physically able to perform. In addition to housing a regular garrison, San Antonio was headquarters for the Department of Texas and its quartermaster depot. At that time several companies of the Sixteenth and Twenty-second Infantry regiments formed the garrison. The post commander was Col. Galusha Pennypacker of the Sixteenth Infantry. Pennypacker is correctly remembered as the youngest general in the Union army during the Civil War, a notoriety commonly attached to George A. Custer. Foster arrived at post on November 16. With no cavalry units stationed there, he was eventually attached to Company E of the Twenty-second for administrative purposes.[62]

It soon became painfully evident that James was unable to perform any kind of active duty, and for that matter was never assigned any specific duties. He spent almost all of his time at San Antonio sick in quarters. The other officers on post were undoubtedly sympathetic to his plight. Still, he was in a strange part of the country, stationed in an unfamiliar garrison, and apparently unable to continue in a useful role in the profession of arms. If the state of his health did improve, he could have possibly remained in the service, no longer in the line, but in one of the supportive branches, quartermaster or commissary departments, or in an administrative position.[63]

In the early spring of 1881 Foster was granted a one month's leave of absence on a surgeon's certificate of disability. His older brother Charles, who was the city editor for the *Evening Chronicle* newspaper in Pittsburgh, came to San Antonio to bring him home. At this point James had taken a turn for the worse, to the extent that Charles did not expect his brother would reach home alive. The Foster brothers left San Antonio on March 25 for the return trip to Pittsburgh. By this time the cause of James's illness was established as "consumption contracted in line of duty." His leave certificate, prepared by Lt. Passmore Middleton, post surgeon at San Antonio, certified that Foster was "suffering from consumption of the Lungs," to which was added "the prospect of ultimate cure is very uncertain." Middleton declared James would not be able to resume duties for less than one year. On the basis of Middleton's certificate, Foster applied for a one-year extension to his leave on April 10.[64]

Department of Texas staff officers approved the leave, which was forwarded to Maj. Gen. John M. Schofield, the commanding general of the Division of the Gulf. Schofield reiterated that Foster's physical condition prevented his performing duty and added his regiment was not serving in the Department of Texas. To keep the record straight, he suggested Foster be relieved from the order which directed him to report to Texas for duty. Gen. Richard C. Drum, the new adjutant general of the army, agreed with Schofield's recommendation and leave extension. His endorsement read "this officer is represented as a gallant & excellent officer and entitled to consideration."[65]

Meanwhile, back in Pittsburgh, Foster's one month leave was running out and he wrote the Adjutant General's Office in Washington inquiring if action was taken on his leave extension. On the twenty-seventh General Sherman ordered that he be relieved from duty in Texas and his leave recommended the next day. The final approval came from Secretary of War Robert Todd Lincoln, the eldest son of Abraham Lincoln.

1 King, *Campaigning with Crook,* 137.

2 Ibid., 138; Regimental Returns, Third Cavalry, August-October 1876. See also Paul L. Hedren, *With Crook in the Black Hills: Stanley Morrow's 1876 Photographic Legacy* (Boulder, CO: Pruett Publishing Co., 1985).

3 For more on the surround, see Jerome A. Greene, "The Surrounding of Red Cloud and Red Leaf, 1876: A Preemptive Maneuver of the Great Sioux War," *Nebraska History* 82 (Summer 2001): 69–75.

4 Robinson, *Bourke Diaries, Vol. II,* 146.

5 Hedren, *With Crook in the Black Hills,* 84.

6 Post Returns, Fort Fetterman, October, November 1876.

7 Regimental Returns, Third Cavalry, October, November 1876; *Cheyenne Daily Leader,* Oct. 29, 1876.

8 Frazer, *Forts of the West,* 180–81; David P. Robrock, "A History of Fort Fetterman, Wyoming, 1867–1882," *Annals of Wyoming* 48 (Spring 1976): 19; Sheridan, *Outline Descriptions,* 98.

9 Robrock, "History of Fort Fetterman," 31.

10 Finerty, *Warpath & Bivouac,* 49. Spitzbergen is the largest island of the Norwegian arctic archipelago of Svalbard.

11 Bourke, *Mackenzie's Last Fight with the Cheyennes: A Winter Campaign in Wyoming and Montana* (Fort Collins, CO: The Old Army Press, 1970), Facsimile edition, 3.

12 Hedren, *Fort Laramie in 1876: Chronicle of a Frontier Post at War* (Lincoln, NE: University of Nebraska Press, 1988): 137.

13 For a recent and comprehensive recounting of the Powder River Expedition, see Jerome A. Greene, *Morning Star Dawn: The Powder River Expedition and the Northern Cheyennes, 1876* (Norman, OK: University of Oklahoma Press, 2003).

14 Ibid., 138.

15 For the history of Cantonment Reno, see Robert A. Murray, *Military Posts in the Powder River Country of Wyoming, 1865–1894* (Lincoln, NE: University of Nebraska Press, 1969): 110–18.

16 Chief Engineer, *Tables of Distances and Itineraries of Routes Between the Military Posts in, and to Certain Points Contiguous to, the Department of the Platte* (Omaha, NE: Headquarters Department of the Platte, December 1877): 20.

17 Special Order No. 172 (SO 172), Ft. Fetterman, Nov. 26, 1876, RG 94 Records of the Adjutant General, NARA.

18 Robrock, "History of Fort Fetterman," 62; Robinson, *Bourke Diaries, Vol. II,* 233.

19 SO 189, Fort Fetterman, Dec. 15, 1876.

20 Thomas R. Buecker, "The Journals of James S. McClellan 1st Sgt., Company H. 3rd Cavalry," *Annals of Wyoming* 57 (Spring 1985): 32; Robinson, *Bourke Diaries, Vol. II,* 234.

21 Robinson, *Bourke Diaries, Vol. II,* 229.

22 SO 33, Fort Fetterman, Feb. 19, 1877.

23 On August 30, 1877, Cantonment Reno was redesignated Fort McKinney. During the summer of 1878 the post was moved to a new site on the Clear Fork, southwest of present-day Buffalo, Wyoming. Murray, *Military Posts,* 117.

24 Maj. Thomas T. Thornburgh later transferred to the Fourth Infantry and was killed on September 29, 1879 in action with Ute Indians at Milk Creek, Colorado. Heitman, *Historical Register,* 958–59.

25 Fort Fetterman Post Journal 1876–77, RG 94, Jan. 27, 1877, Feb. 8, 1877.

26 SO 55, Mar. 21, 1877; Post Journal 1876–77, Mar. 22, 29, 1877; SO 83, Apr. 23, 1877; Robrock, "Fort Fetterman," 66.

27 "Sketch of A Plan for Proposed Cavalry Stable at Fort Fetterman W.T., Jan. 8, 1877," Quartermaster Consolidated Correspondence File 1867–1890.

28 SO 98, May 15, 1877.

29 Tom Lindmeier, *Drybone, A History of Fort Fetterman, Wyoming* (Glendo, WY: High Plains Press, 2002): 40.

30 SO 113, June 11, 1877; SO 136, July 14, 1877.

31 SO 157, Aug. 13, 1877.

32 Sec. of War, *Regulations*, 16–17; ANJ, Aug. 18, 1877.

33 Foster to AGO, Washington, Aug. 31, 1877, ACP 1873.

34 Utley, *Frontier Regulars*, 61–63; Whitman, *The Troopers*, 106–17.

35 King, *Trials of a Staff Officer* (Philadelphia, PA: L. R. Hammersley & Co., 1891): 12.

36 Billings, *Circular No. 8*, 349.

37 GO 56 1877. For example, none of the monthly Post Returns prepared by Foster were returned for correction.

38 King to Foster, April 14, 1878; Robinson to CO Co. I, Apr. 5, 1877. Both letters are from Post Adjutant, Fort Fetterman, 803–14 Incoming Letters and Telegrams.

39 Wilhelm, *A Military Dictionary*, 64; SO 6, 128, 71 1877; SO 86 1878; SO 18 1877; SO 50 1878.

40 Ibid., 64; SO 160 1876; SO 74 1878.

41 Robrock, "History of Fort Fetterman," 71; SO 46 1878.

42 Wilhelm, *Military Dictionary*, 12; General Order 7 1879; GO 41 1878; SO 50, 90 1878; SO 14 1879.

43 Coffman, *The Old Army*, 277–78.

44 Foster to AG, Mar. 10, 1879; Endorsement of General Sherman, April 8, 1879, Letters Received by the Adjutant General, 1871–1880, RG 94, NARA. Although the use of whistles to transmit orders never really took hold, Maj. Guy V. Henry used whistle signals to command his battalion in the 1890–1891 Pine Ridge Campaign. *ANJ*, Dec. 6, 1890.

45 Foster to Adjutant General, June 30, 1878, ACP 1873.

46 Billings, *Circular No. 8*, 352–53.

47 Medical certificate dated Apr. 15, 1879, and letter, Foster to AGO, Apr. 16, 1879, both ACP 1873.

48 Post Returns, April & May 1879; SO 44, May 8, 1879; Regimental Returns, Third Cavalry, June 1879.

49 Foster to AGO, Oct. 25, 1879, and certificate of H. P. Peebles, Oct. 25, 1879, ACP 1873.

50 Foster to AAG, Oct. 25, 1879; "Case of 2nd Lt. James E. H. Foster," Oct. 30, 1879; Hoff notation on medical certificate, Nov. 2, 1879.

51 Foster to AGO, Nov. 8, 1879; Telegram, AAG to Foster, Nov. 10, 1879; Letter, Yates to AG, Wash., Jan. 5, 1880, ACP 1873.

52 Senate, *Journal of the Executive Proceedings of the Senate of the United States of America from March 21, 1879, to March 3, 1881, Inclusive, Vol. XXII* (Washington, DC: Government Printing Office, 1901), 125, 135, 164, 168; Foster to AG, Feb. 4, 1880, ACP 1873.

53 1880 Mortality Schedule, Records of the U. S. Census 1880, RG 29, NARA.

54 James E. H. Foster, "The Battle of the Kiskiminetas" *The United Service* 2 (April 1880): 424–49.

55 Foster, "The Battle of the Kismininetas," 449.

56 Frazer, *Forts of the West*, 185; Post Returns, Fort Sanders, June 1880. Fort Sanders was located about three miles south of present day Laramie, Wyoming.

57 U. S. Census 1880, RG 29, NARA; Post Returns, Fort Sanders, June–July 1880.

58 *Cheyenne Daily Sun*, Aug. 17, 1880; Regimental returns, Third Cavalry, August 1880; Robinson, *Bourke Diaries, Vol. IV*, 101.

59 Letter, Foster to AG, Aug. 20, 1880; Certificate by Kimball accompanying letter of Aug. 20; Endorsement by Johnson accompanying the letter, all ACP 1873.

60 *ANJ*, Sept. 11, 1880.

61 Endorsements on letter, Foster to AG, Aug. 20, 1880, ACP 1873.

62 *ANJ*, Oct. 30, Nov. 13, 1880; Post Returns, San Antonio, November 1880–March 1881.

63 Sections 7–10 of the 1878 Army Appropriation Bill (H. R. 4867) proposed and passed by the House provided for the replacement of longtime staff officers with company grade line officers. *ANJ*, May 25, 1878.

64 Letter, Chas. G. Foster to AG, April 24, 1882, ACP 1873; "Certificate for Absence" from P. Middleton, Apr. 15, 1881, ACP 1873.

65 "Case of Jas. E. H. Foster," Apr. 25, 1881, ACP 1873.

CHAPTER 7

"The Vigor of Youth Passed By"

James was home under the attentive care of his family. The Foster residence was a two-story frame house, with an outbuilding for carriage and stable to the rear. It was located in Bellefield, in a rural/suburban area, three or four miles from the congestion of the main city. His medical care was supervised by "the best physicians," which, combined with his "natural supply of grit," did somewhat improve his condition. One alarming factor of his illness was his dramatic loss of weight. When in full health, Foster stood five feet, ten inches tall and weighed 140 pounds; on June 21 his weight was recorded as 99 pounds. He had a long way to go for recovery.[1]

Emaciation, debility, cough, and purulent expectoration were all symptoms of pulmonary phthisis, today known as tuberculosis. At the time the disease was believed to be caused by inflammatory processes in the lungs, such as bronchial catarrh, long before diagnosed as Foster's health affliction. Treatment for phthisis, commonly called consumption, followed three courses of action. First, the patient was to be kept in a cold, dry climate with exposure to continuous fresh air and exercise. Secondly, the patient was to take prescribed medications of counter irritants to relieve pain, and opiates and mineral acids for coughs and diarrhea. Finally the patient was well fed; good nutrition was a necessity for full recovery.[2]

For the next months, Foster was confined to the house in a weak, bedridden condition. His mother and sisters followed the standard treatments, and prepared his meals and provided continual nursing care. By this point he was desperate for any medical recommendation that might improve his condition. In the late fall his physician emphatically advised him to escape Pittsburgh's damp and polluted winter climate. He warned that spending the winter months there would prove seriously injurious if not fatal to Foster's fragile respiratory condition. In November James followed his advice and traveled to St. Paul, Minnesota, believing that a change to a cleaner winter climate was "the only means of saving his life." His physician had insisted it was absolutely necessary to send a nurse with him so he could receive constant attention and care. So as not to travel alone and have to depend on strangers in St. Paul, one of his younger sisters accompanied him.[3]

At this same juncture, an army administrative decision was made that would cause anxiety on his further application for leave. In November Foster's company was transferred from Fort Robinson to Fort Leavenworth, Kansas, in the Department of Missouri, changing the chain of command for approval. Consequently, after he was relieved from San Antonio, his proper duty station was Fort Leavenworth and no longer in the Department of the Platte.

In early March 1882, Foster and his sister returned to Pittsburgh because of "extremely painful family events" which required the presence of the accompanying sister. Their return was necessitated by an unknown domestic problem in the family of an older married sister. At any rate, the weather in St. Paul had been rainy for some days, and probably would continue. Foster's doctor advised he might as well return to Pittsburgh and be confined to his home there. The Fosters returned home on March 10.[4]

On March 30 Foster applied for a further extension of six months to his absence granted back in April 1881. Dr. J. H. McClellan, his physician, provided a certificate stating he needed more time on leave and required careful nursing and a special diet. He was not able to rejoin his troop, at least not before fall and probably not before spring. Foster's extension application was passed through channels and received the appropriate approvals, until it reached General Crook. He correctly pointed out that because Lieutenant Foster's troop was currently stationed at Fort Leavenworth, the Department of Missouri had to make the leave decision. That headquarters forwarded the extension request to the AGO in Washington for decision.

While Foster waited for word on his leave extension, the time on his approved leave was running out. On April 24 he received a telegram from the Adjutant General in Washington that his absence would expire on May 15, when he was required to rejoin his troop at Leavenworth, his proper duty station. Without James's knowledge, brother Charles wrote Adjutant General Drum, pleading to having his leave extended. Charles pointedly declared his brother could not stand the trip to the Plains; in his present condition, James could not even walk two hundred yards in the open air. At best he might go west, and return shortly afterward without performing any duty, however light. In closing he wrote James's health was injured in the 1876–77 Sioux War, and that he could have been a healthy man "had not his love for his profession led him to defer going off duty until disease had got such a grip on him" that he could not return to duty.[5]

On May 2 Foster received notification from the Adjutant General's Office in Washington that the order for him to report to his troop by May 15 had been revoked by General of the Army Sherman. His future absences could be covered by furnishing the usual monthly certificates. With no army medical officer in Pittsburgh, Foster was permitted to modify the printed "Form of Certificate for Absence on Account of Sickness" to appear as his own form, filled out and signed on his honor. An endorsement to Charles's request expressed support for his brother and noted, "Lt. Foster is a good officer." But, it also added the hard reality that everybody seemed to know: "I don't believe he will ever be fit for much duty."[6]

During his last year, Foster's personal statements on his certificates of absence read as a sad litany of his forlorn insistence of improvement and the actual deterioration of his health:

> July 15, 1882 — My strength does not seem to increase, and in the past months I have lost weight.
> October 1, 1882 — An examination made Sept. 23 . . . shows that the left lung to be still in a bad condition . . . For the past month or two a steady though slight improvement is noticeable, both as to strength, and in the decrease in quantity of mucus thrown off by expectoration.
> November 1, 1882 — Since date of my last report I have lost ground, being somewhat weaker.
> January 1, 1883 — I am enabled to report a slight general improvement during the past month.
> February 28, 1883 — Progress during month, favorable.[7]

For most of this time, he continued to insist that his illness was as originally diagnosed — catarrh of the air passages, from which he had suffered for the past several years. He seemingly ignored any mention of consumption.

Finally, on March 1 and 14, Foster received examinations by McClellan and Dr. William Daily, an expert in pulmonary cases. For some time Foster had been induced (or wanted to believe) his eventual recovery was probable. What he learned after his most recent examinations gave him a very different report as to the condition of his lungs. McClellan and Daily confirmed the diagnosis previously made by army surgeons: he was suffering from Consumption of the Lungs, "Fibrous Phthisis" which infected both lungs. But, by this time the disease had spread to two thirds of the left lung and one quarter of the right. In addition he was suffering from chronic catarrh of the air passages. Foster knew it was his duty to report this assessment of his condition to army headquarters. He immediately sent word of his continued affliction to the Adjutant General, and added in near defiance, ". . . I do not wish to be understood as <u>desiring</u> retirement."[8]

However, it was time for Foster to face the bitter reality that he would never again "stride the cavalry saddle." On his final certificate of absence that James filed, he admitted he would not be able to return to active duty. He modified the printed statement of condition on the form to read (underlined portions modified in Foster's hand): ". . . and that in consequence therefore <u>I am</u>, in my opinion, unfit for duty, and not able to travel without endangering <u>my</u> ultimate cure. I further declare my belief that <u>I</u> will not be able to resume <u>my duty</u>." Although for the past two years he had been confined to home, Foster's hope of return to active service kept his spirits up. But after his last consultation, family members noticed he gave up all hope of "returning to the active service he loved so well."[9] Foster did however brighten up when he received letters from friends in his regiment.

James gave no indication of impending death until the evening of May 7. About 10 o'clock he suddenly suffered violent pain and the family physician was called. His suffering was quickly relieved, but it became evident death was near. According to attending family members, he expressed his last wishes with clarity, and sent messages to his friends at home and in the army. In the words of brother Charles, ". . . and finally the brave spirit left the poor emaciated body, so emaciated indeed that there was nothing left in it apparently but the big heart that had so nobly throbbed in response to the desires of a sturdy loyal soul."[10] James E. H. Foster died at 8:05 on Tuesday morning, May 8. Charles sent a telegram to the Adjutant General that announced his death. The post commander at Fort Leavenworth did the same after reading of his death in the papers.

In addition to the local papers, news of his passing was announced in other papers and publications, which included the *Army & Navy Journal*, *San Francisco Times*, *New York Times*, *The United Service*, and *Army Register*. The *Pittsburgh Dispatch* remembered that before he entered the army he was a bright and active member of the city press, and "a genial companion."

FIG. 7.1. James Foster's grave marker in Allegheny Cemetery.

Several obituaries made note of the fact that he was complimented for his part in the Battle of the Rosebud, "... in which he charged with his troop the savage enemy no less than five times in quick succession."[11]

His funeral was private at the family residence on Thursday afternoon, with burial in the Allegheny Cemetery, the largest and one of the oldest cemeteries in Pittsburgh. He was buried in the family plot between the graves of his father and oldest brother. His simple marker read:

JAMES EVANS HERON

FOSTER

LIEUT. 3rd U. S. CAVALRY

BORN

JUNE 4, 1848

In the official record, Foster's death moved every officer behind his date of commission up one notch. All over the country, army officers took down their copies of the *Army Register* and drew a line through his name.

* * *

As the senior brother residing at home, Charles Foster took care of James's final affairs. As requested by the Adjutant General's Office, he provided the army with an official cause of death from the Pittsburgh Board of Health: Fibrous Phthisis, and the secondary, Apnoea, contracted during the Sioux War of 1876. After that he cleared his brother's final pay with the office of the Second Auditor of the Treasury, which was responsible for pay due deceased officers. The hardships of the Big Horn & Yellowstone Expedition took its toll on the rank and file of Crook's troops. In looking back, one chronicler of the campaign wondered after the toilsome marches and drenching bivouacs "how some men stood it as they did."[12] In later years John Bourke summed up the brutality of the campaign:

> I made out a rough list of the officers present on this expedition, and another of those who have died, been killed, died of wounds, or been retired for one reason or another, and I find that the first list had one hundred and sixteen names and the second sixty nine; so it can be seen that of the officers who were considered to be physically able to enter upon that campaign in the early summer months of 1876, over fifty per cent. are not now answering to roll-call on the active list, after about sixteen years' interval.[13]

Along with Foster's obituary published in the *Army & Navy Journal*, the following poem was submitted as "Written by 1st Lieut. J. E. H. Foster, 3d Cavalry, a few months before his death, and when he had began to give up hope of returning to the active service he loved so well."[14]

"RETIRED," — TO THE REGIMENT

NEVER again in the saddle to wear the buff and blue;
Never again in the saddle to march with the troop in review;
Never again to hear with joy the boom of the morning gun
As it sends its salutation to the rising of the sun.

Dead are the hopes of life's morning,
    The vigor of youth passed by;
Oh, comrades! It's harder retiring;
    Better, far better, to die!

Broken, worn out, and useless,
    No longer to play in life's game;
'Tis hard, yet alive, to be buried;
    To me it means just the same.
Better to have fallen in action
    When the heart beat is strong and high;
Oh, comrades! It's harder retiring;
    Better, far better, to die.

Never again to follow on the savage enemy's path,
Never again to meet the foe and face his hellish wrath;
Never again to lead the troop with its thundering hoofs behind,
With pistols out, and charging shout, and guidon flying to wind.
Dead to all things of the future;
    Only to eat, sleep, and sigh;
Oh, brothers! it's harder retiring,
    Better, far better, to die.

Never again on the prairie, to see the sunset's glow,
O'er the sober brown of the heather, a bloodlike crimson throw;
Never again in the mountains, to see the lordly pine,
Or the flashing gleam of the crystal stream as it leaps and foams
    like wine.
My hope is beyond the sunset;
    When the stream of life runs dry;
Oh, comrades! It's harder retiring;
    Better, far better, to die.

As a final note, during the 1890s, after time passed from the battles of old, a need was seen to recognize the deeds of the soldiers, both alive and deceased, who performed so ably in the combats of the western campaigns. In 1890, Maj. Guy V. Henry wrote commendations for both Capt. William H. Andrews (died June 1880) and 2nd Lt. James Foster, "for conspicuous gallantry at Rosebud, Montana, June 17, 1876."[15] James would have been proud.

* * *

James Foster served as an officer in the regular army from his date of commission on October 1, 1873, until his death on May 8, 1883, making a total service time of nine years, eight months, and eight days. Out of this time span, he was on leave of absence, sick in quarters, absent sick, or on sick leave for a total of four years and nine months, about half of his time in the army. Foster's illnesses originated in his first days of duty and worsened because of his hard service in the Great Sioux War. The other half of his service time was spent on active duty. Out of this, he spent nearly twenty-two months on field service or on detached service. The rest of his duty time was on garrison duty, where he learned and performed the daily routine of the army.

Foster remains a minor footnote in American history. Nevertheless, minor players contribute to the big picture. He witnessed critical events in that history, including the end of the Civil War and the end of hard years of struggle for control of the northern plains. But he also saw the continued rise of his home city into a great industrial capital. His record of service in the U. S. Army is preserved through military records of the era, and can also be traced through civilian records and newspapers.

Foster used his personal abilities to help record the experience of the army in the West. In 1875 he was on the Black Hills Expedition, where he honed his skills as a surveyor and topographer, and learned the art of road building for movement of wagons and troops. He personally trekked through and mapped vast areas of the Hills, contributing to the public's knowledge of that important geological and geographical feature. Additionally, his ability as a sketch artist provided the public with some of the first views of Black Hills scenery and the surrounding region.

During the 1876 Sioux War, he served through the trying summer and fall campaigns and took part in the major engagements with plains tribesmen. Foster's experience under fire demonstrated his leadership and also his ability to follow orders. A gifted writer, Foster authored a detailed account of the famous Rosebud battle, and kept at least one personal journal of his experiences in the West for future reference. Undoubtedly others of his writings could have existed but are lost to time and posterity.

In the meantime, he was proud to be a commissioned officer in the regular army. As a junior subaltern, he held positions of responsibility and administration and could perform both mundane garrison duties and lead troops in harm's way. He also understood legalities enough to serve as judge advocate for court martial duty. He proved a capable, loyal soldier with a promising career. He was interested in professional improvement and confidant enough to write a stinging critique of the state of national defense for a peer audience in *The United Service* journal.

Foster took full advantage of his opportunities to command and serve. He was a man interested in his place and time in American history. Had he been able to continue his army career, he doubtless would have commanded a regiment or higher in the Spanish-American War or Philippine Insurrection, and retired after the turn of the century with a star on his shoulder straps. Had he survived in years, he would have written one of the classics of the Indian Wars, like his contemporaries, John Bourke, Finerty, and Charles King.

Foster's experiences increase our knowledge of the American West and the important role played in it by the frontier army. His was a story worthy to be told. Unfortunately for us, he died too early to tell it in full.

1   Charles Foster to AG, Apr. 24, 1882, ACP 1873; "Certificate for Absence on Account of Sickness," July 15, 1882, ACP 1873.

2   Richard J. Dunglison, *A Dictionary of Medical Science . . . New Edition Enlarged and Thoroughly Revised* (Philadelphia, PA: Henry C. Lea, 1874), 792–93.

3   Charles Foster to AG, Apr. 24, 1882; Foster to AGO, May 4, 1882, ACP 1873. His youngest sister Eleanor (Nellie) probably accompanied him to St. Paul.

4   Foster to AGO, May 4, 1882; Charles Foster to AG, Apr. 24, 1882, ACP 1873.

5   Charles Foster to AG, April 24, 1882.

6   Endorsement to Foster letter to AG, Apr. 24, 1882. Unfortunately, the initials of the officer writing the endorsement are illegible.

7   "Certificates for Absence," ACP 1873.

8   "Certificate for Absence," Mar. 31, 1883, ACP 1873; Foster to AGO, Mar. 31, 1883, ACP 1873.

9   "Certificate of Absence," Apr. 30, 1883, ACP 1883; *ANJ*, May 19, 1883.

10   *ANJ*, May 19, 1883.

11   *Pittsburgh Dispatch*, May 9, 1883; *Lawrence Guardian*, May 18, 1883.

12   King, *Campaigning with Crook*, 141.

13   Bourke, *On the Border with Crook*, 359.

14   *ANJ, May 19, 1883*.

15   ACP 1873.

Bibliography

MANUSCRIPT MATERIALS

National Archives and Records Administration, Washington, DC

RG 29 Records of the Bureau of the Census: U. S. Census, 1840, 1850, 1860, 1870, 1880

RG 94 Records of the Adjutant General: ACP 1873 (Appointments, Commissions, Personal File); General and Special Orders, Fort Fetterman, 1876–1879; Letters Received by the Adjutant General, 1871–1880; Post Journal, Fort Fetterman, 1876–1877; Post Returns, Fort McPherson, 1873–1875, Sidney Barracks, 1875–1876, Fort Fetterman, 1876–1879, Fort Sanders, 1880, Fort D. A. Russell, 1880, Post at San Antonio, 1880–1881; Records of Enlistments, First Battalion Pennsylvania Light Artillery, 155th Pennsylvania Infantry; Register of Enlistments in the U. S. Army, 1778–1914; Returns from Regular Army Cavalry Regiments, Third Cavalry, 1873–1883; U. S. Military Academy Cadet Application Papers, 1805–1866

RG 393 Records of the United States Army Continental Commands: Black Hills Expedition, General and Special Orders

Pennsylvania State Archives, Harrisburg, Pennsylvania

RG 19 Records of the Department of Military and Veterans' Affairs: 155th Pennsylvania Infantry; Pennsylvania Army National Guard

UNPUBLISHED MATERIALS

No Author. "A Historic Resources Study: The Civil War Defenses of Washington, Parts I & II." Chevy Chase, MD: CEHP Incorporated.

John D. McDermott. "Gen. George Crook's 1876 Campaigns: A Report Prepared for the American Battlefield Protection Program." Sheridan, WY: Frontier Heritage Alliance (June 2000).

GOVERNMENT PUBLICATIONS

Adjutant General's Office. *Army Registers.* Washington, DC: Government Printing Office, 1874–1884.

———. *Index of General Orders, 1874.* Washington, DC: General Printing Office, 1875.

———. *Official Army Register of the Volunteer Force of the United States Army, Part III.* Washington, DC: Adjutant General's Office, 1865.

Chief Engineer. *Tables of Distances and Itineraries of Routes between the Military Posts in, and Certain Points Contiguous to the Department of the Platte.* Omaha, NE: Headquarters, Department of the Platte, December, 1877.

Engineer Department. *Report upon United States Geographical Surveys West of the One Hundredth Meridian, Vol. I, Geographical Report.* Washington, DC: Government Printing Office, 1889.

Heitman, Francis B. *Historical Register and Dictionary of the United States Army.* Reprint of 1903 edition. Urbana, IL: University of Illinois Press, 1965.

Senate. *Journal of the Executive Proceedings of the Senate, Vol. XIX, XXII.* Washington, DC: Government Printing Office, 1901.

Sheridan, Philip H. *Outline Descriptions of the Posts in the Military Division of the Missouri.* Reprint of 1876 edition. Fort Collins, CO: The Old Army Press, 1969.

Surgeon General's Office. *A Report on the Hygiene of the United States Army, with Descriptions of Military Posts.* New York: Sol Lewis, 1974. Reprint of 1874 edition.

War Department. *Regulations for the Army of the United States, 1881.* Washington, DC: Government Printing Office, 1881.

———. *The War of the Rebellion: A Compilation of the Official Records of the Union and Confederate Armies.* Washington, DC: Government Printing Office, 1880–1901. Series 1, Vol. I, Parts 1 & 2.

NEWSPAPERS

Army & Navy Journal (New York)
Cheyenne Daily Leader
Cheyenne Daily Sun
Chicago Tribune
Hazard's Register of Pennsylvania (Philadelphia)
Lawrence Guardian (Pennsylvania)
New York Daily Graphic
New York Herald
New York Tribune
North Platte Enterprise (Nebraska)
Omaha Daily Bee (Nebraska)
Pittsburgh Dispatch

BOOKS AND ARTICLES

Abrams, Marc H. *Sioux War Dispatches: Reports from the Field, 1876–1877.* Yardley, PA: Westholme Publishing, 2012.

Albert, George D., *History of the County of Westmoreland, Pennsylvania.* Philadelphia, PA: L. H. Everts & Co., 1882.

Bates, Samuel P. *History of Pennsylvania Volunteers 1861–65.* Harrisburg, PA: B. Singerly. State Printer, 1869.

Boucher, John N. *History of Westmoreland County, Pennsylvania, Vol. I & II.* New York, NY: The Lewis Publishing Co., 1906.

Bourke, John G. *Mackenzie's Last Fight with the Cheyennes: A Winter Campaign in Wyoming and Montana.* Reprint of 1890. Edition Fort Collins, CO: Old Army Press, 1970.

———. *On the Border With Crook.* New York, NY: Scribner's Sons, 1891.

Buecker, Thomas R. "Fort Sidney: Its Role on the Upper Plains." *C.A.M.P. Periodical* 11 (March 1982): 381–98.

———. "The Journals of James S. McClellan 1st Sgt., Company H, 3rd Cavalry." *Annals of Wyoming* 57 (Spring 1985): 21–34.

———. "The Letters of Caroline Frey Winne from Sidney Barracks and Fort McPherson, Nebraska, 1874–1878." *Nebraska History* 62 (Spring 1981): 1–46.

———. "The Post of North Platte Station, 1867–1878." *Nebraska History* 63 (Fall 1982): 22–36.

Carroll, John M., ed. *The Papers of the Order of Indian Wars.* Fort Collins, CO: Old Army Press, 1975.

Coffman, Edward M. *The Old Army: A Portrait of the American Army in Peacetime, 1784–1898.* New York, NY: Oxford University Press, 1986.

Collins, Charles D., Jr. *Atlas of the Sioux Wars, Second Edition.* Fort Leavenworth, KS: Combat Studies Institute Press, 2006.

Cooling, Benjamin Franklin, III and Walter H. Owen, II. *Mr. Lincoln's Forts: A Guide to the Civil War Defenses of Washington.* Shippensburg, PA: White Mane Publishing Company, 1988.

Diffenbacher, J. F. *Directory of Pittsburgh and Allegheny Cities.* Pittsburgh, PA: J. F. Diffenbacher, 1879–1883.

Dunglison, Richard J. *A Dictionary of Medical Science . . . A New, Enlarged and Thoroughly Revised.* Philadelphia, PA: Henry C. Lea, 1874.

Finerty, John F. *Warpath and Bivouac.* Chicago, IL: John F. Finerty, 1890.

Foster, Alexander W., compiler. *Codified Ordinances of the City of Pittsburgh.* Pittsburgh, PA: W. S. Hoven, City Printer, 1860.

Foster, James E. H. "The Battle of Kiskiminetas." *The United Service* 2 (April 1880): 424–49.

Foster, Stephen C. & Foster, Morrison. *Biography, Songs, and Musical Compositions of Stephen C. Foster.* Pittsburgh, PA: Percy F. Smith, 1896.

Frazer, Robert W. *Forts of the West: Military Forts and Presidios and Posts Commonly Called Forts West of the Mississippi River to 1898.* Norman, OK: University of Oklahoma Press, 1965.

Gray, John S. *Centennial Campaign: The Sioux War of 1876.* Ft. Collins, CO: Old Army Press, 1976.

———. *Custer's Last Campaign.* Lincoln, NE: University of Nebraska Press, 1991.

Greene, Jerome, A. *Battles and Skirmishes of the Great Sioux War, 1876–1877: The Military View.* Norman, OK: University of Oklahoma Press, 1993.

———. *Morning Star Dawn: The Powder River Expedition and the Northern Cheyenne, 1876.* Norman, OK: University of Oklahoma Press, 2003.

———. *Slim Buttes: An Episode of the Great Sioux War.* Norman, OK: University of Oklahoma Press, 1982.

———. "The Surrounding of Red Cloud and Red Leaf, 1876: A Preemptive Maneuver of the Great Sioux War." *Nebraska History* 82 (Summer 2001): 69–75.

Harris, Isaac. *Harris' Pittsburgh Business Directory.* Pittsburgh, PA: Isaac Harris, 1837–1847.

Hedren, Paul L. *Fort Laramie in 1876: Chronicle of a Frontier Post at War.* Lincoln, NE: University of Nebraska Press, 1988.

———. *Great Sioux War Orders of Battle: How the United States Army Waged War on the Northern Plains, 1876–1877.* Norman, OK: The Arthur H. Clark Co., 2011.

———. *Ho! For the Black Hills: Captain Jack Crawford Reports the Black Hills Gold Rush and Great Sioux War.* Pierre, SD: South Dakota State Historical Society, 2012.

———. *With Crook in the Black Hills: Stanley Morrow's 1876 Photographic Legacy.* Boulder, CO: Pruett Publishing Co., 1985.

Kime, Wayne R., ed. *The Black Hills Journals of Colonel Richard Irving Dodge.* Norman, OK: University of Oklahoma Press, 1996.

———. *Col. Richard Irving Dodge: The Life and Times of a Career Army Officer.* Norman, OK: University of Oklahoma Press, 2006.

King, Captain Charles. *Campaigning with Crook.* Norman, OK: University of Oklahoma Press, 1964; second printing 1967.

———. *Trials of a Staff Officer*. Philadelphia, PA: L. R. Hamersley & Co., 1891.

Leech, Margaret. *Reveille in Washington, 1860–1865*. New York, NY: Harper & Bros., 1941.

Lindmier, Tom. *Drybone: A History of Fort Fetterman, Wyoming*. Glendo, WY: High Plains Press, 2002.

Mangum, Neil C. *Battle of the Rosebud: Prelude to the Little Bighorn*. El Segundo, CA: Upton & Sons, 1987.

Martin, Col. Edward. *The Twenty-eighth Division: Pennsylvania's Guard in the World War*. Pittsburgh, PA: 28th Division Publishing Co., 1924.

Mark E. Miller. *Military Sites in Wyoming 1700–1920: Historic Context*. Laramie, WY: Wyoming Department of State Parks & Cultural Resources, 2012.

Morneweck, Evelyn Foster. *Chronicles of Stephen Foster's Family, Vol. II*. Pittsburgh, PA: University of Pittsburgh Press, 1944.

Murray, Robert A. *Military Posts in the Powder River Country of Wyoming, 1865–1894*. Lincoln, NE: University of Nebraska Press, 1969.

Newton, Henry and Jenney, Walter P. *Report on the Geology and Resources of the Black Hills of Dakota*. Washington, DC: Government Printing Office, 1880.

Rickey, Don. *Forty Miles a Day on Beans and Hay*. Norman, OK: University of Oklahoma Press, 1963.

Robinson, Charles M., ed. *The Diaries of John Gregory Bourke, Vol. I, November 20, 1872–July 28, 1876*. Denton, TX: University of North Texas Press, 2003.

———. *Vol. II, July 29, 1876–April 7, 1878*. (same), 2005.

———. *Vol. III, June 1, 1878–June 22, 1880*. (same), 2007.

———. *Vol. IV, July 3, 1880–May 22, 1881*. (same), 2009.

Robrock, David P. "A History of Fort Fetterman, Wyoming, 1867–1882." *Annals of Wyoming* 48 (Spring 1976): 5–76.

The 155th Regimental Association. *Under the Maltese Cross: Antietam to Appomattox*. Pittsburgh, PA: 1910.

Thrapp, Dan L. *Encyclopedia of Frontier Biography*. Lincoln, NE: University of Nebraska Press, 1988.

Thurston, George H. *Directory for Pittsburgh and Allegheny Cities*. Pittsburgh, PA: George H. Thurston, 1856–1876.

Turchen, Lesta V. and McLaird, James D. *The Black Hills Expedition of 1875*. Mitchell, SD: Dakota Wesleyan University Press, 1975.

Utley, Robert M. *Frontier Regulars: The United States Army and the Indian, 1866–1891*. New York, NY: Macmillan Publishing Co., 1973.

Vaughn, J. W. *The Reynolds' Campaign on the Powder River*. Norman, OK: University of Oklahoma Press, 1961.

———. *With Crook at the Rosebud*. Harrisburg, PA: The Stackpole Co., 1956.

Whitman, S. E. *The Troopers: An Informal History of the Plains Cavalry, 1865–1890*. New York, NY: Hastings House Publishers, 1962.

Wilhelm, Thomas A. *A Military Dictionary and Gazetteer*. Philadelphia, PA: L. R. Hamersly & Co., 1881.

Willert, James. *March of the Columns: A Chronicle of the 1876 Indian War, June 27–September 16*. El Segundo, CA: Upton & Sons, Publishers, 1994.

Wilson, Erasmus, ed. *Standard History of Pittsburgh, Pennsylvania*. Chicago, IL: H. R. Cornell & Co., 1898.

Woodward & Rowland. *Pittsburgh Directory*. Pittsburgh, PA: W. S. Hoven, 1852.

Index

Foster, James Evans Heron (*continued*)
promotion of, to 1st lieutenancy, 170;
recognition for, 96, 108, 125, 135, 155, 185;
rejection of stable plan of, *161*; rejection of whistle signaling of, 167, 177n44;
retirement poem by, 184–85; at Sidney
Barracks, 4, 107, *112*, 113; significance of,
1, 3, 186–87; and Slim Buttes fight, 145;
on Starvation March, 146, *147*, 152–54; in
St. Paul, 180; in Tongue River fight, 120;
tuberculosis of, 173, 175, 179, 181, 182, 184;
United Service article by, 171, 186. *See also*
Journal (of Foster)

Foster, J. Heron (uncle of James E. H.), 9–11,
18, 23

Foster, Pearson G. (bro. of James E. H.), 9,
10, 23; enlistment of, 11; grave of, 171, 183

Foster, Stephen C. (composer), 9

Foster, William (great-grandfather of James
E. H.), family of, 7

Foster, William Barclay (cousin of Alexander William, Sr.), 9

Foster's Butte, naming of, 91, 110n31

Fourteenth United States Infantry, Crook's
troops joined by, 139

Fourth United States Cavalry, at Red Cloud
and Red Leaf surround, 154

Fourth United States Infantry: at Ft. Fetterman, 155, 161–64, 166, 168; at Ft. Sanders,
172

Frank Leslie's Illustrated Newspaper: Big
Horn and Yellowstone Expedition's
sketches for, *120, 121, 124*

Fredericksburg, Battle of, 155th Pennsylvania Inf. at, 17

Freeland, George H. (Cpl.), hunt by, on
Dismal River Scout, 53, 69n38

Freeze out. *See* Poker

French, William H. (Lt. Col.), on officer
examining board, 28

French Creek: Big Horn and Yellowstone
Expedition along, 153; Camp Harney
near, 88; gold miners along, 96

Galveston (TX), Foster's arrival in, 173, 174

Gambling. *See* Poker

General Orders No. 8, for ending Big Horn
and Yellowstone Expedition, 154–55

General Orders No. 27, for army promotions and appointments, 58

"Genuine Pate" (liquor), 40, 46, 68n18

Gettysburg, Battle of: 155th Pennsylvania
Inf. in, 17; Knap's Battery in, 14; Pittsburgh relieved by, 12

Gibbon, John (Col.), Montana Column
under, 117

Gillmore Canyon, Foster in, during First
Jump of '74, 57, 70n62

Glendive Creek, supply depot at, 143

Gold (in Black Hills), 114; discovery of, 73,
96; eviction of miners of, 100; Morrow's
photos of, 154

Goose Creek, 119, 121, 125, 126

Goose Creek Camp, 121, 125, 137; dateline
of, for Foster's account of Battle of the
Rosebud, 126

Grand Review, of postwar Union troops,
18, *19*, 21

Grand River, Starvation March along, 143

Grant, Ulysses S. (Gen.): army commissions
approved by, 27, 28, 58–60; inaugural
parade of, 24; Washington's defenses
weakened by, 12, 15

Graves: of Foster, *183–84*; of Foster's family, 73, 171, 183; of Indians, 84; of John
Burke, 55, 70n48; of soldiers, 125, 135

Gray, Armor, murder charge against, 55–56,
70n52, 70n56

Great Sioux Reservation, 73; forts around,
160; nonagency Lakota Sioux on, 116

Great Sioux War of 1876–77, 4; army strategy
for, 118; beginning of, 116; Foster's hardships during, 181, 184, 186; Foster's letters
on, 139; launching point for, 117; turning
point of, 154, 157; veterans of, at Ft. D. A.
Russell, 174. *See also* Rosebud, Battle of
the; Slim Buttes fight; Starvation March;
Stern Chase; Tongue River fight

Greensburg (PA), Foster's roots in, 7–9

Gregg, Thomas J. (1st Lt.), in 1874 Sioux
Expedition, 55, 70n44

Grinnell (KS), Foster's service at, 64, 66

Groesch, Andrew (Sgt.), wounding of, in
Battle of the Rosebud, 136–37

Grouard, Frank (scout): on Sibley Scout,
138; in Slim Buttes fight, 144

One-hundred-day units, Washington defended by, 12, 14, 16

One Hundredth Pennsylvania Infantry, Pearson G. Foster's service in, 11

One Hundredth Meridian, at Cozad, 62, 71n71

Ord, E. O. C. (Gen.), Foster's duty application to, 174

Oumet, Fred, saloon of, at Ft. McPherson, 55, 56

"Our Army in Flanders" (soldiers' profanity), 44, 69n24

Overland Stage, station ruins of, 62

Overland Trail, 158

Owl Creek. *See* Moreau River

Palestine Exploration Society, Holy Land mapped by, 2, 35

Pallardie, Leon Francois ("The Wolf"): on Dismal River elk hunt, 46–51; on Dismal River Scout, 38, 40, 43, 45, 53, 54, 68n12

Parker, — (Lord), hunting camp of, 52

Paul, Augustus C. (1st Lt.), *147*; at Ft. D. A. Russell, 174; at Post of North Platte Station, 40–41, 68n20

Paul, Reunie (child of Augustus C.), 40–41

Pawnee Creek: Dismal River Scout's march to, 53, 69n37; Plum Creek Scout's march to, 61

Pawnee Indians, on Powder River Expedition, 157

Pawnee Scouts, at Red Cloud and Red Leaf surround, 154

Pawnee Springs, 54, 69n39; Indians near, 66

Peal, James T. (1st Lt.), in 1874 Sioux Expedition, 55, 70n44

Pearson, Alfred L. (Pennsylvania National Guard), Foster's commission application endorsed by, 26

Peebles, H. P. (Dr.), Foster treated by, 169–70

Peninsular Campaign, Knap's Battery in, 14

Pennsylvania Light Artillery (First Battalion of): computation of service time for, 168; disbanding of, 16; Washington defended by, 12–16

Pennsylvania National Guard, 25; formation of, from militia units, 25; Foster's endorsement from, for army

commission, 26; Foster's service in, 1. *See also specific units*

Pennypacker, Galusha (Col.), at Post of San Antonio, 174

Petersburg (VA), 18

Philadelphia (PA), 7

Philippine Insurrection, 8, 187; officers in, 30

Photography: by Guerin, 73, 91, 96, 98, 99, *104*, 115; by Morrow, *147, 152, 153, 154*

Phthisis. *See* Tuberculosis

Pine Ridge, Jenney Expedition in, 80

Pioneer duty (on the march): for Big Horn and Yellowstone Expedition, 119; for Jenney Expedition, 74, 80–82

Pittsburgh (PA): Civil War defense of, 8, 11–12, 14, 20; Civil War industry of, 11; fictional British attack on, 171; Foster's 1877 return to, 163, 170, 171; Foster's early career in, 23–28, 32; Foster's final days in, 175, 179–82; Foster's roots in, 7–11, 17; suburban growth of, 8, 10, 186. *See also* Allegheny Arsenal; Camp Reynolds (Pittsburgh); Fort Pitt Foundry

Pittsburgh Colonization Society, 9

Pittsburgh Dispatch, 9; Foster family's work for, 23; Foster's obituary in, 182

Pittsburgh Evening Chronicle, under Charles G. Foster, 175

Pittsburgh Light Guards (militia), Foster's enlistment in, 23, 24

Platte River, 36, 38, 57, 64, 155; bridging of, 35, 62, 71n72; maps of, *48, 59, 63. See also* North Platte River; South Platte River

Plum Creek Bridge, over Platte River, 62, 71n72

Plum Creek Scout, Indian scare investigated by, 60–62

Poker, playing of, on Dismal River Scout, 45

Pollock, Edwin (Maj.), at Cantonment Reno, 160

Post of North Platte Station, 115; 3rd Cav. at, 31; Dismal River Scout relieved from, 40–41, 42–44; Foster's service at, 54, 55; scouts from, 64, 174

Post of San Antonio, Foster's service at, 173–75

Royall, William B. (Lt. Col.), *147*; in Battle of the Rosebud, 122–24, 125, 127, 129, 130–33; on Big Horn and Yellowstone Expedition, 119, 138–39; escort of, to Ft. Laramie, 168

Russell, Gerald (Capt.), Indians pursued by, 66

Salt Lake City (UT), Ft. Douglas near, 139

Sand Bluffs, Foster's description of, during Jenney Expedition, 76

Sandhills: elk hunt in, 4, 47, 50, 51, 57, 66; maps of, *48, 65*; scouting in, *36*, 44, 46; snowstorm in, 40

San Francisco Times, Foster's obituary in, 182

Saucier, Phil (store clerk), 55, 70n50

Schofield, John M. (Maj. Gen.), Foster's sick leave approved by, 175

Schwatka, Frederick (2nd Lt.), *134, 147,* 155; at Ft. McPherson, *36*, 55, 135; in medical school, 2; in polar regions, 2; at Post of North Platte Station, 41, 42, 64; in Slim Buttes fight, 144

Scott, Hugh, career longevity of, 2

Scouting patrols (from Ft. McPherson), 31–32, 37; maps from, *48, 59, 63, 64, 65. See also* Dismal River Scout; Plum Creek Scout

Second lieutenants: appointment list for, 30; commissions for, 20, 27, 28, 58–60; forage for, 31; leaves for, 31, living quarters for, 31; pay for, 31; promotions for, 140; subsistence for, 31

Second United States Cavalry (former Second Regiment of Dragoons), 40; in Battle of the Rosebud, 122, 127, 133, 150n45; on Big Horn and Yellowstone Expedition, 117–19; in Dept. of the Platte, 31; at Ft. Fetterman, 155; on Jenney Expedition, 73, 76, 84, 87; at Post of North Platte Station, 55

Sentinel Buttes, Indian skirmish near, 142

Seventeenth United States Infantry, in Dakota Column, 117

Seventh United States Cavalry, 72; on Big Horn and Yellowstone Expedition, 117; Foster's proposed promotion to, 139–40;

at Little Big Horn, 139; souvenirs from, 144, 157

Seventh United States Infantry, in Montana Column, 117

Seymour, Richard ("Bloody Dick," "Red Dick"), on Dismal River Scout, 44, 45, 52, 69n26

Shenandoah Valley, Early's Confederates along, 15, 16

Sheridan, Philip (Gen.), 153; Crook's report to, of surround, 154; Foster's sick leave approved by, 169; impatience of, with Crook, 139; instructions of, to Crook and Terry, 117

Sherman, William T. (Gen.): armies of, 20, 181; Foster's commission application reviewed by, 26; Foster's sick leaves reviewed by, 175, 181; whistle signaling rejected by, 167

"Shorty," on Plum Creek Scout, 61

Shoshoni Indians: in Battle of the Rosebud, 125, 127, 133, 137, 149n39; on Big Horn and Yellowstone Expedition, 121, 122; with Crook after Little Big Horn, 139

Sibley, Frederick W. (Lt.), on Sibley Scout, 138

Sibley Scout, failure of, 138

Sick leave (for Foster), 186; in Florida, 67, 74; at Ft. Fetterman, 159–61, 163, 164, 168–69; at Ft. Leavenworth, 180–81; at Ft. McPherson, 66–67; at Ft. Sanders, 172; in Nassau, 170; at Post of San Antonio, 175, 180

Sidney (NE): description of, 114; Foster's drawing of, 4, *112, 113, 115,* 116

Sidney Barracks: 3rd Cav. at, 31, 118, 155; description of, 113, 118; Foster's service at, 4, 107, 113, 115; Foster's sketch of, 4, *112, 113, 115*; Morton's return to, 105, 109

Sidney Bridge, Foster's drawing of, 115–*16*

Sidney-Deadwood Trail, to Black Hills, *112,* 114

Sidney Telegraph, Foster's drawings for, 116

Simpson, James E. (2nd Lt.), *147, 152,* 153; newspaper coverage of, 155

Singer, Caroline C. (Mrs. Alexander William Foster, Jr.), 9, 10